THE BIBLICAL MYSTERY TOUR

THE
BIBLICAL
MYSTERY TOUR

Coming to take you away
to where the televangelists won't!

By: Rev. Tom Muzzio (resigned)

Territorial Enterprise Foundation
P.O. Box 16
Virginia City, NV 89440

Library of Congress Control Number: 2015908267

ISBN-13: 978-0-9969628-0-3

ISBN-10: 0-9969628-0-8

Edited by Edith Zdunich

TABLE OF CONTENTS

Part 1: Prerogatives and Preconceptions

Part 2: Patriarchs and Pagans

Part 3: Promises and Protests

Part 4: Property and Propriety

Part 5: Priests and Palaces

Part 6: Poetry, Passions and Praise

Part 7: Prophets and Principles

Part 8: Parables, Prophecy and Punishment

Itinerary

Hop on the bus, Gus!

Welcome to our tour of the Holy Bible. I will be your guide. My name is Tom and I will be taking you on a trip through the pages of the world's number one bestseller of all time ... a book possessed by many, but read carefully by few. It is a book oft quoted and thumped, but rarely understood. Hopefully I can fix that. So find yourself a nice comfy seat on the Biblical Mystery Tour bus. Relax and let me do the driving.

Like all tours we need an agenda—a schedule—a plan. Here is ours: We will follow the Bible narrative fairly closely. We will go from one well-known story to the next, examining each in turn. These accounts are of a primitive people, their early hand-me-down history, and their campfire tales of dim antiquity. Gradually, we will see the rise of a sophisticated culture and a philosophy or mindset that has gradually come down to us today ... whether we like it or not!

In your brochure you'll notice that the scriptures are always printed in **boldface** type. Anything in boldface is a direct quotation from the Bible itself. And, given my ministerial background, I have taken pains to follow each with the exact specific reference—chapter and verse. This is so that you can do an instant fact check.

Another important thing to know is that all direct quotes are taken from the *New International Version* of the Bible, which was first published in the 1970s. I've always preferred it, cuz I don't believe that the Bible fell down out of the sky in the quaint 1611 English that is called the *King James Version*, also known to many old duffers as the "Authorized Version." Yeah, authorized by King James. Duh. However, I do like to quote that antique translation from time to time for comic relief. But I'll let you know when I am doing so : -)

There will be some vocabulary builders along the way and I'll carefully define them for you right on the spot instead of sending you to a glossary at the end. However, there will be a test! Okay, I think that is enough of an intro, so let's get started. First stop: Creation ... otherwise known as "The Little Bang."

Part 1

Prerogatives
and
Preconceptions

God got sick of sitting around in the dark void, so he created the
Sun and Moon :-) After he created the plants and livestock, that is!

Creation

OMG—What a totally fucked up way to create a universe!

The first stop on our tour is "In the beginning." Perhaps you have heard of the Big BANG! Well, the Bible account is more like a little bang, or a fizzle, or kind of a dry fart. If you look out your tour bus window, you will notice that it is dark. That's because God hasn't created the rest of the Universe yet. No, he creates the Earth first. **Now the Earth was formless and empty, darkness was over the surface of the deep and the Spirit of God was hovering over the waters.** (Genesis 1: 1-3). Now the planet, which is floating in total darkness, is formless and void. Let me tell you—it is really dark cuz at this point there are no stars or anything to provide light. But there is water! Huh?

Then, Hallelujah: "Let there be light," and there was light. Yea! This is really great, but notice that we don't know where this light was coming from, as the Sun and Moon and stars haven't been invented yet! Hmm. In any case, there was light from somewhere and it was good. Works for me :-)

Okay, now there is light—from somewhere—and it was good. I'll say. **God called the light "day," and the darkness he called "night." And there was evening, and there was morning—the first day.** (Gen. 1: 5). **And God said, "Let there be an expanse between the waters to separate water from water." So God made the expanse and separated the water under the expanse from the water above it. And it was so. God called the expanse "sky." And there was evening, and there was morning—the second day.** (Gen. 1: 6-8).

Now let me get this straight. God made the sky to separate the water *beneath* it from the water above it? ...Okay. So there is water above the sky. I am sure there is a logical explanation for that. But one thing for sure—when a space probe finally manages to get above the sky, they will surely be amazed to find water! (Spoiler alert: It is all explained when we get to the Book of Job.) Actually, I think I do know what this is all about. Ancient men looked up and thought the sky was sort of a ceiling above their heads. They saw the sky as children do. When I was small, I too looked up into the blue and saw the sky as a sort of hard, roof-like dome. Obviously, it was round, as it melted away at the edges and came down at the horizons equally in all directions. It was like the

Astrodome. The sky was hard, fixed in place, and it was painted blue on the underside facing down toward the Earth.

I distinctly recall lying on my back on a warm summer day and commenting to a friend about a certain fir tree just across the fence on our neighbor's farm. Surely, I noted, that tree must be the tallest tree in the world; it must have grown right up through the sky. We mused as to how much higher it really was, out of sight above the blue dome. Although I had read the tale of "Jack and the Beanstalk," I knew that was just a fable. *This* was obviously true. No child can be faulted for thinking like that. Look up. What do you see? A solid blue ceiling. It seemed logical at the time. From the perspective of the ancients, it likewise made sense. It was big, it was blue, and it was impressive. They too wondered what lay "beyond the blue!"

What indeed? Our ancestors figured it out. Water! There had to be water up there somewhere, because—duh—it rains! Where does that falling water come from? Obviously, it comes from a source out there above the sky. They surmised that there must be a "storehouse" for the rain, hail, and snow. Naturally, we cannot see anything, as it is beyond the blue ceiling. **And God said, "Let the water under the sky be gathered to one place, and let the dry ground appear." And it was so. God called the dry ground "land," and the gathered waters he called "seas." And God saw that it was good.** (Gen: 1:9,10).

The Genesis concept of the Earth is sort of like a pizza. It is round and flat, with an uneven surface. The dry ground—the land—floats on the seas. Beneath the dry ground is water. Ancient men knew this by digging down into the dry ground to get water. We call those things *wells*. All that being said, it is no wonder that the Bible writers assumed that there was water above and beneath the land upon which they were walking.

Then God said, "Let the land produce vegetation: seed-bearing plants and trees on the land that bear fruit with seeds in it, according to their various kinds." And it was so. The land produced vegetation: plants bearing seed according to their kinds and trees bearing fruit with seed in it according to their kinds. And God saw that it was good. And there was evening, and there was morning—the third day. (Gen. 1: 11-13).

This third day has always baffled me. For years there has been a debate going on among religious scholars (and non-scholars) about this business of the use of the word "day." The literalists—who claim the Bible is flawless— use their favorite word on this topic: *inerrant* (without errors). If it says "days" it means just that—*days*. God doesn't make mistakes. The Universe and the Earth were all created in six literal 24-hour days. The more interpretive types have argued that this is silly; these "days" are actually eons of time—epochs or something. This last idea is supposed to allow for dinosaurs, fossils, evolution, and all sorts of other prickly questions oft posed by nearly anyone who casually reads Genesis. I can certainly not be accused of being a literalist when it comes to this, but even the most liberal interpreters run into problems with day three no matter how you try to explain it.

Okay, granted, there is light from some source—sky, water, and land, with water above the sky and beneath the land. In any case, there are all these trees and various sundry types of vegetation covering the Earth by day three, but the Sun doesn't make its debut until day four. (Or eon four! Take your pick.) Either way, there isn't much accounting for photosynthesis, is there? Finally! **And God said, "Let there be lights in the expanse of the sky to separate the day from the night, and let them serve as signs to mark the seasons and days and years, and let there be lights in the expanse of the sky to give light on the earth." And it was so.** (Gen. 1: 14,15).

I'm confused again. We have already read that the light has been separated from the darkness, and that there has been enough light around already to grow plants and trees and shrubs and things. (Whether it is for a day or a zillion years.) Besides, there have already been "days" all along. Anyway, this is day four. So creating a sun and moon in order to mark the seasons, and delineate days and years, seems a bit late in coming. Now we read: **God made two great lights—the greater light to govern the day and the lesser light to govern the night. He also made the stars. This was the fourth day.** (Gen.1: 16).

Long before the astronauts walked on the Moon, scientists had pointed out that the Moon is not actually a light at all, but merely reflects light from the Sun. But the inerrantists insist that if the Bible says it is a light, then—by god—it is a light! So there! Well, at least now, with the entrance of the Sun and Moon... At least we finally have the days and nights in a more realistic perspective.

So the Sun was created to govern the day, and the Moon to govern the night. Fair enough. After getting the Sun and Moon in place, God finally gets around to making the stars. Whew, that makes me feel better. Let's talk about stars here. They get a lot of mention in the Bible, as well as in ancient texts all over the world. Since antiquity men have been fascinated with the stars. Some thought of them as little lights in the sky, which is quite dark at night, as we well know. And, for some reason, the Moon periodically fails to appear to govern the night as is his task. But, fortunately, on moonless nights we do still have the stars to guide us. That makes me feel good to know.

Actually, some of the ancients thought that those little lights were hanging on the inner surface of the blue dome. They figured this because from time to time one or more got bumped off and fell to the ground. We often still refer to meteors as "falling stars," don't we?

On the other hand, in order to make the story work, other wise men of old concluded that the stars were actually little holes in the solid dark sky. The dome was quite like an inverted kitchen colander. The first and most obvious reason is because it rains! The Bible already made it clear that there is water above the sky, so naturally it has to fall through those tiny holes to make rain drops. But there is another reason as well. God lives out there on the other side of the sky dome and his glory shines through those itsy-bitsy holes ... teasing us and urging us to aspire to share in that brilliant glory some day when we die. Cool, huh?

Oh yes ... day five. This provides plenty of material for controversy between contending schools of thought. Fish and other sea creatures are created now on this day, as are the birds. Science says that birds came later. But since over half of all Americans today believe the Bible over science, let's give them the bird. LOL. Anyway, by day six the land is now producing living creatures **—namely ... livestock, creatures moving along the ground, and wild animals, each according to its kind.** (Gen. 1: 24).

Out of order again. And even though we are told that the Bible is true, accurate and factual, on the one hand ... on the other, many things are reversed from what we are taught in school. For example, on day six, God creates livestock. I presume that means sheep, goats, cattle, and pigs. Livestock. I find it interesting that livestock are invented before wild animals.

At least the wild animals get a mention. But what has me scratching my head is that the livestock are around before man is. I was taught in school that mankind domesticated wild animals, making them into livestock. Maybe my teachers weren't inerrant, but one thing seems clear to me … all these sundry creatures—regardless of the order in which they were created—definitely needed somebody to *rule* over them!

At last! **Then God said, "Let us make man in our image, in our likeness, and let them rule over the fish of the sea and the birds of the air, the livestock, over all the earth, and over all the creatures that move along the ground." So God created man in his own image, in the image of God he created him; male and female he created them.** (Gen. 1: 26). Interesting— is it not—that God is now referred to in the plural? "Let us make man in our image."

Christians point out that this refers to the presence of Jesus Christ with the Father at creation, although I have a feeling that the Jews might disagree. I presume that Mary, the mother of God, would have been there too, along with the "heavenly host" of angels, cherubim and seraphim, and various sundry fallen angels floating around up there somewhere too. But that comes later in the story, so let's go on.

As to man … **God blessed them and said to them, "Be fruitful and multiply; fill the earth and subdue it. Rule over the fish of the sea and the birds of the air and over every living creature that moves on the ground." And it was so. God saw all that he had made, and it was very good. And there was evening and there was morning—the sixth day.** (Gen. 1: 28-31). Whew!

Considering all the various commands and charges that God has given to mankind in the Bible, these two given on the sixth day of creation have certainly been taken to heart. We surely have been fruitful enough, having overpopulated the planet quite well already. And to be sure, we have managed to really subdue the Earth as well. In fact, it has just about been subdued to death—wouldn't you agree? I wonder if this is what he had in mind. That's hard to fathom. All in all, I can't say much for God's organizational skills in creating the Universe in the most bass-ackwards way possible. But, hey, he got the job done!

God and Adam searched throughout the garden looking for a "suitable" helpmate. When they failed, God created the woman.

Adam and Eve in the Garden

On the seventh day he rested.

Now that everything is up and running, our story moves on. From the cosmos we come down to *Earth*—so to speak—and pick up in the Garden of Eden. **Thus the heavens and the earth were completed in all their vast array. By the seventh day God had finished the work he had been doing; so on the seventh day he rested from all his work. And God blessed the seventh day and made it holy, because on it he rested from all the work of creating that he had done.** (Genesis 2: 1-3).

Theologians and non-theologians both love to speculate as to the nature of God. Literalists insist that God is *omnipotent*. That means he is all-powerful. That makes sense to me. After all, he put this Universe together—albeit, in a rather discombobulated fashion—in a week. But what bothers me is … why would an omnipotent God need to rest? I mean, after all, he is all-powerful. If the creative process tired him out to the point where he needed to rest then he wouldn't really be omnipotent, would he? He would be almost omnipotent perhaps. Well, I am sure I cannot supply an answer for this, so—suffice it to say—he rested. In any case, he thereby created the seven-day work week and, "God knows," we all need a day of rest now and then.

But the second chapter of Genesis isn't all about resting. It has more to do with creation again. Now, the fundamentalists and other literalists make a point of saying that the Bible is perfect *as is* and that it is inviolable. So I will not recommend an editor, but one could really help straighten out chapter two for us—perhaps by putting it before the end of chapter one!

Actually, it was pointed out years ago that the hodgepodge presentation of the creation story is due to the fact that it had multiple authors. Scholars and careful observers have in fact already managed to recut the story and reorganize it in a much more sensible way. But to quote a tried and true sentiment, "If God wanted it to be any other way, he would have written it thusly." We dare not presume to become editors, as our tour is just an overview. But if the literalists are right—and God dictated it word for word, exactly in the form that we now find it—I do believe he could have used one. An editor, that is. And after all that, a cocktail perhaps.

In chapter one God created man and woman. This was on the sixth day. Chapter two is concerned with the details of that creation ... before he rested. And chapter two gives us more details about the Earth, before the plants got going on day three.

When the Lord made the earth and the heavens, no shrub of the field had yet appeared on the earth and no plant of the field had yet sprung up; the Lord God had not sent rain on the earth and there was no man to work the ground, but streams came up from the earth and watered the whole surface of the ground. (Gen. 2: 4-6).

This strains my imagination a bit, but no more than some of the other things we are likely to encounter as we proceed. Anyhow, God planted a garden in the east, in Eden. And there he put the man he had formed. We are all familiar with the story of the Garden of Eden (kind of). It contained all sorts of neat plants and trees. It is not clear if the garden was planted on day three, when the plants in general were being created, or whether it was on day six, simultaneous with the creation of man. But one thing is for sure; the garden was *before* the creation of woman, since God put the man into the garden to ... **work it and take care of it.** (Gen. 2: 15). Wherever the garden actually was is immaterial, I suppose, but Bible scholars love to speculate. It was in the "East"—wherever that is. East of what?

A river watering the garden flowed from Eden and from there it divided; it had four head-streams. The name of the first is the Pishon; it winds through the entire land of Havilah, where there is gold. (Gen. 2: 10-12). I have always wondered why gold is mentioned here. What has that got to do with the garden? Oh well. The second river is called Gihon; the third and fourth are the now famous and well known Tigris and Euphrates. That narrows it down a bit anyway. We all know from recent events that these rivers are in Iraq. What an ideal place for paradise!

The Lord God took the man and placed him in the Garden of Eden to work it and take care of it. And the Lord commanded the man, "You are free to eat from any tree in the garden; but you must not eat from the tree of the knowledge of good and evil, for when you eat of it you will surely die." (Gen. 2: 15-17). You see, in the middle of the garden was a special tree unlike all the other trees and shrubs... It was forbidden. Adam, the man that God had created out of the dust that day, was assigned to his task of tending God's garden right off the bat. He was to *work* in the garden.

Some paradise! Actually, I don't read anywhere in that section anything that says the garden was paradise as we have come to imagine it. The way I read it, God created man and then immediately put him to work. The man was also assigned to name all the various animals that were created on that same day. God brought these animals to the man. That sounds like a hell of a day's work to me. In any case it was obvious to the omnipotent God (who could have easily named all the animals himself if he had a mind to) that the man was a ditz on his own. How was he ever going to do all this thinking up of names for countless animal species, and tend to the garden as well? Obviously a "helper" was called for—and right away.

So the man gave names to all the livestock, the birds of the air and all the beasts of the field. But for Adam no suitable helper was found! (Gen. 2: 20). What? No *suitable* helper was found!? Duh! Where exactly did they look? Among the livestock, the birds, and the beasts? Like where *else* was there to look? I love that word. *Suitable*. Suitable for what?

He had to have finished naming the animals somehow. But it must have been a helluva job indeed, since there are 10,000 varieties of bears alone on our planet, not to mention different cat, dog, and deer species (to name a few). And then there was the livestock issue. Like, were horses wild or domesticated at this point? (Or both?) In any case, my favorite group is the dinosaurs. Half of all Americans do not believe in evolution. They believe this account: The Earth was created in six literal days, and God brought all the animal species to Adam to name. So I suppose he likely started out with the easy stuff like the Aardvark and ended up with the Zebra. But then God trotted out the Allosaurus, the Brontosaurus, the Diplodocus and—of course—the star of *Jurassic Park* fame, the T-Rex. Oh, how fun :-) Those fellows must have left the garden in a terrible mess—what, trampling down all the grass and shrubs and stuff.

What a job Adam had after all that! Obviously, God could see the damage caused by all those animals tromping through paradise. It was clear that help was severely needed. But instead of bringing on a crew of low-wage Hispanics to do the job, he gave Adam one helpmate! Just *one*! So God created a woman to be the helper. But, unlike the creation of the Earth and the sky and the waters (spontaneously from nothing) and unlike the birds and the beasts (from the ground, and the man from dust), he created woman differently...

He caused Adam **to fall into a deep sleep; and took one of his ribs and closed up the place with flesh. Then the Lord God made a woman from the rib he had taken out of the man, and he brought her to the man. The man said: "This is now bone of my bones and flesh of my flesh; she shall be called woman for she was taken out of man."** (Gen. 2: 21,22).

Very eloquent for a man who was just created that very day, exhausted after naming all the animals and dinosaurs, and facing a major clean up and garden replanting job, to boot. But wait, there's more! Before we get out of chapter two we are confronted with this non-sequitur ...**For that reason a man will leave his father and mother and be united to his wife, and they will become one flesh. The man and his wife were both naked, and they felt no shame.** (Gen. 2: 25).

What have fathers and mothers to do with any of this? We have already noted that God created both male and female on the sixth day. And all the events of chapter two appear to have happened before God rested. This whole episode with the naming of the animals, the charge to tend the garden and not to touch the Tree of Knowledge, and the creation of woman, all took place on day six. So where did this talk of fathers and mothers come from? Up to this point, it seems to me that nobody has yet even *had* a father or mother. I know full well that the fundamentalists of our day love this verse and often quote it. This, however, is an odd location for it. Looks like somebody has been editing along the way. The whole order of the story is totally out of whack.

Then, to make the whole thing even weirder, the obvious is stated: They were *naked*. Duh. They had been alive less than 24 hours; and—the matter of clothes notwithstanding—why the mention of *shame*? Obviously, as we shall see during our journey's progress, guilt and shame are very important throughout the biblical narrative. I'll tell you one thing... If it had been me there—less than a day old, and exhausted from naming animals and reptiles all day, stark naked, and facing a massive cleanup operation in the garden—I would have grabbed

OMG. They realized that they were buck naked—and they felt shame! So they whipped together some fig leaves to cover themselves. Very effective, huh?

the little woman right then and there and headed out of the garden straight for Pishon in the Land of Havilah (where there is gold)!

But instead, they stuck around tending the garden. Then they encountered their first problem. They met up with "the serpent." We will run into him from time to time as we go along on our tour. The story needs a "baddie" to make the whole thing work, and the serpent proves worthy of the role. In fact, he was rotten (to the core).

Now the serpent was more crafty than any of the wild animals the Lord God had made. He said to the woman, "Did God really say, 'You must not eat from any tree in the garden'?" She replied: "We must not eat from the tree in the middle of the garden, for if we touch it we will die." (Gen. 3: 1-3). **"You will not surely die," the serpent said to the woman. "For God knows that when you eat of it your eyes will be opened, and you will be like God, knowing good from evil."** (Gen. 3:4,5).

Without so much as an introduction, the serpent appears and discourses with the woman. They discuss God's prohibition against eating from the magic tree. We have been told over the years all about this tree by priests, rabbis, preachers, and televangelists. They tell us all about it—what it is like, what it represented, and why God put it there. Oddly enough, the Bible does not state any of this. The problem is that this particular story is so critical to the entire message of the Bible, and without an explanation it makes no sense. So, over the years writers and thinkers, philosophers and theologians, have built for us an elaborate explanation of what it all means.

God, they say, intended man to be good. God did not mean for humans to even know of evil. So he put a tree right in the middle of the garden that would offer this knowledge. Then he warned man not to touch it lest he die. Well, this is heavy stuff for a man who is only a day or so old. Many, like me, have wondered whether the point was that God needed it because he wanted man to love him, and that by putting the temptation there in the first place it would give man free will to choose to love God. By choosing not to touch the fruit, man was proving his love for God. See, because if God didn't provide the temptation in the first place, man would more or less be obligated to love God since there would be no alternative. On the other hand, even the word love has not even yet entered the scene at all. There is no talk of love, choice, or anything at all ... just the command: Don't touch the fucking tree! Period.

For those of us accustomed to hearing sermons expounding on what God was *actually* doing, thinking, and intending, this can make sense. However, if we just read it as is and stop editorializing, we are left in the dark. As on most tours, we are apt to learn a new word here and there. This is a case in point. It's time for a vocabulary builder. The word is *eisegesis*. It is defined by Webster's Online Dictionary as: *the interpretation of a text (as of the Bible) by reading into it one's own ideas.* And this—often referred to as the apple story—is a classic example. Although the Bible gives us no details at all as to the rationale or meaning of any of this, whole libraries have been spilled out over the centuries explaining it all to us in infinite detail. (Eisegesis)

Anyway, just sticking to the text, we definitely know a couple of things for sure: The serpent was crafty; the woman was either not too bright or mighty gullible; Adam was rather dull too—to be sure. So, the serpent smooth-talked them into taking a bite from the fruit of the forbidden tree. Well, suddenly they recognized that they were buck naked and they were embarrassed. They felt biblical-style shame. Thereupon, they quickly sewed some handy fig leaves together to cover themselves. I don't know about you, but little details like the sewing often trip me up. Like, where did they get the needle and thread in the garden? I guess wherever they got the hoes and shovels and rakes needed to tend it.

Anyhow, the plot then thickens. The man and wife heard the sound of the Lord as he was walking around in the garden. Quick, hide! But God called out (to the man): **"Where are you?" He answered, "I heard you in the garden, and I was afraid because I was naked; so I hid.** (Gen. 3: 9,10). If you pay attention to the ubiquitous religious programming on television today, you will surely know that there is an endless debate about the nature of God. We have already encountered the vocabulary word: *omnipotent*, which means all-powerful, and, now, *omniscient*, meaning "all-knowing." And finally we encounter a new word: *omnipresent*, everywhere at the same time! Pretty cool, huh? Only problem here is that he exhibits none of these qualities here in the garden. He is walking around in the garden like a human.

Cursed is the ground because of you.
So get the hell out of the garden and don't come back!

Isn't he supposed to be everywhere-present? He calls out to Adam: "Where are you?" Duh, shouldn't an omniscient god know already? After all, he is all-knowing. Well, you get the picture. We will get into this more specifically as we go along, so for now, suspend your disbelief and enjoy the movie.

Another question follows: **"Who told you that you were naked?"** (God is upset.) **"Have you eaten from the tree that I commanded you not to eat from?"** (Gen. 3: 11). Well, obviously they ate the fruit (but just a little bite). This is sort of like a parent asking a child if he ate any of the cookies from the cookie jar, easily noting the crumbs on the face and clothes. In the case of Adam and Eve, I think it was the fig leaves that gave them away. **"The woman you gave me—she gave me some fruit from the tree, and I ate it."** Then God says to the woman: **"What is this you have done?"** What indeed? But she passes the buck further... **"The serpent deceived me, and I ate."** (Gen. 3: 12,13).

God really didn't need to ask all these questions. We are told that he is omniscient; so he would have already known what they had done. He would have known it before they did it. He would have known that they were going to do it a-gazillion years before they were even created. After all, an omniscient god would certainly know the future if he knows everything. Therefore, if he already knew, why did he even bother to ask? In fact, if he knew in advance that they would eat the fruit, why did he put the temptation in front of them anyway? In fact, if he knew that mankind was going to totally trash the Earth, why even bother with the creation at all?

A contemporary debate swirling around in religious circles for the past several years asks this question: If God knew the future, was he obligated to *make* it happen? If he was obliged to make it all happen, then was he *powerless* to do otherwise? If he was powerless to do otherwise, is he then, in fact, *not* all-powerful after all? If he is not all-powerful... Oh, forget it. Arguments and debates like this have been vexing religious thinkers for centuries. Most folks who are troubled with stuff like this simply throw up their hands and declare, "We'll understand it all by and by." What a cop out! IMHO

Suffice it to say, that at this point God is pissed. He curses the serpent first. Now it has to crawl on its belly and eat dust forever. **"Cursed are you above** the livestock and all the wild animals! You will crawl on your belly and you will eat dust all the days of your life." (Gen. 3: 14). Then God curses the woman: "I will greatly increase your pains in childbearing; with pain you will give birth to children." (Gen. 3: 16). Then comes the first really great biblical sexist put-down … "Your desire will be for your husband, and he will rule over you." (Gen. 3: 16).

Women get a raw deal throughout the Bible as we shall see. Over the years, when men have felt it necessary to "put women in their place," they usually dredge up this old story of the forbidden fruit. "It's all your fault! … You started it!" Ah, but this is just the beginning. Okay, God cursed the snake and the woman. So, who's next? The man, of course. But not only that; while he   is at it, he curses the Earth as well! So much for divine environmentalism.
Here we go …

"Cursed is the ground because of you; through painful toil you will eat of it all the days of your life. (Gen. 3:17). Bear in mind that Adam is already assigned to tend the garden. From his first day of life, man was cursed to labor. But now it is going to be even more difficult, as the Earth will now produce thorns, thistles, and all manner of evil things to make life more complicated and unpleasant. All that over a measly piece of fruit! The words "love" and "justice" are found in the Bible, in relation to God, as are words like "forgiveness" and "loving kindness." *But not here.* Maybe God was having a bad day or perhaps he just needed another rest. Who knows? Well, those of the eisegesis persuasion can explain a whole lot here that is not revealed in any Bible. God simply curses all mankind to a bitter miserable existence and then death. *Life's a bitch and then you die.* Right out of the Old Testament.

"By the sweat of your brow you will eat your food until you return to the ground, since from it you were taken; for dust you are and to dust you will return." (Gen. 3: 19). Then: "He must not be allowed to reach out his hand and take also from the tree of life and eat, and live forever." (Gen. 3: 22).

This is the first hint of the issue of life and death, about which the Bible has a lot to say. Scholars and theologians tend to agree that from these verses we are able to assume that mankind was entitled to eternal life until they ate the apple. Thereupon, God cursed them to a mortal life of torture, pain, and eventual physical death. No hint of eternal life is promised or implied hereafter for quite a while. Instead man is promised to be returned to dust in the end. But after all the cursing, at least Adam finally decided to give the woman a name. **Adam named his wife Eve, because she would become the mother of all the living.** (Gen. 3: 20). **Then God made garments of skin for Adam and his wife and clothed them.** (Gen. 3: 21).

Obviously those tacky fig leaves just wouldn't do. Then he kicked them out of the garden! He didn't want them sneaking back in either, so he put a guard on duty to see that they stayed out. So, did he put up a *No Trespassing* sign? Heck no. He had a way cooler thing in mind. **On the east side of the Garden** (God put) **cherubim and a flaming sword flashing back and forth to guard the way to the tree of life.** (Gen. 3: 24). I have always wondered what ever happened to that flaming sword.

Millions of modern men and women of the 21st Century—living with computers, space laboratories, Moon and Mars landings, jet travel and satellite communications—still believe this tale literally. These are not closed-off monks in some dark forgotten abbey in a backwater mountain range in Moldavia somewhere. These are your relatives, friends, and neighbors who attend churches in your neighborhood on Sunday and sit next to you at work on Monday. They are also likely to be campaigning to have Genesis taught alongside science on Tuesday. Most are not really uneducated kooks. Some are actually school teachers, attorneys, and politicians. Some may even represent you in congress. Many of these people have the power to alter our world, our laws, and our lives. They take the Bible very seriously.

To them these accounts are real and the implications for us all are important. They contend that their scriptures are inerrant and factual in all matters of doctrine, philosophy, of history, and of science. And, even in the face of overwhelming evidence to the contrary, they still claim that we must believe it all as fact. In their black and white world it is simple. Either you believe it or you can go straight to hell. But we will get to all that as our tour rolls on.

Abel brought fat portions from the firstborn of his flock.
Cain got a quick lesson: God does not want cereal. He wants fat!

Cain and Abel

Am I my brother's keeper?

The nice thing about Genesis—in my opinion—is that the first half is full of neat and incredible stories, most of which we know already in some form or other. It falls off sharply after that, and we have to skip large portions to get back to familiar territory. But the nice thing about having a guide is that he is able to skip and skim for you, so as to avoid a lot of unnecessary verbiage, while making sure that you don't miss any of the good stuff. There is no doubt that the next story is definitely one of the good parts. Most of us have heard the story of Cain and Abel. But what really happened and what was it really all about? Let's see...

Adam lay with his wife Eve and she conceived and gave birth to Cain. Later she gave birth to his brother Abel. Abel kept flocks. (Genesis 4: 2,3). We don't know exactly where they were, but definitely not in the garden. Obviously, some of the livestock were expelled from the garden as well. Cain worked the soil. No further mention is made of what Adam did, but I presume he worked the soil as well, since God had cursed him to do so back in the garden. Remember that?

In the course of time Cain brought some of the fruits of the soil as an offering to the Lord. But Abel brought fat portions from some of the firstborn of his flock. The Lord looked with favor on Abel and his offering, but on Cain and his offering he did not look with favor. So Cain was angry and his face was downcast. (Gen. 4: 3-5).

God does not appear to be a vegetarian. After all, he was pleased with the fat offering of slain meat by Abel, but thought the cereal offering of Cain to be unacceptable. I have always thought this to be petty on God's part. He was pissed at Adam for eating one piece of fruit, and pissed at Cain for offering similar fare as an offering! And who instituted these offerings anyway? Up to this point nothing whatsoever is said of offerings. Obviously, no one explained to Cain that fruits of the soil were not going to make God happy. He wants fat! But God assumes that Cain knows better.

He chides Cain thusly: **"Why is your face downcast? If you do what is right, will you not be accepted? But if you do not do what is right, sin is crouching at your door; it desires to have you, but you must master it."** (Gen. 4: 6,7). What? Poor Cain. Just like his father, he runs afoul of God who tosses out this "if you do right" line, and condemns Cain with it even though there has been no indication yet of what "right" is. Then he points out that there is "sin" crouching at his door even though that has not been defined either. To top it all off, he is expected to "master" it. That is a tall order. For years theologians have pointed out that this verse implies that humankind "inherited" knowledge of good and bad, "right" and "wrong," and sin. For this reason, all are cursed and have no excuse, *because they should know better.* All are condemned like Cain. It becomes a major theme throughout the Bible and has been a great debate throughout the ages. We will encounter it again and again. You'll see.

The theologians and preachers love to editorialize about the next point. They say Cain offered out of his abundance only a small portion and Abel gave of his best ... The Bible does not say that. It says Cain offered some cereal and Abel offered some fat. God liked one and not the other. Period. It implies that Cain knew better and that was why he was mad at Abel. Somehow I think God was just having another one of his bad days. He never did like Cain as much as Abel anyway. Besides, if God were omniscient he would have already known that Cain was going to kill Abel, so it makes sense that he would be God's favorite. And as we will see, God definitely and often plays favorites.

Suffice it to say that Cain killed Abel out of jealousy. Then the Lord does the same number on Cain that he did on Adam ... (Remember this?) He asks: **"Where is your brother, Abel?"** (Gen. 4: 9). What kind of question is that? Obviously an omniscient god would already know. Playing cat and mouse with Cain, God asks further: **"What have you done?"** (Gen. 4: 10).

Finally, God gets tired of this guessing game, whereupon he curses Cain and drives him from the ground. What was the curse? Get this: No longer will he have a green thumb. Nothing will grow for him. (I know the feeling.) He is cursed to be a restless wanderer on the Earth. **"My punishment is more than I can bear! I will be a restless wanderer on the earth, and whoever finds me will kill me!"** (Gen. 4: 14). What? Who in the world is going to find him? Isn't he one of only three people on the planet at this point? Duh.

"My punishment is more than I can bear!" Cain wails. So he heads out
to the land of Nod and takes a wife there. ...Where did she come from?

This is the first mention in the Bible of other people. Who are they and where did they come from? Hmmm. The theologians say these other people refer to Eve's other offspring, as she was the mother of all the living. In order for the whole story to work as is, we have to go along with that. Okay. Assuming that is the case, Cain went out from the Lord's presence and lived in the land of Nod, east of Eden. A bit of geography here: Since we know Eden was in Iraq, and Nod is east of there, presumably he ends up in Iran! This story... Gotta love it!

Cain lay with his wife and she gave birth to Enoch. Much ado has been made about his wife. Well, if there were others out there to kill him, they were of necessity his brothers; his wife is of necessity his sister. The fundamentalists today would pillory anyone even hinting at incest, as it is expressly forbidden by the Bible (found in Leviticus 20: 17). Yet here it is in black and white. In any case, Cain and one of his sisters took up residence in the Land of Nod. I have often wondered if they were the first ones to get there and if they were the ones to name it or if others were there already. I have also wondered if they stopped off en route to Nod to visit the flaming sword flashing back and forth to guard the way to the tree of life there in Eden. I guess we will never know.

The Land of Nod. Now that's a catchy name. I have always liked that. In fact, it is appropriate as from that point on I usually begin to *nod* off, myself. In fact, this gets really boring as we go on because these people lived so long! For example ... **When Adam had lived 130 years, he had a son in his own likeness, in his own image; and he named him Seth. After Seth was born Adam lived 800 years and had other sons and daughters. Altogether Adam lived 930 years, and then he died.** (Gen. 5: 3).

It goes on and on. I don't think it takes much of a mathematician to figure out that these early sons of the Earth were doing something right. If I could figure out how they managed to live to be over 900, I would definitely give that a shot. And in addition to living that long, they were screwing like crazy up to the end. The population of the Earth increased dramatically and, according to the record in chapter six, so did *wickedness*. Huh, what's that? We'll run into that word a lot as we go on. **The Lord saw how great man's wickedness on the earth had become, and that every inclination of the thoughts of his heart was only evil all the time. Then the Lord grieved that he had made man on the earth and his heart was filled with pain. (Gen. 6: 5,6).**

So God has a heart? If we read it literally, he must. If he has a heart, that implies that he has the rest of a body somewhere. But that flies in the face of the omnipresent theory, doesn't it? Naturally, a regular body would be confined within space and time, whereas a spirit could conceivably be omnipresent. But, we continue to note, God seems to have other quite human attributes. He sees, he hears, he walks and talks, and now he feels. If he sees, does he have actual eyes? How about ears to hear, a nose to smell, and all that? If he has a heart, does he have the full complement of other organs to go along, making a regular human body?

Actually, these are called *anthropomorphisms*. They are not to be taken literally. Why not? They want us to take everything else literally. Well, they have a problem here and it is not easily explained away. On the one hand, they insist that the Bible is literal. But in some cases—like these—it is *not really* literal ... just *sort of* literal. What it boils down to is that one has to know when it is being literal and when it is being figurative. How does one know these things? It is obvious, they say. An omnipresent god cannot be limited by the confines of a flesh and blood body. An omnipresent god does not have a literal beating heart. That is figurative.

Okay, then who is to say that the serpent in the garden was not figurative as well? OMG no, they chant. That is *real*. That is to be taken literally. Oh, I see. Nevertheless, we do know that God has a temper. What got his dander up in this case? Well, here it is...

When men began to increase in number on the earth and daughters were born to them, the sons of God saw that the daughters of men were beautiful, and they married any of them they chose. (Gen. 6: 1,2). What? The Nephilim were on the earth in those days—and also afterward— when the sons of God went to the daughters of men and had children by them. (Gen. 6:4).

Theologians, Bible students, preachers, and televangelists, have never agreed on who the *Nephilim* actually were. Some say angels; some giants; others say extraterrestrials. Anyway, sort of like the Greek gods from Olympus, they "came down" from beyond the sky and mated with Earth women. It says that they really had the hots for the beautiful ones especially. Of course, they had children by them too. The Holy Bible refers to these offspring as: **The heroes of old, men of renown.** (Gen. 6:4).

I have always wondered what ever happened to those guys. Well, sort of like that flaming sword guarding the east gate of the Garden of Eden ... gone but not forgotten. But, true to form, God is upset with this arrangement. He does not seem to go for this interplanetary marriage between the Nephilim and Earth women. So what does he do? He cuts down man's lifespan!

"My spirit will not contend with man forever, for he is mortal; his days will be a hundred twenty years." (Gen. 6: 3). Nice try. But that really didn't help much, did it? **The Lord saw how great man's wickedness on the earth had become, and that every inclination of the thoughts of his heart was only evil all the time.** (Gen. 6:5).

I have always loved the quaint King James Bible's fossilized choice of words here. It says God "repented" at having made mankind. God had blown it. He made a mistake. Now he was going to have to undo what he had done.

It has often been asked how an omniscient god could make a mistake like that. The Fundies say that it was not really a mistake. Others point out that he would have already known that he was going to be upset with mankind, and could clearly see into the future, and know that he would have to do something; so he was forced to act. You know the argument already. If he was obliged to do it on the basis of his foreknowledge, was he then not powerless to do otherwise? If powerless, how could he be all-powerful? The Ol' Biblical Catch-22. It comes up again and again in pages ahead. See if you can catch them :-)

Either way ... **The Lord was grieved that he had made man on the earth and his heart was filled with pain. So the Lord said, I will wipe mankind, whom I have created, from the face of the earth—men and animals, and creatures that move along the ground, the birds of the air—for I am grieved that I have made them.** (Gen. 6: 6,7).

And wipe them out he did! For that story we need to meet a new character. Noah is one of the truly beloved men of renown in the Bible. His famous ark-building and animal-gathering experiences are legendary. The story of Noah's Ark is the next stop on our tour. So get out your umbrellas. It's gonna rain :-)

God promises never again to destroy the world with water.
Next time it's going to be fire!

Noah's Ark

Noah found favor in the eyes of the Lord!

Noah was a righteous man, blameless among the people of his time, and he walked with God. (Genesis 6: 9). God walked in the garden and Noah walked with God. The literalists are stuck with a lot of baggage, and this tale is one of those unbelievable accounts they are stuck trying to defend as actual fact. Really, it is so preposterous as to be no fun at all. Everybody has taken pot shots at the ark story over the years. For that reason I'll just take a "once over lightly" approach since we will definitely find far more esoteric folly ahead. Anyway, Noah was about 600-years-old (despite the 120-year life limit) when God told him that he was sick of all the sin and corruption on the Earth.

God said to Noah: "I am going to put an end to all people, for the earth is filled with violence because of them. I am surely going to destroy both them and the earth. So make yourself an ark of cypress wood; make rooms in it and coat it with pitch inside and out. This is how you are to build it: (Cubits converted to feet) ... **The ark is to be 450 feet long, 75 feet wide and 45 feet high.** Note: That would make it, like, half the size of the *Titanic.*

I am going to bring flood waters on the earth to destroy all life under the heavens, every creature that has breath of life in it." The Lord said to Noah, "Go into the ark, you and your whole family, because I have found you righteous in this generation. Take with you seven of every kind of clean animal, a male and its mate, and two of every kind of unclean animal, a male and its mate, and also every kind of bird, male and female, to keep their various kinds alive throughout the earth. Seven days from now I will send rain on the earth for forty days and forty nights, and I will wipe from the face of the earth every living creature that I have made." (Gen. 6: 13-21). **And Noah did all that the Lord commanded him.** (Gen. 6: 22).

Okay, stop and just think about this. Noah and his three sons had six days to build a ship the size of the Titanic ... out of *wood*! Then God brought all animal species; mammals, amphibians, and reptiles (including dinosaurs) to Noah. He brought the birds as well. Nothing is said of fish or aquatic mammals, I always wondered how they got there and how their dietary needs were met for such an extended stay on that pitch-covered boat.

Years ago, as a young believer, I tried to run this story through my fairly pliable mind. Coming up short on ideas and excuses, I read a book entitled *The Genesis Flood*. It answered all my simpleminded questions, like: How did the pandas from China and the koalas from Australia all manage to get to the ark at the exact same time to file in two by two? The author surmised that they would have had to start walking and swimming years in advance of the actual date. But even by then I was aware that Pandas only eat a certain type of bamboo, and that the koala's diet is exclusively eucalyptus leaves. Of course, neither he nor the Bible addressed the question of what all these creatures were supposed to eat during their epic voyage. But just ignore that for now as we will understand it all by and by. So the story continues...

According to the weather report, it rained for forty days and nights. And it flooded the entire Earth, killing everything. **The waters rose and increased greatly on the earth, and the ark floated on the surface of the water. They rose greatly on the earth, and all the high mountains under the entire heavens were covered. The waters rose and covered the mountains to a depth of more than twenty feet.** (Gen. 7: 18).

Every living thing that moved on the earth perished—birds, livestock, wild animals, all the creatures that swarm over the earth, and all mankind. Everything on dry land that had breath of life in its nostrils died. Only Noah was left, and those with him in the ark. The waters flooded the earth for a hundred and fifty days. (Gen. 7: 21). Another point of interest that any decent tour guide would likely draw your attention to is that in addition to rain, water bubbled up from under the Earth. Or as the Bible puts it, **"The springs of the great deep burst forth!"** (Gen. 7:11).

Remember, under the flat pizza-like Earth (or dry land as scripture calls it), there is water. So, after forty days and nights of rain and a total artesian extravaganza, the Bible says that the ark came to rest on Mt. Ararat—which is in Turkey. So, let's talk about mountains. Likely, the writer of this fairytale never had seen a mountain higher than, say, the Mount of Olives in Jerusalem. It is a grand total of 380 meters (2500 ft.) high. Wow. Haha, those aren't even foothills compared to the Alps, the Andes, and—above all—the Himalayas. Not to be too nitpicky here, but it does say emphatically that the water covered *all* the mountains under heaven. All means *all* to literalists—and me.

Mt. Everest and K2 are both over 29,000 feet high. Water that deep would be the equivalent of the depth of the deepest part of any world ocean, namely the Mariana(s) Trench. Now that's a *lot* of water! Scientists refer to that as "crush depth." At least the writer got one thing right: *Nothing* could have survived that inundation. But where did the water go?

Now the springs of the deep and the floodgates of the heavens had been closed, and the rain had stopped falling from the sky. The water receded steadily from the earth—for one hundred and fifty days. (Gen. 8: 2,3).

I am quoting from a modern translation here but, in this case, I like the earlier versions better, where they say that the water simply "ran off." Remember, the Earth is a flat pizza, so for centuries this explanation presented no problem. Everybody at the time "knew" that all that water could simply run off the edge of the Earth and fall off into empty space.

This problem for the modern mind is enough to make even the most fundamental literalist squirm in his or her pew. And there are many who *claim* to believe this still. Of course, I too once upon a time tried to believe this, and paid lip service to it, but just wasn't really buying it. One time when I was doing missionary work in the Philippines, my wife and I attended an evangelistic rally featuring a "world famous" preacher. I was not impressed with him or his message. But I had been assigned to escort him and his wife from the rally site to his hotel, and take them to a late dinner after the shindig was over.

Later I learned that, as the "young guy," I had to put my time in, entertaining various traveling kooks. Nobody else wanted to do it, so I was elected. Anyway, during the course of a rather tense dinner, the subject of the flat Earth came up. He was adamant that it was indeed flat if the Bible said so. He trotted out that cliché: "I don't try to understand or interpret the scripture. I just read it and believe it." I said nothing more. But later that night I mentioned to my wife how odd it was that a flat-Earther could be making an "around-the-world" speaking tour.

The problem here is one that we have already encountered during the wacko, out-of-order creation story. If the Bible makes a statement that is provably untrue, and a literalist admits that it is wrong, it begs the next question: Well then, what else may be untrue, wrong, or false? As anyone might imagine, that could bring the whole house of cards down. Believe me, we will encounter this conundrum many times along our tour, so just think about it as we go on. Most of us think Noah's story just ends here with all the various animals merrily hopping away to procreate and repopulate the Earth. That would be a nice, tidy Hollywood ending, but Noah's story goes on and then ends in a rather disturbing way. Let's see what happened next.

All the animals and all the creatures that move along the ground and all the birds—everything that moves on the earth—came out of the ark, one kind after another. Then Noah built an altar to the Lord and taking some of the clean animals and clean birds, he sacrificed burnt offerings on it. The Lord smelled the pleasing aroma and said in his heart: "Never again will I curse the ground because of man, even though every inclination of his heart is evil from childhood. And never again will I destroy all living creatures, as I have done." (Gen. 8: 19-21).

So Noah was happy. He built an altar and—slaughtering some "clean" birds and animals, dripping their blood all over the place—set it alight. God was thrilled. He accepted the offering as he had received Abel's fat offering. At least Noah knew not to offer *cereal*. We know what happens then. Anyway, moving right along... Then God blessed Noah and his sons, saying to them:

"Be fruitful and increase in number and fill the earth. The fear and dread of you will fall upon all the beasts of the earth and all the birds of the air, upon every creature that moves along the ground, and upon all the fish of the sea; they are given into your hands. Everything that lives and moves will be food for you." (Gen. 9: 1). Oh, but there is one more rule...**"You must not eat meat that has its lifeblood still in it. And for your lifeblood I will surely demand an accounting. I will demand an accounting from every animal. And from each man too I will demand an accounting for the life of his fellow man."** (Gen. 9: 4,5). What?

God is going to demand an accounting. What the hell is an accounting? What is it for? Moreover, what are the animals supposed to account for? This is really vague and unclear. And it is just left there without any further explanation. Of course, that is the televangelist's job ... to fill in the blanks and tell us what he or she thinks it means (according to their own preconceived ideas and notions, that is). Remember the word *eisegesis*? Hmmm. And as long as they are positing about accountings (both human and animal), here is a nonsequitur that is just another biblical hanging chad: **"Whoever sheds the blood of man, by man shall his blood be shed; for in the image of God has God made man."** (Gen. 9: 6). This sounds fair, I guess. What goes around comes around, right? In other words, don't kill anybody or you're going to get it yourself. Advice from someone who has just killed all mankind and all the animal kingdom in the previous chapter of scripture. Go figure.

Now, I don't know if God was truly sorry that he drowned everybody on the planet—save Noah's clan and all those cute fuzzy animals as well. Maybe Noah's blood sacrifice/burnt offering was pleasing to the point of a reconsideration. But we do know that God made an agreement with Noah—and by extension, to all mankind—never again to kill all Earthlings with a flood. And God said, **"This is the sign of the covenant I am making between me and you and every living creature with you, a covenant for all generations to come. I have set my rainbow in the clouds, and it will be the sign of the covenant between me and the earth. Whenever I bring clouds over the earth and the rainbow appears, I will remember my covenant between me and you and all living creatures of every kind."** (Gen. 9: 12,13).

A *rainbow*? What a beautiful sign! What a gorgeous symbol! You would think that Christians would dance with joy. God chose a rainbow to remind him of his promise to respect life from then on. But they hate the rainbow symbol, as it has become in recent years, the symbol of gay pride and diversity ... two things rip-snorting Fundies hate the most. Well, I guess while they were warping themselves into pretzels over abortion and gun rights, the gays simply stole their symbol right out from under them! Haha.

But all that aside ... the story of Noah, the guy who walked with God, didn't really end well for a lot of us. Here's what happened next: Noah and his sons came out of the ark, and Noah, being a man of the soil, planted a vineyard. Well, where there is a vineyard there are grapes; and where there are grapes there is wine; and where there is wine, can scandal be far behind?

"When he drank some of its wine, he became drunk and lay uncovered inside his tent." (Gen. 9: 21).

Okay, so Noah got drunk and passed out in his tent ... stark naked. So? This is the first mention of both drunkenness and nakedness in the same breath. Mankind had been getting drunk and naked for years, fulfilling God's earlier admonishment to be fruitful and multiply. Then God got pissed at them for doing what he had ordered them all to do, and killed everybody because they were wicked. The fundamentalists say that wickedness is sex-based, but here we have the most righteous man on Earth falling down drunk, embarrassing his boys. So what do they do?

Ham, the father of Canaan, saw his father's nakedness and told his two brothers outside. But Shem and Japheth took a garment and laid it across their shoulders; then they walked in backwards and covered their father's nakedness. Their faces were turned the other way so that they would not see their father's nakedness. (Gen. 9: 22,23). They were discreet.

Perhaps we should ask a televangelist to interpret this for us. I really don't see what all the fuss was about. Noah passed out nude in his tent and two of his kids covered him up (without peeking). Big deal. Simple enough. But when he woke up he was furious. He was livid. Hell, he was pissed.

When Noah awoke from his wine and he found out what his youngest son had done to him, he said, "Cursed be Canaan! The lowest of slaves will he be to his brothers." He also said, "Blessed be the Lord, the God of Shem! May Canaan be the slave of Shem. May God extend the territory of Japheth; may Japheth live in the tents of Shem, and may Canaan be his slave." (Gen. 9: 24-27).

Cursed be Canaan! What? Canaan, Ham's son and Noah's grandson, had absolutely nothing to do with this story at all. He wasn't even there! So why did Noah curse him? The answer is simple: Nobody knows. I have heard preachers, priests, pastors, rabbis, and other miscellaneous teachers, theologians, and "Bible scholars" all try to explain this weirdity. And I have read countless Bible commentaries—among them the massive *Liberty Bible Commentary* by Jerry

After surviving those long days in the ark, Noah gets rip-roaring drunk and passes out (stark naked). Fortunately, his boys covered him up—without peeking!

Falwell. The whole lot of them, including Jerry himself, just dance around and around, and, in the end, expose their total ignorance. Another biblical mystery.

Well, anyway, at least we can point out that this is the first mention of *slavery* in the Bible. But, believe me, it won't be the last. In fact, on our tour this subject will come up frequently and most disturbingly. The institution of slavery was introduced on the Earth by Noah, the man who walked with God. Noah was still so in with God that he could curse his own grandson and his descendants into slavery, and be sure that God would adjudicate it on his behalf. Talk about God playing favorites. And there are more of those ahead. I call them God's pets.

Anyway, Noah lived another 350 years (despite the 120-year limit) and, at 950, he died. But his curse went on and on. We will leave it at that for now as we will encounter it with a vengeance later on our tour, and I don't want to spoil it for you :-(This story blends into the next; but keep in mind that Noah had other sons, most notably Cush, another of the brothers. He had a son called Nimrod who grew to **be a mighty warrior on the earth. He was a mighty hunter before the Lord.** (Gen. 10: 9).

This is the first use of the word war/warrior in the Bible, another theme we will encounter constantly along our tour route. When we read this section we are sorely tempted to compare this primitive enchantment with hunters and warriors to accounts from other ancient tribal peoples. The Bible, however, emphatically states that the sons of Noah repopulated the Earth after the flood; and since God had killed everything with breath in its nostrils during the flood, there were no other peoples on the Earth with which to compare these sons. So, if Nimrod was such a heavy duty warrior, with whom did he make war? The only possibility would be his brother's kids—his nephews and their offspring.

So, be prepared ... we will return to the Biblical fascination with warriors and war a lot as our tour moves on to the next issue: *misunderstanding*. Or more specifically, misinterpretations. We read ... **These are the descendants of Ham by their clans and languages, in their territories and nations.** (Gen. 10: 31). Note the use of the word "languages" (plural). Moving right along... Next stop, Babel!

God confuses the languages of mankind to prevent the completion of the Tower of
Babel, and, simultaneously, sows the seeds of endless misunderstandings.

The Tower of Babel

"Come, let us go down and confuse their language
so they will not understand each other."

Now the whole earth had one language and a common speech. (Genesis 11:1). What? Didn't we just read in the last chapter about Ham's descendants, their territories, nations, and languages (plural)? Oh well, ignore that. The Bible is inerrant. Ask the nearest televangelist to explain it. Believe me—he or she will, even if they have to make something up.

As men moved eastward, they found a plain in Shinar and settled there. They said to each other, "Come, let's make bricks and bake them thoroughly." They used brick instead of stone, and tar instead of mortar. Then they said, "Come, let us build ourselves a city, with a tower that reaches to the heavens, so that we may make a name for ourselves and not be scattered over the face of the whole earth." (Gen. 11: 2-4).

So, it appears that mankind after the flood, in some fashion, has his collective act together. He has a common language and is repopulating the Earth. Some men had the idea to stop plodding eastward nomadically, and to settle down and build a city. Sounds fine to me. God hated this idea.

By this time, several other cities are mentioned, including Nineveh, Ir, Claha, Resen, and Rehoboth (not to be confused with the beach resort in Delaware). God doesn't seem to be upset with the idea that these cities have sprung up. We already note that certain men are tilling the land, gleaning whatever meager sustenance they can from it, living out God's curse on Adam—feeding their faces by the sweat of their brows. Others appear to be nomadic, like Abel, tending flocks (livestock). Others, like Nimrod, were "mighty hunters before the Lord." Presumably, they were hunting wild animals and not their relative's livestock :-) Still others appear to congregate in cities like Nineveh and Rehoboth.

God seems to have tolerated these urban areas, but all of a sudden, in typical God-like fashion, he sees men building a city and is threatened. **But the Lord came down to see the city and the tower that the men were building. The Lord said, "If as one people speaking the same language they have begun**

to do this, then nothing they plan to do will be impossible for them. Come, let us go down and confuse their language so they will not understand each other." (Gen. 11:5-7).

"Let us go down" ... So they came *down*. Hmmm, let us—who is "us?" Most modern preachers say that God brought Jesus down with him to inspect the construction project. Like a lot of stuff in the Bible that we will encounter on our tour, this is not clear. It could just as easily have been Satan or an angel or two. And down from where? Would an omnipresent being even need to use prepositions like up and down? Remember, that new vocabulary word means *everywhere*-present! Hmmm.

So, why all these questions? The way I look at it, this just proves that the God of the Bible is not in fact omnipresent at all, but, rather, that he is confined to place—occupying only one place at a time and not everywhere at the *same time*. Nevertheless, the real neat thing about these verses is that they give us another indication of the nature of the Almighty as portrayed in the Holy Bible. He is threatened. And by *man*! Wow, that's heavy. The men of Babel are not just building a city, but a *tower*! OMG, the cheek! How dare they? And why were they building this terrible tower in the first place? To make a name for themselves. Wow, I am totally unimpressed. But God was flabbergasted. We simply cannot have all this cooperation and robust ambition. It simply must be stopped.

The Lord said, "If as one people speaking the same language they have begun to do this, then nothing they plan to do will be impossible for them." (Gen. 11: 6). Think about this for a minute. Corporately, man is pulling himself up after being annihilated by God's flood. He is subduing the Earth as God commanded, ruling over the wild animals and the livestock, and being fruitful and multiplying. Sounds rather compliant to me. He is being a farmer, a shepherd, and a hunter/warrior. Now he tries his hand at being an architect. But that is going too far! He will have to be stopped—thwarted.

Nothing they plan to do will be impossible for them! Does God have mankind's best interest at heart here? What conceivably could man possibly plan that could so threaten the omnipotent, almighty God? In this age of increasing desire for unity and understanding, it rankles that God intentionally thwarted man's best efforts to plan something grand and expansive on his own.

Looking back as we can from our cities of hundred-plus-story buildings of steel and glass, this offensive tower of brick and tar seems a bit lackluster a thing to raise God's ire to such an extent. But it did! God came down and took a look at that tower and concluded that mankind was way too ambitious. If man could achieve something of this magnitude on his own, just imagine what things he might possibly accomplish. Just think of what he might think up next! Ooo.

I have always been a bit upset by God's meddling here. "Nothing they plan will be impossible for them." Well, what is wrong with that? Think of all the great things man could have planned, but God had to throw a monkey wrench into things. Why? He is nonplussed, threatened. He doesn't want mankind to be able to think for himself—to accomplish, to imagine, to innovate. And I have heard a lot of sermons on this very topic, praising God for dissuading man from getting too big for his britches and making all sorts of newfangled things when we would all be better off without modern stuff like cars, computers, and central heating (to name a few). Haha, and I thought Republicans were reactionary! Obviously, they learned from the big guy himself.

God seems to have a vested interest in making sure that some things are impossible for man. So to make sure, he says, **"Let us go down and confuse their language so they will not understand each other."** (Gen. 11: 7).

God sees mankind accomplishing really big things ahead, like cooperating in a building program that is sure to be the ultimate human achievement. Man is building a tower of brick and tar that is going to reach up to the heavens! If this omnipotent god were indeed who the scriptures claim he is, he would have just chuckled at man's paltry efforts to reach up to the heavens with such a lame attempt. But instead, he reveals his insecurity when he fears man's capacity and sets out to throw stumbling blocks in his way.

So the Lord scattered them from there over all the earth, and they stopped building the city. (Gen. 11: 8). Bummer. Man's one unified language is garbled and many appear. As a result, man ceases work on the city and the tower. God is happy. He is still top dog. Man is unhappy. He is now scattered all over the planet and is unable to understand his fellow man. So, whereas mankind was on a cooperative trajectory, with the ability to understand each other and follow through with getting things done, now there is chaos. Clans, tribes—all speaking different languages—began to misunderstand one another, and then distrust each other. They do not understand the intent of the heart. Fear and suspicion grow. They begin to fight, to kill and to die, all because of the language barrier that God implemented. All because of that stupid hokey tower of bricks and tar.

You know, even the grandest of man's architectural achievements—whether in stone, steel, or some modern alloy—all look puny from the air. This tower was made of bricks and tar, but, due to God's paranoia, has cursed man to endless misunderstandings and conflicts.

Too bad God didn't just let man keep going until the whole thing collapsed under its own weight like what happened to one of the first Egyptian pyramids. I have always loved that account. Many scientists also point out that an ark the size of the one described in the last chapter—built of wood and held together by pitch—could not possibly sustain its own weight without collapsing. Well, at least we all got a really cool word out of the Egyptian construction incident. The builder of the doomed structure was named (get this) Snafu. Total LOL! *Snafoo!*

God establishes a far-reaching covenant with Abraham. **Any uncircumcised male will be cut off**... (Exiled). **He has broken my covenant.** (Gen. 17:14) Whew!

Abraham

"I will make your offspring like the dust of the earth."

Have you noticed that God has this propensity for selecting humans and letting them get away with crimes, while cursing others? I guess it's just a quirk, but Abraham is a case in point. This fellow starts out life as "Abram" and God changes his name half way through our story—so don't get confused. I'll point out when that occurs.

The Lord said to Abram, "Leave your country and go to the land I will show you. I will make you into a great nation and I will bless you; I will make your name great, and you will be a blessing. I will bless those who bless you and whoever curses you I will curse; and all peoples on earth will be blessed through you." (Genesis 12: 1-3).

God himself sets the stage for future conflict. He promises a man, Abram, that he will bless him and curse his enemies. So much for the myth that *all men are created equal*. Whether or not Jefferson was referring to the Bible when he wrote that into the *Declaration of Independence*, is not clear. But even on a quick tour like ours through the "good book," obviously it is not true.

So, Abram left, as the Lord had told him; and Lot went with him. Abram was seventy-five years old when he set out from Haran. He took his wife Sarai, his nephew Lot, and his possessions they had accumulated and the people they had acquired in Haran, and they set out for the land of Canaan, and they arrived there. (Gen. 12: 4,5).

Abram owned slaves. And that subject is of great importance throughout the Bible, but we will come back to it later on and look at it more in-depth. His slaves aren't a big part of this story, but notice how casually they were mentioned. We will devote a whole chapter to that gut-wrenching issue ahead.

Now there was a famine in the Land, and Abram went down to Egypt to live there for a while because the famine was severe. As he was about to enter Egypt, he said to his wife Sarai, "I know what a beautiful woman you

are. When the Egyptians see you they will say, "This is his wife." Then they will kill me but will let you live. Say you are my sister so that   I will be treated well for your sake and my life will be spared because of you." (Gen. 10: 13).

To save his own skin, Abram concocted a lie. If anyone else had done so, God would likely have condemned him right there on the spot because ... **The Lord detests lying lips, but he delights in men who are truthful.** (Proverbs 12: 22). Notice, Abram gets special treatment from God. When we regard Biblical double standards, we can think of Abel, now Abram... (And just wait till we get to David!)

Anyway—sure enough—the Egyptians saw that Sarai was beautiful and immediately whisked her off to Pharaoh's den of iniquity, commonly known as a harem. I have always figured that she must have really been a knockout, as she would have been around 65 at this time. But what did righteous Abram do? He took full advantage of his "bad" situation and saw how he could profit from his sad predicament. In fact, Pharaoh made sure of it. **Pharaoh treated Abram well for her sake, and Abram acquired sheep and cattle, male and female donkeys, menservants and maidservants and camels.** (Gen. 12:16).

Abram acquired beasts and slaves (adding to those he brought with him from his last gig in Haran). He seemed totally cool with this. He took full advantage of his lucrative situation. All the while God is sanctioning this. Nowhere does God say that slavery is wrong or immoral. Nowhere does he tell Abram that he should not lie or that he should free those whom he owned. But—suffice it to say—in addition to humans, Abram also got some good camels out of the deal. I am impressed.

What bothers me about this section is that God is so *willing* to give human slaves into Abram's greedy hands ... and Abram is so willing to trade off his wife for some cattle, sheep, and camels. When I consider the gut-wrenching agony that the slavery issue wrought in the US alone in the past... Shouldn't it bother us that God was not only willing to let Abram's lie stand, but that he gave him all sorts of loot as a reward? If you think that is unfair, take note of what comes next.

But the Lord inflicted serious diseases on Pharaoh and his household because of Abram's wife Sarai. (Gen.12: 17). We recall that when God drowned all of humanity and the animal kingdom in the great flood, he had a reason at least. They were all "wicked," so they deserved to die. But here he inflicts illness on totally innocent people. It happened because Pharaoh took Sarai, Abram's wife, unknowingly. The way I see it, God and Abram and Sarai were all promoting a lie; and just because God can do whatever he wants, he slaps disease on Pharaoh and his family and subjects. When we get to the story of Job we will see another example of God inflicting disease, but in that case he ravaged one of his most ardent admirers. Much ado is made in Exodus about God sending plagues on Pharaoh when he refused to liberate the Israelites from bondage in Egypt, but that's all ahead. Meanwhile, and finally, Pharaoh confronts Abram with the lie.

"What have you done to me?" he said. "Why didn't you tell me she was your wife? Why did you say, 'she is my sister,' so that I took her to be my wife? Now then, here is your wife. Take her and go!" Then Pharaoh gave orders about Abram to his men, and they sent him on his way with his wife and everything he had. (Gen. 12: 18-20). I am sure the preachers on TV and "Christian" radio have all sorts of reasons and excuses for God's appalling behavior in this case. But I doubt that they would convince me. Okay, time for another of God's "covenants." And you're going to like this one. Or, likely, it will leave you scratching your head. Here we go ... **God took him outside and said, "Look at the heavens and count the stars—if indeed you can count them. Then he said to him, "So shall your offspring be."** (Gen. 15: 5).

God promises at this point to give Abram and his descendants a particular piece of real estate which, of course, is already occupied by somebody else. The interesting thing to note here is that at this juncture, God sows the seeds of future conflict, which are still causing bloodshed in the Middle East to this day. But as in the unfair and ruthless treatment of Pharaoh, God just arbitrarily favors Abram and promises him that he will occupy the land. When Abram questions whether he will really be able to gain possession of it, God replies in a most bizarre way (dig this):

"Bring me a heifer, a goat and a ram, each three years old, along with a dove and a young pigeon. Abram brought all these to him, cut them in two and arranged the halves opposite each other... (Gen. 15: 9,10). I have always wondered what sort of thrill God got out of killing heifers, goats, doves, and the like. I have also wondered why in this particular case each had to be exactly three years old! Weird, huh? But wait, there's more!

When the sun had set and darkness had fallen, a smoking fire pot with a blazing torch appeared and passed between the pieces. On that day the Lord made a covenant with Abram and said, "To your descendants I give this land…" (Gen. 15: 17). What do you suppose was the significance of the smoking fire pot and the blazing torch? I wonder if it had anything to do with the flaming sword flashing back and forth at the entrance to the Garden of Eden, when Adam and Eve were evicted. Oh, no big deal. There's more like that to come, so on with our story.

The problem for Abram was that he had no children. Now that was a big problem in ancient tribal societies. Anyway, Abram was about 85 at the time, way back when he was not scheduled to live that long—unlike Noah and all those who lived into their 900s—and was already an oldster by now. So, when he told his wife Sarai that God had promised their kids would kick everybody else out of "the promised land," she was perplexed and thought of an angle. She states the obvious … **The Lord has kept me from having children. Go, sleep with my maidservant; perhaps I can build a family through her."** (Gen. 16: 2-4). Wishful thinking?

So Hagar bore Abram a son, and Abram gave the name Ishmael to the son she had born. Abram was eighty-six years old when Hagar bore him Ishmael. (Gen. 16: 15,16). Now the covenant… **When Abram was ninety-nine years old, the Lord appeared to him and said, "I am God Almighty; walk before me and be blameless.** (Gen. 17: 1). Keep this command in mind as later we shall discover that according to the Bible it is impossible! Would God issue an order that he knew no man could follow? Of course. Or at least it seems so. Regardless, the Bible continues …

"I will confirm my covenant between me and you and will greatly increase your numbers." (Gen. 17: 2). There it is. The covenant has to do with the creation of a race of people. This is neat. And like many civilizations, the Hebrews trace their origins back to a mythical source. But, we notice, there is a twist: Ishmael, the product of a surrogate, is to be the chosen vessel! (You're supposed to say "hmmm.") **"As for Sarai your wife, you are no longer to call**

Abraham was really old and Sarah was "worn out" as well. So she gave
him her servant. And that was bound to come out well, huh? No shit.

her Sarai; her name will be Sarah. I will bless her and will surely give you a son by her. I will bless her so that she will be the mother of nations; kings of people will come from her." (Gen. 17: 15,16). So then Sarai becomes Sarah and Abram becomes Abraham. This is where they both got a name change. And then the last stipulation of the covenant is announced: Circumcision! What?

Yup. God charges Abraham to be circumcised and to cut all the males of his household as a sign of the covenant between him and the chosen people. Talk about an obvious sign! But I am intrigued, however, with God's command to circumcise the slaves as well. Obviously, these people who were "bought with money from foreigners" (and gifted by Pharaoh) were not related to Abraham in any way. But they had to have the procedure as well. Go figure. And, mind you, this is a big deal. **"Any uncircumcised male, who has not been circumcised in the flesh, will be cut off from his people; he has broken my covenant."** (Gen. 17:14).

Okay now, let's take a break and discuss this term, "cut off." It is used throughout the Bible, and sounds innocent enough, but is a de facto death sentence. To be cut off, or abandoned by one's own people, is tantamount to capital punishment, minus the traditional biblical means like stoning, beheading, and being run through with a sword. Way back then one could not simply take a Greyhound to another city and start all over again. There was really nowhere else to go. All alone without the security of the tribe? Impossible. Clearly being uncircumcised was a capital offense.

Circumcision is a big deal to God and throughout the Bible. We will revisit the subject again and again, so get ready. I do, from time to time, quote "true" Bible scholars and commentators like Jerry Falwell and Pat Robertson. But, on this topic, I really need to quote a certain Gleason A. Archer, who is best known as a Biblical apologist. That is, he makes apologies (excuses) for all the crap we find in the "holy book" as they keep thumping away on it. He says...

The right of circumcision, i.e., (surgical removal of the prepuce) was intended as a sign and a seal of the covenant relationship between God and the believer. The sacramental removal of this portion of the male organ was a blood-sealed testimonial that the believer had turned his life over to the Lord, with the commitment to live for Him and in dependence on His grace for the rest of his earthly life. As a seal the act of circumcision amounted to a stamp of ownership of the Old Testament; it testified that he belonged not to this world, Satan, or self, but to the Lord, Yahweh, who had provided for his redemption. (Archer p. 94).

A blood-sealed testimony of ownership. There you have it. Archer goes on to call the foreskin an "instrument of unholiness" in that same place. And whether it is real or just symbolic, it is definitely seen in the Bible as "evil." No wonder the Prophet Jeremiah quoted God thusly: **"Circumcise yourselves to the Lord and the removal of the foreskins of your heart, men of Judah and inhabitants of Jerusalem, lest my wrath go out like a fire because of the evil of your deeds."** (Jeremiah 4: 4).

Anyway, Abraham, Ishmael, and the guys all got circumcised on that same day. Abraham was ninety-nine and Ishmael was thirteen. Note, Arab/Muslim boys are circumcised at age thirteen, unlike newborn Jews. But before we leave Ishmael altogether, I think we should point out here that the Arab world claims Ishmael as its source. Hagar was an Egyptian slave, so Ishmael would have been a Jewish-Arab hybrid. He really gets dumped on later as the story progresses. Here's what happened…

The Lord visited Abraham again a couple of chapters later. Out of sequence, like lots of entries in the Bible—he was sitting under a tree when God "came down" for a chat. Abraham fed him and two angels whom he had in tow. Then, out of the clear blue sky, the omniscient God simply had to ask where Sarah was. To which Abraham replied: **"There in the tent,"** he said. **Then the Lord said, "I will surely return to you about this time next year, and Sarah your wife will have a son."** (Gen. 18: 9,10). Sarah overheard the dialogue and snickered: **"After I am worn out and my master is old, will I now have this pleasure?"** (Gen. 18: 12). God was rather put off by her doubt and left with a parting … "You'll see." And guess what? He was right!

Now Sarah became pregnant and bore a son to Abraham in his old age, at the very time God had promised him. Abraham gave the name Isaac to the son Sarah bore him. When his son Isaac was eight days old, Abraham circumcised him, as God commanded him. Abraham was a hundred years old when his son Isaac was born to him. (Gen. 21: 1-5).

Well, as the story goes, it didn't take Sarah long to grow tired and resentful of Hagar's half-breed son, Ishmael. What was her solution? **"Get rid of that slave woman and her son, for that slave woman's son will never share in the inheritance with my son Isaac."** (Gen. 21: 10). Well, Abraham was kind of freaked out, as he knew that Ishmael was really his own son, as well. Like *Sophie's Choice*, he didn't know what to do.

But God said to him, "Do not be distressed about the boy and your maidservant. Listen to whatever Sarah tells you, because it is through Isaac that your offspring will be reckoned." (Gen. 21: 11). **"I will make the son of the maidservant into a nation also, because he is your offspring."** (Gen. 21: 13). So Abraham ditches them in the desert the following day—but not without a parting shot. Even though he is destined to be the founder of the Arab race, the Bible describes him in these glowing terms ...

He will be a wild donkey of a man; his hand will be against everyone and everyone's hand against him, and he will live in hostility toward all his brothers. (Gen. 16: 12). No wonder there are tensions in the Middle East to this day! Our nation's hostility toward the Arab world is to some degree born out of this Biblical slur. When I hear Bible belt fundamentalists fuss and fume about the "A-rabs," at least I know where they got their prejudices from.

And speaking of prejudice, the next stop on our tour is a town much maligned by our Fightin' Fundie friends and foes. The "wicked" folks of Sodom lived not too far away. So let's go on and see what that's all about.

Part 2

Patriarchs
and
Pagans

Lot and his two ugly daughters flee the burning city. Mrs. Lot innocently turns around
and is turned into salt. However, the fun part of the story happens later.

Sodom and Gomorrah

That's a Lot to Swallow

Then the Lord said, "The outcry against Sodom and Gomorrah is so great and their sin so grievous that I will go down and see if what they have done is as bad as the outcry that has reached me. If not, I will know." (Genesis 18: 20). The outcry is so great. I will go down and see. If not, I will know. What? The omniscient god is once again befuzzled and unsure. He somehow hears an outcry from somewhere, from someone, about bad goings-on down on Earth. So he decides to "go down" and check it out for himself. Obviously, he doesn't know what all the fuss is about, but he is determined to get to the bottom of it.

The traditional explanation is that Sodom and Gomorrah were hotbeds of homosexual activity. However, the Bible does *not* say that. It only says that God heard a rumor from some quarter and is going down to investigate.

Sort of like back in Noah's day when God got fed up with some sort of general undefined wickedness, he gets his knickers in a twist over some undisclosed malady on the planet. We are told that it was *obviously* homosexuality. Obvious to whom? It may be as clear as day to the "theologians," preachers and pseudoreligious politicians of our day, but if we just read what is there and forget the personal interpretations and eisegesis, the fact is that it says nothing at all.

What is obvious, however, is that God is willing to murder untold numbers of people (the flood), condone slavery (Canaan's curse), as well as lying (Abram to Pharaoh), incest (Cain and his sister), and murder (we will meet Moses soon). So the holy deity is upset with the undefined wickedness of two cities of the plain, and sets out to annihilate them.

Evangelicals and fundamentalists of all stripes love this story, as it adjudicates their preconceived prejudices, biases, and hatreds. Somehow, to them, this brief account proves God hates fags so much that their death and destruction are deserved. I've even heard it preached that gays were responsible for the Genesis flood, which you may recall, resulted in total destruction of everything with breath in its nostrils—animals and all. Of course, the Bible does not say that, but there is that editorializing again. If God had given the Ten Commandments already (or any guidelines for living whatsoever) he would have already defined what was good and what was wicked behavior. At least then he would have been justified in being angry, should men contravene his laws and rules.

Up to this point, no divine rules or regulations for human behavior have been sent down from on high. How were they supposed to know what was wicked and what was not? Heck, they didn't even know—let alone, have a chance—to modify their bad behavior. God was on the war path and he was en route to destroy them all. So there.

Now preachers and priests for ages have told us that we all *instinctively* know what is right and wrong. We are born with a deep-seated understanding that some things are okay and others just wrong! When you ask these learned men of the cloth what this foreknowledge covers, they will confidently say: murder, adultery, lying ... and, of course, gay sex.

Meanwhile, although we are supposed to know not to do these things, the Almighty murders whomever he pleases; sends disease on whomever he wants to; or sends down fire, water—or whatever he wants to—onto a human race totally in the dark as to why. If we were simply born with a built-in knowledge of right and wrong already, why would God need to give the Ten Commandants and all the myriad rules and laws that he hands down later? Surely we would know right from wrong already. But that is all coming up later on the tour, so stay tuned.

Anyhow, God decides to destroy the cities. Abraham, who just happens to be on hand for God's arrival, is appalled. **"Will you sweep away the righteous with the wicked?"** he is aghast. **"What if there are 50 righteous people in the city? Will you sweep it away and not spare the place for the sake of the 50 righteous people in it? Far be it from you to do such a thing—to kill the righteous with the wicked, treating the righteous and the wicked alike. Far be it from you! Will not the judge of the earth do right?"** (Gen. 18: 25).

Aha! What a question! Will not the judge of all the Earth do right? This is the first mention of the word "judge." Suddenly we are confronted with a new concept:

judgment. The omnipotent God is about to murder a significant number of people because he is mad, but Abraham calls to his attention that there may be some good people in town. Like duh. God hadn't thought of this.

And Abraham asks: **"Will not the judge of all the Earth do right?"** What is right? It looks to me like God doesn't actually know. Then Abraham takes the questioning a step further ... **"What if there are fifty righteous people in the city?"** And God replies: **"If I find fifty righteous people in the city of Sodom, I will spare the whole place for their sake."** (Gen. 18: 26). Here the omniscient God admits that he would have to locate fifty good guys in town to justify sparing it. Of course, an all-knowing god would naturally already know how many righteous people there were in Sodom. But Abraham persists ... **"What if the number of the righteous is five less than fifty? Will you destroy the whole city because of five people?"** (Gen. 18: 28). Then, as they continue negotiating, he talks God all the way down to ten. Exasperated, God finally fumes: Oh, alright! **"For the sake of ten I will not destroy it."** (Gen. 18: 32).

I have oft wondered if Noah, had he been a bit brighter and bolder, might have posed the same questions to God himself before taking up his hammer to build that ridiculous ark. No such luck. Noah was no Abraham. And you have to admit, Abraham had chutzpah! **When the Lord finished speaking with Abraham, he left, and Abraham returned home.** (Gen. 18: 33). But wait, there's more.

Then two angels arrived at Sodom in the evening, and Lot was sitting in the gateway of the city. When he saw them, he got up to meet them and bowed down with his face to the ground. (Gen. 19: 1).

Who were these angels? Well, anyway, they arrived at night and Lot bowed appropriately. How did he know to do that? Maybe his inborn knowledge told him that it was the right thing to do. Who had programmed him? Whatever. He says to them: **"My Lords, please turn aside to your servant's house. You can wash your feet and spend the night and then go on your way in the morning."** (Gen. 19: 2). Apparently he had no clue as to their actual mission. They were doing reconnaissance—laying plans to blow up the place. **"No, we will spend the night in the square."** (Gen. 19: 2) They defer. **But he insisted so strongly that they did go with him and entered his house. He prepared a meal for them, baking bread without yeast, and they ate.**

(Gen. 19: 3). So—without a doubt—angels can eat, sleep, get dirty feet, and change their minds. But then the real fuss starts.

Before they had gone to bed, all the men of Sodom—both young and old —surrounded the house. They called to Lot, "Where are the men who came to you tonight?" (Gen. 19: 4). Now, we know that they were angels. But those wicked men of Sodom thought they were just men—strangers. They must have been really hot, because it says that *all* the men (young and old) wanted them. Or so we are told by the preachers on Sunday morning TV. But how do we actually know any of that? Answer: We don't. The clergy of various stripes and denominations have for years just made this up and sold it to us as fact. Sure. Well, anyway...

Lot went outside to meet them and shut the door behind him and said, "No, my friends. Don't do this wicked thing. Look, I have two daughters who have never slept with a man. Let me bring them out to you, and you can do what you like with them." (Gen. 19: 6-8). Well, the wicked men of Sodom would have none of that! In fact, they moved forward to break down the door! **But the men inside reached out and pulled Lot back into the house and shut the door. Then they struck the men who were at the door of the house, young and old, with blindness so that they could not find the door.** (Gen. 19: 10,11).

Verse one says they were angels. Verses six through eight refer to them as men. But either way, they caused massive blindness. This has bugged me for a long time. The ostensible reason for the blinding of the entire male population was to prevent them from finding the door. Like, hello, they were already pounding on it. Looks to me like they had found it already. Hmmm.

We hear so much about the men of Sodom—their lust, the door pounding and the blinding ... But what of the women? Were they all just as wicked as their husbands, fathers and brothers? Our preachers love to speculate as to the nature of the sin of Sodom, but I have always wondered if the women and children as well deserved the rain of fire that was soon to come.

Moreover, there is the issue of Lot's offer to give his virginal daughters over to the sex-crazed mob. Okay, it's certainly an innovative solution to the problem.

Yet, whenever I hear evangelists and other preachers extol the virtues of sinless, blameless Lot, I often wonder if any of *them* would offer their teenage daughters up to a horny crowd of wild-eyed sodomites. Somehow I doubt it.

Then the two men said to Lot, "Do you have anyone else here—sons-in-law, sons or daughters, or anyone else in the city who belongs to you? Get them out of here, because we are going to destroy this place. The outcry is so great that he has sent us to destroy it." (Gen. 19: 12,13). Ironically, Lot's two sons-in-law (to be) decline to leave! I have often thought that those two daughters must have been real dogs. First of all, the sex-crazed mob doesn't want them; then, their own betrothed don't either. Huh. Then, with the coming of the dawn, the angels urged Lot, saying: **"Hurry! Take your wife and your two daughters who are here, or you will be swept away when the city is punished."** (Gen. 19: 15). Ooh, punished. But were we ever actually told why? It couldn't be because of the mob, as the angels had been dispatched by God long before that door-pounding incident. No. It is still all about that nebulous "outcry."

Naturally, there's more to the story. And this part is also well known and expounded upon. By sunup, Lot, the Mrs. and the two ugly daughters flee to the mountains. Then a memorable thing happens: Mrs. Lot looks back toward the burning city, and is instantly turned into a pillar of salt. Most churchgoers are familiar with this story. They have been told that she deserved to be salinized because she looked back. This, they say, "symbolizes" disobedience and a longing to return to the wicked old ways for which the city was being punished at that very time.

This really begs the next question. If that event is symbolic, what else in the Bible is just that—symbolic? We will encounter this enigma over and over. Most literalists insist that she did instantly become a salt lick for wandering wildlife. Others believe it just represents a yearning for a sinful past lifestyle. But she was one of the righteous—those allowed to depart and escape the devastation. Why did God snuff her in particular? Was this real or symbolic? Go ask your pastor or priest, but—let's face it—either way, her *death* was real!

The story of righteous Lot has a real twisted ending. I love it. And hopefully you will get something out of it as well. A chuckle at least. You will rarely ever hear a sermon preached from any text from verse thirty onward. I doubt that most pew sitters have even read this section. The blameless Lot, who fled into the hills with his two daughters, ends up living with them in a cave just outside Zoar, which was presumably out of bombing range. Anyway, a most peculiar thing happened there...

One day the older daughter said to the younger, "Our father is old, and there is no man around here to lie with us. Let's get our father to drink wine and then lie with him and preserve our family line through our father" (Gen. 19: 13, 32). **So both of Lot's daughters became pregnant by their father. The older daughter had a son, and she named him Moab; he is the father of the Moabites of today. The younger daughter also had a son, and she named him Ben-Ammi; he is the father of the Ammorites of today.** (Gen. 19:36-38).

So the much touted righteousness of Lot reveals itself. Lot and the two ugly daughters commit incest. After all the hoopla about the righteousness of Lot, we see this bizarre twist. Those same preachers who extol Lot's virtues and cheer the destruction of Sodom, utter nary a peep about this part of the story. Despite the fact that the girls might have nipped over to Zoar to find a man, they preferred in the end to live happily ever after with their dad in their own private ménage à trois.

The story of the destruction of Sodom gets a lot of press from Evangelical pulpits these days. But I know another story found in the Book of Judges that rarely gets a mention. It's an example of wise old duffers sitting around the campfire and getting their stories mixed up. Want a laugh?

This is the account of an old man living in a town named Gilbeah, and an itinerant Levite priest (it is found in Judges Chapter 19). The stranger, passing through Gilbeah, happens upon the old man who is remarkably like our old friend, Lot. He addresses the wayfarer:

"You are welcome at my house," the old man said. "Let me supply whatever you need. Only don't spend the night in the square." So he took him into his house and fed his donkeys. After they had washed their feet, they had something to eat and drink. While they were enjoying themselves, some of the wicked men of the city surrounded the house. Pounding on the door,

they shouted to the old man who owned the house, **"Bring out the man who came to your house so we can have sex with him."** (Sound familiar?) **The owner of the house went outside and said to them, "No, my friends, don't be so vile. Since this man is my guest, don't do this disgraceful thing. Look, here is my virgin daughter, and his guest's concubine. I will bring them out to you now, and you can use them and do to them whatever you wish. But to this man, don't do such a disgraceful thing. But the men would not listen to him.** (Judges 19: 20-24).

I don't know what the writer of this tale was smoking, but it sounds like he was a bit stoned. On the other hand, unlike the Sodom story, this one has a very different ending.

So the man took his concubine and sent her outside to them, and they raped her and abused her throughout the night, and at dawn they let her go. At daybreak the woman went back to the house where her master was staying, fell down at the door and lay there until daylight. (Jud. 19: 25,26). (Thereupon she croaked.)

Obviously these wicked men of Gilbeah were not wild wicked homosexuals, as they were more than happy to accept, rape, and abuse the man's concubine all night. You don't hear theologians and preachers in the Bible Belt railing against the wickedness of Gilbeah, do you? Why? I think the women on our tour should be asking this question.

Typical of the sexism found throughout the Bible, this is a good example of its acceptance of the degradation of women. It is unacceptable to rape and abuse the male visitor as a form of humiliation; this is "vile and disgraceful." But it is okay to rape and abuse the female concubine. Note that the men of Gilbeah were straight sexually, as they accepted the female offering with relish. You hear endless sermonizing against Sodom, but not a peep against Gilbeah. Why? I think it's because this story has an even more disgusting ending than the pillar of salt incident. Moving on... **When her master got up in the morning and opened the door of the house and stepped out to continue on his way, there lay his concubine, fallen in the doorway of the house, with her hands on the threshold. He said to her, "Get up; let's go." But there was no answer. Then the man put her on his donkey and set out for home. When he reached home, he took a knife and cut up his concubine, limb by limb,**

into twelve parts and sent them into all the areas of Israel. (Jud. 19: 27-29). UPS or FedEx? You wonder.

What? After sleeping comfortably all night while this poor woman was being ravaged by the townspeople, he finds her dead on the doorstep. "Come on, let's go," he demands. Oh, sure. Duh. She's dead! So what does he do? He tosses her corpse onto his donkey and heads for home like nothing happened.

Then, when he gets there, he dismembers her body and sends the parts to all the areas of Israel. What in the hell is that about? Well, since I don't have a clue, let's see what the late Jerry Falwell tells us in his infamous book, the *Liberty Bible Commentary*:

"The Levite sent the twelve pieces of her body to the twelve tribes of Israel in an effort to rally the nation out of its lethargy and to a willingness to acknowledge its responsibility." (LBC p. 512).

Wow, that sure clarifies everything, doesn't it? How any woman can read the Bible and not be infuriated by all the blatant sexism, I'll never know. But, then again, it seems to me that anybody who would look to drivel like the LBC for an explanation, is living on the planet Kusbane or Kolobsomething.

"Let me go for it is daybreak," the angel implores Jacob. Heck, I thought only
vampires had to be in before sunrise!

Isaac, Jacob, et al.

The Great Sacrifice

Most people start wearing out right about now, when reading the Bible page by page like a regular book. You don't have to do it that way. A problem with the Bible is that the further into it you get, the longer and wordier the stories become. For that reason, we will compress several overlapping stories and concentrate on some of the really fun stuff.

Whereas up to now we have been dealing with great stories like the creation of the Universe, murders, mayhem, and building a really cool tower, the terrain flattens out when we get to Isaac. Now the narrative begins to get more mundane—dealing with Isaac and his wives and childbearing—like in most nature/fertility based tribal societies.

Most of us remember Isaac as a child—Abraham's son by Sarah. As you might recall, Abraham had a son (Ishmael) by Hagar, the slave of Sarah. Well, Sarah never did like that slave, nor her son either. And when well into their nineties, Abraham and Sarah finally produced their own son, Isaac, they were overjoyed. They really doted on this one as God had promised to make a great nation out of him and his offspring. They shuffled Hagar and Ishmael off into desert exile and turned their full-time attention to Isaac.

Isaac is a little kid when God decides that he has to test Abraham's dedication and devotion. The omniscient God who knows everything, apparently feels the need to see for sure if Abraham loves him best. So God sends Abraham up into the mountains to sacrifice Isaac in order to prove his love and dedication. We already know from the Cain and Abel story how important sacrifices are to God. We know grains and cereals don't compare to slaughtered animals. And we are about to learn that slaughtered animals don't compare with human sacrifices. (How very Aztec.)

So God sends Abraham with the express mission to kill the boy, slit his throat like a goat, and offer him up as a human sacrifice. The sick thing about this story is that Abraham is *willing* to do it! He is so devoted to the God who sends floods and fires, and turns people into pillars of salt, that he is willing to kill his long-awaited son—the one who is going to carry his own precious genes on into the future. God is pleased that Abraham is about to kill the child, but stops the execution in the nick of time. Now God knows for sure. Yea!

Anyhow, Isaac is spared being charbroiled, but his near miss does not fully address the issue of human sacrifice in the Bible. We have to turn to the account of a fellow named Jephthah to find out more. Human sacrifice has been largely ignored by Bible readers and preachers. They simply point out that Isaac was spared at the last moment. God obviously doesn't condone human sacrifice. That would be pagan—barbaric. We need, therefore, to turn to a more ignored passage once again to bring the issue into a more critical view. The story of Jephthah is rarely, if ever, mentioned from the pulpit. Here is his story...

Jephthah was a thug. Son of a prostitute, he was driven away from home at an early age by the elders of Gilead, and fell in with a gang in the land of Tob. He became the leader of the pack. Sometime later, when the Ammonites made war on Israel, the elders of Gilead went to get Jephthah from the land of Tob. **"Come," they said, "Be our commander so we can fight the Ammonites."** (Judges 11: 6).

Well well well, now the shoe was on the other foot! Whereas earlier they drove him away, now they need him. So the negotiation begins. **"Didn't you hate me and drive me from my father's house? Why do you come to me now when you're in trouble?"** (Jud. 11: 7). Good question! Then he asks, logically enough, what's in it for me? To which they reply that if he wins the battle, they will make him head honcho of all Gilead. It was an offer he just couldn't refuse.

After futile negotiations with the Ammonites, **the Spirit of the Lord came upon Jephthah. He crossed Gilead and Manasseh, passed through Mizpah of Gilead, and from there he advanced against the Ammonites.** (Jud. 11: 29). Now comes the wrinkle. Jephthah like really wanted to beat the Ammonites and get the job as mob boss of Gilead. So he came to the Lord with a proposal: **And Jephthah made a vow to the Lord: "If you give the Ammonites into my hands, whatever comes out of the door of my house to meet me when I return in triumph from the Ammonites will be the Lord's and I will sacrifice it as a burnt offering."** (Jud. 11: 30).

Needless to say, Jephthah really kicked some Ammonite ass. Well, God had done his part of the deal. He had "given" the Ammonites into Jephthah's hand, so now it was Jephthah's turn to come through and fulfill his part of the vow. He indeed came home in triumph. Yea! Everybody's happy—except for one thing... **When Jephthah returned to his home in Mizpah, who should come out to meet him but his daughter, dancing to the sound of tambourines! She was an only child. Except for her he had neither son nor daughter.** (Jud. 11: 34). Uh-oh. What was he going to do? What was God going to do? **When he saw her, he tore his clothes and cried, "Oh! My daughter! You have made me miserable and wretched, because I have made a vow to the Lord that I cannot break."** (Jud. 11:35).

See the problem that this poses for Jephthah? For God? For modern believers? In Deuteronomy we read: **You must not worship the Lord your God in their way, because in worshiping their gods, they do all kinds of detestable things the Lord hates. They even burn their sons and daughters in the fire as sacrifices to their gods.** (Deut. 12: 31). Further, we read: **Let no one be found among you who sacrifices his son or daughter in the fire** ... (Deuteronomy 18: 10).

Now what is he going to do? On the one hand, he faces the above mentioned prohibitions against pagan sacrifices of sons and daughters to the fire; but on the other, he has made a vow! And God has no intention of letting him off the hook. He goes through with it. The story could probably be shuffled under the rug by modern fundamentalists and other true Bible believers ... except for one problem. Jephthah is mentioned again in the *New Testament* as a "hero of the faith" in one of the most famous chapters in the Bible, namely Hebrews chapter 11! Christians read and parrot this chapter endlessly. The problem for them (and me) is this: If Jephthah made such a stupid vow in the first place, fulfilled it in the second, and God adjudicated it in the third ... how on Earth could he be considered on par with the other "heroes of the faith" mentioned in that notorious chapter in the Book of Hebrews? How indeed?

Meanwhile, back to Isaac. There is yet another account involving him that we don't hear about much. I find it quite interesting as it has a certain familiar ring to it. See if you recognize it. **So Isaac stayed in Gerer. When the men of that place asked him about his wife, he said, "She is my sister" because he was** afraid to say, "She is my wife." He thought, "The men of this place might kill me on account of Rebekah, because she is beautiful." (Gen. 26: 6).

When Isaac had been there a long time, Abimelech, king of the Philistines, looked down from a window and saw Isaac caressing his wife Rebekah. So Abimelech summoned Isaac and said, "She is really your wife! Why did you say, "She is my sister?" Isaac answered him, "Because I thought I might lose my life on account of her." (Gen. 26: 8,9). Then Abimelech said: "What have you done to us? ..." Yatta Yatta Yatta. You remember how it goes. Haven't we read this story already? Oh, yeah, that's exactly what his dad Abraham tried to pull on Pharaoh. Is King Abimelech really that stupid? Would he really have fallen for that exact same line? The way I see it, either he was a real dunce or maybe (just maybe) somebody got their stories mixed up somewhere along the line.

Let's face it—this stuff supposedly happened long long ago in a desert far away. These folks were not scholars. They were hunter/warrior types with a smattering of shepherd and farmer tossed in. From the flood up until this time we have had no mention of any writing whatsoever. It seems that for the most part these are just illiterates, telling and retelling stories around the campfire at night. I have always called it an ancient version of the common children's game of "telephone." As the original story is whispered from ear to ear it gets garbled and confused. The Bible is full of such stories told and retold for years and then edited by Italian monks centuries later. They caught a lot of the flaws and did quite a bit of their own eisegesis to try to make it work. But in the end they really didn't help much. It is still totally whack.

Anyway, Isaac had a son named Jacob. Some may remember him and his twin brother, Esau, and their sibling rivalry. Their adventures and misadventures span many chapters and become wordier and wordier. I guess my favorite is a marvelous tale of a personal account of an encounter between Jacob and God. Or was it God? Here's the Bible's rendition: **That night Jacob got up and took his two wives, his two maidservants and his eleven sons and crossed the ford of Jabbok. After he had sent them across the stream, he sent over all his possessions. So Jacob was left alone and a man wrestled with him till daybreak. Then the man said, "Let me go for it is daybreak." But Jacob replied, "I will not let you go unless you bless me." The man asked him, "What is your name?" "Jacob," he answered.** (Gen. 32: 22-27).

Then the man said, "Your name will no longer be Jacob, but Israel, because you have struggled with God and with men and have overcome." Jacob said, "Please tell me your name." But he replied, "Why do you ask my name?" Then he blessed him there. So Jacob called the place Peniel, saying, "It is because I saw God face to face, and yet my life was spared." (Gen. 32: 28-30).

These verses just sort of show up here sandwiched in among all sorts of superfluous detail, but this is a real zinger! Let's look at it. At first it doesn't make clear with whom he is wrestling. In fact, it specifically says he wrestled with a *man* all night. But later it specifically refers to his opponent as God *himself.* Even Jerry Falwell's renowned *Liberty Bible Commentary* casts doubt on which it was. You'll just love this: *"Assuming* the deity of the messenger, God *allowed* himself to be overcome." (LBC: p. 84). What? Note the use of the word "allowed." I vividly recall a magnificent brouhaha in Evangelical circles some years ago about this specific notion.

It sort of went like this: If God is all-knowing and all-powerful, why would he need to come down and tangle with Jacob in the first place, and why would he have to ask Jacob his name? As in Jerry's tome, he "assumes" the deity of the opponent and posits that the deity "allowed" himself to be overpowered by a mere mortal.

This is actually a very old controversy, but simply put, if God is all-knowing he would already know all our fates—our destinies. So if he already knows whether we are going to be saved or damned, is that foreknowledge causative? In other words, are we all predestined to heaven or hell, and, if so, is God powerless to do anything but what he knows is going to happen to us all anyway? Big problem.

So, some American "theologians" began preaching the popular-sounding doctrine that came to be called "limited foreknowledge." In other words, as in the case of his wrestling match with Jacob, he *chose* to lose and let Jacob win. And then it follows that in order to avoid being obligated to save or condemn us because he already knows our fate, he has chosen not *to know* certain things, thus giving humankind free will. To our first time visitors on our tour this may sound weird, silly, or even outright ridiculous. But I do assure you, assure you, it really caused as much grief to the Fightin' Fundies as abortion or gay rights ever has.

Now, there is a connection here as we move along into far less complicated machinations. **"Let me go for it is daybreak."** Like, what does this have to do with anything? I always thought that only vampires had to get out of sight by then. Jacob comes back with a version of *No way, Jose*: **"I will not let you go unless you bless me."** (Gen. 32: 24-26). Alright already! God *has* to bless Jacob in order to get out of the full-Nelson, and then decides right then and there to change his name, à la Abram and Sarai. Now, he is henceforth to be referred to as Israel, which means "God's Fighter." Note that the deity won't tell Israel *his* name. Why should he? After all, he is God Almighty and isn't obligated to prove anything to anybody. So there. However, it is interesting to note that despite the name change, the Bible continues to refer to him as Jacob. Hmmm.

Onward and upward on our tour. This whole thing about "God's Fighter" is important to note, as the theme of the next five hundred plus pages of the Old Testament is wrapped around fighting, killing, wars, and all the trappings of ancient hunter-warrior societies. God's participation in the stories of the Old Testament ranges from unleashed fury and anger—as in the flood—to total bumbling ignorance and confusion over matters such as how many righteous people should be enough to spare a city like Sodom. No matter what ... even the most clueless, unobservant, unquestioning Bible reader should be able to see this.

Jacob/Israel may have been God's fighter, but even he could not fight famine. The remainder of Genesis more or less concerns itself with the circumstances that bring the Israelites into captivity in Egypt. Several chapters that follow deal with Jacob and his sons, especially Joseph the dreamer. As the story goes, basically he got too big for his britches, and all his older brothers ganged up on him and sold him into bondage. They never could stand that arrogant little snot anyway. But, he saves the entire family years later after they have all fled famine in Canaan. This is another of those stories most favored by writers of children's books. It is simpleminded and well within the grasp of even the densest Bible believer. As fairy tales go, it is a classic. But the interesting thing about it is that there's a distinct break in the narrative—namely Genesis chapter 38—which doesn't really fit. But it is fun and challenging. Let's take a look and see that, despite the fact that it seems out of place, it actually does push the storyline along in a most amusing way.

Totally out of sequence with the rest of the story, the account of Judah and Tamar is sandwiched in the middle of Joseph's story. Judah's birth was already mentioned in Genesis 30. He was a rogue—the brother who instigated the selling of Joseph into slavery in chapter thirty-seven. His story is particularly important as it launches the "tribe" of Judah, which has a significant place in Jewish history right up to, and including, the birth of Jesus in Matthew chapter 1. It also presents another example of an Old Testament law being applied that would totally freak out modern Bible believers should it ever have to apply to them today. It goes like this ...

Judah had three sons. The first was named Er. His second son was named Onan. And the third was named Shelah. Er was all set to marry this woman named Tamar. She was ready and willing. **But Er, Judah's firstborn, was wicked in the Lord's sight; so the Lord put him to death.** (Gen. 38: 7). Just like that! Poof. He's dead. God killed him.

This did not present a problem. It was the second son's responsibility to take over where his brother Er left off. This is a tradition formalized in Deuteronomy 25, referring to brothers, one of whom dies without a son to continue the family line. Get this: **His widow must not marry outside the family. Her husband's brother shall take and marry her and fulfill the duty of a brother-in-law to her.** (Deut. 25: 5).

So, what if the second brother is not interested or willing? To me, this is some of the Old Testament at its best (and most humorous). Here's what she has to do in this case: **His brother's widow shall go up to him in the presence of the elders, take off one of his sandals, spit in his face and say, "This is what is done to the man who will not build up his brother's line. That man's line shall be known as the Family of the Unsandaled."** (Deut. 25: 9,10). Isn't that a hoot? I wonder how often that has been tried in Dallas First Baptist or Tulsa First Assembly of God.

Anyway, Onan was uncooperative. He would have none of this. **He knew that the offspring would not be his; so whenever he lay with his brother's wife, he spilled his seed on the ground to keep from producing offspring for his**

brother. What he did was wicked in the Lord's sight; so he put him to death also. (Gen. 38:9,10).

This form of birth control was totally unacceptable to God, who killed Onan right then and there, on the spot, for *his* wickedness. I can't help but wonder which is more outrageous—the sexual preferences of the sons or their murder by God. In any case, after all that, Judah was reluctant to give his third and last son to Tamar. I can't say that I blame him really. The third son, Shelah, was way too young anyway, so Judah promised to give him to her when he grew up. But Judah backed out of the deal and Tamar was livid. She decided to get back at him. And I love the way she did it.

She dressed up as a hooker to entice him! **When Judah saw her, he thought she was a prostitute, for she had covered her face. Not realizing that she was his daughter-in-law, he went over to her by the roadside and said, "Come now, let me sleep with you."** (Gen. 38: 15,16). In exchange for her sexual favors, Judah paid her in junk jewelry and the promise of a goat to be delivered to her later. What a deal!

Three months after that she came up pregnant. Obviously, they were not just *sleeping* there along the roadside. Judah was outraged. He was furious. In fact, he was royally pissed. He storms: **"Bring her out and have her burned to death!"** (Gen. 38: 24). Note: It is okay for him to use a prostitute, but he did not know it was Tamar. God isn't the least bit ruffled. She, on the other hand, is to be burned at the stake. It is unclear why. Because she was pretending to be a prostitute or because she was pregnant?

Nevertheless, she saves her own neck by producing the jewelry that Judah had given her (much to his embarrassment. Wonder if she brought the goat as well...). Interestingly, the twins who were born to them (Perez and Zerah) as a result of that little tryst, are mentioned in the genealogy of Jesus in the New Testament (Matthew chapter 1). There will be a lot more about Judah ahead.

So Joseph wraps up his career in Egypt, having gotten even with his brothers. Jacob blesses his twelve sons who are to sire the twelve tribes of Israel ... then he dies. Joseph does likewise shortly thereafter. The problem is that they are all living in Egypt by this time, and their population has taken off. Their situation in Egypt gets more and more difficult as all the original brothers die

The line of Judah (and Jesus) had a rather dubious beginning. It all started when a
certain "whore" named Tamar tricked Judah into getting her pregnant.
What could go wrong? LOL.

off. Their Pharaohs are elected and policies keep changing with each new administration. Finally, at some point, the Israelites (AKA Hebrews) get the drift. "Hey, guys, we're captives of the Egyptians!" They are stuck in a bad situation and it is getting worse. Not only are they captives, but "Hell, let's face it, guys. We're slaves!" Total bummer. And that begs the next question. Without Jacob and the boys, how will they ever escape so that they can fulfill God's promise to Abraham (to populate the Earth with their seed, that is)?

Answer: They need a deliverer. So enter our next hero. And what a whopper of a story his is! Let's all give a big welcome and a round of applause for ... Moses!

Part 3

Promises
and
Protests

Moses is always portrayed as quite the patriarch.
In reality, he was a stuttering fool who never knew which end was up.

Moses

I am who I am ... And who I am needs no excuses!

The story of Moses and the flight of the Hebrews from Egypt is wonderful. It is beyond just a simple children's story in a coloring book. It has inspired feature films with big time actors! Since most of us have seen Cecil B. DeMille's version, our tour will take a little extra time to fill in the blanks. The film has shaped the consciousness of people worldwide for years. But it took a lot of liberties with the Bible account. I am not so concerned with what fluff it added, but with all the stuff it left out on purpose.

We left off with the Jews (or Israelites or Hebrews) in slavery in Egypt. Their lives were increasingly miserable. The leaders of Egypt feared that such a populous minority within their borders might pose a threat, so decided to restrict their population growth potential by eliminating the young male population by a hundred percent.

Then Pharaoh gave this order to all his people: "Every boy that is born you must throw into the river, but let every girl live." (Exodus 1: 22). Well, Moses' mom hid him for three months, then floated him off into the Nile River in a basket—so the story goes. By happenstance, Pharaoh's daughter, the princess, was bathing in the muddy fetid crocodile-infested waters of the River Nile at the time. She rescued the baby and decided to adopt it and raise it as her son. Moses then grew up in an aristocratic environment with all the advantages of royalty—including an education (one would assume)!

The adult life and career of Moses begins with a murder. He observes an Egyptian taskmaster beating a Hebrew and in a fit of rage kills the guy. He must know full well that such a thing is wrong, because he hides the body! Then, the following day, he encounters two Hebrews fighting and, when he attempts to intervene, one says, **"Who made you ruler and judge over us? Are you thinking of killing me as you killed the Egyptian?"** Whereupon Moses realized: **"What I did must have become known"** (Ex. 2: 14). Like, duh. No kidding. Busted!

Unwilling to face up to his crime, he flees out into the Sinai desert where he spends the next forty years herding sheep. I think that is where they get the expression "I think I'll go herd sheep." :-) He found a woman in the desert named Zipporah and married her. They had a son. ... Details later on the tour.

Meanwhile, back in Egypt, the old Pharaoh dies. Moses is forgotten. But God notes the pain and suffering of the Hebrew people under the Egyptian yoke. Now the story heats up.

Moses is quietly tending his flock on Mt. Horeb when suddenly: **There the angel of the Lord appeared to him in flames of fire from within the bush. Moses saw that though the bush was on fire it did not burn up. So Moses thought, "I will go over and see this strange sight—why the bush does not burn up." When the Lord saw that he had gone over to look, God called to him from within the bush, "Moses, Moses!"** (Ex. 3: 2-4).

These few verses are a cause for question for some and great joy for others, as it is unclear from the text who the two personalities in the bush really are. Who's who? The Bible states: **The Lord would speak to Moses face to face, as a man speaks with his friend.** (Ex. 33: 11). And a few verses later it says: **"You cannot see my face, for no one may see me and live."** (Ex. 33: 20). Well? Huh? Our friends, the Fundies are absolutely sure that the "angel of the Lord" personality is really Jesus. Okay.

Anyhow, the Lord informs Moses that he is aware of the sufferings of the Hebrews in Egypt. God tells him that he plans to liberate them and that it is going to be Moses's mission to do the liberating. Moses is horrified! Who me? **"Who am I that I should go to Pharaoh and bring the Israelites out of Egypt?"** (Ex. 3: 11). I mean—like, come on—who is going to believe the burning bush story anyway? Besides, Moses is still on a "wanted" poster for murder back in Egypt. God totally ignores all that. Big deal. Not only does he promise Moses that the people will be freed from their slavery, but promises to let them rip off the Egyptians on their way out. **"And so you will plunder the Egyptians!"** (Ex. 3: 22). But Moses still isn't buying.

"What if they do not believe me or listen to me and say, the Lord did not appear to you?" (Ex. 4: 1). At this point God is getting fed up. So he shows Moses three great tricks that are sure to convince the people that he is legitimate. He has Moses throw down his staff, which God turns into a snake and then back again. Cool. He then has him reach into his cloak so he can turn his hand leprous and back again. Wow. And finally he instructs him to throw a container of water from the River Nile onto the ground that then turns into blood. I mean, let's be real. That would convince even me! (Especially since the Nile is hundreds of miles from Mt. Horeb in the Sinai!) Matters not. Moses is still dragging his feet. Oh, come on.

He whines, **"O, Lord, I have never been eloquent, neither in the past nor since you have spoken to your servant. I am slow of speech and tongue."** (Ex. 4: 10). My question is how could he have been raised in Pharaoh's court, with all those educational opportunities and possibilities, and still feign such ignorance and poor penmanship?

God is getting pissed off. And when he gets that way, watch out! He roars at Moses**, "Who gave man his mouth? Who makes him dumb? Who gives him sight or makes him blind? Is it not I, the Lord?"** (Ex. 4: 10). Whoa! In his haste to prove his power to give Moses speech facility, he actually confesses to causing deafness, dumbness and blindness! The Almighty God is taking credit for *making* people handicapped. Hallelujah!Yea!

Kicking and screaming, Moses begs God to send somebody else. What a wimp! After God showed him all those keen tricks to impress the court of Pharaoh, he is still unsure of himself (and God). He is such a namby-pamby handwringer. Finally, God blows up. He says ... "Oh, alright already!"

"What about your brother, Aaron the Levite? I know he can speak well." (Ex. 4: 14). I just love stuff like this in the Bible. God is perplexed and frustrated with this doofus, Moses. So he rounds up his long lost brother, Aaron (of whom Moses could not possibly know), and offers to let this guy speak on behalf of Moses and God himself.

Okay, anyway—somehow, Moses—who was cast out into the river, was rescued and raised as an Egyptian playboy—now, all of a sudden, has a *brother* who has managed to somehow become a Levite priest in Egypt when they were killing little Jewish boys. Come on—who is buying this? But it gets better! God informs Moses that his brother, Aaron (whom he has never met and who is articulate), is en route to Mt. Horeb in Sinai at that very moment. (Now that would be a story I'd like to hear.) God announces: **"He is already on his way to meet you, and his heart will be glad when he sees you. You shall speak** to him and put words in his mouth; I will help both of you speak and will teach you what to do. But take this staff in your hand so you can perform miraculous signs with it."** (Ex. 4: 15-17). Let's face it—the miraculous signs should do the trick. But did they?

Now the story takes a bizarre twist. God reminds this dimwit, Moses, one more time: **"When you return to Egypt, see that you perform before Pharaoh all the wonders I have given you the power to do. But I will harden his heart so that he will not let the people go."** (Ex. 4: 21). What? Here God tips his hand! He is confessing that he is going to make Pharaoh *not* cooperate. Huh? He is going to collude with Moses in the same way he did with Abram, Sarai, Isaac, and Rebekah. He is simply going to lie. He even tells Moses that he is going to do it! No wonder Moses isn't interested in participating in this charade.

In effect, God is saying, "Go show Pharaoh all these signs and demand that he let my people go. Tell him that if he doesn't, I am going to send all sorts of disgusting plagues on him and his land. But don't be surprised when he refuses, as he really doesn't have a choice because I am going to harden his heart; and then I get to send down all these really neat plagues anyway." I don't know about you, but this seems really warped to me. The Bible apologists say rather weakly that Pharaoh had hardened his heart *already*. ... And where does it say that?

When you next find yourself in a position to ask a clergyman a Biblical question, try this one on him for size ... (I love it). Get this: **At a lodging place on the way, the Lord met Moses and was about to kill him. But Zipporah took a flint knife, cut off her son's foreskin and touched Moses' feet with it. "Surely you are a bridegroom of blood to me," she said. So the Lord let him alone.** (Ex. 4: 25).

What in the world is going on here? This incident defies imagination. It is true that being uncircumcised is a violation of the Abrahamic covenant, and the penalty for it was death by exile. **Any uncircumcised male, who has not been circumcised in the flesh, will be cut off from his people; he has broken my covenant.** (Genesis 17: 14). It was a capital offense. True enough, Moses *could* have been uncircumcised, as he was raised an Egyptian—but, obviously, his son was uncut at the time. Even so, why would God want to kill *Moses* in that case? Anyway, Zipporah to the rescue. She zips out a flint knife and whacks off the foreskin of her son's penis right then and there, thus saving her husband's life. After all, he had to fulfill the mission to liberate his people, the Hebrews.

Sure enough, just as the Lord of the burning bush predicted, Moses and Aaron teamed up to show off their bag of tricks to Pharaoh. The people were wowed. But Pharaoh wasn't. We already know that God had pre-hardened his heart so that he would not believe.

Instead, Pharaoh makes the Hebrew slaves work even harder by increasing their work load and brick-producing quotas, pissing them off in the process. So they bitch at Moses! Whereupon, Moses *returns* to the Lord. It is unclear where God is at the time—back in Sinai or in Egypt. In any case, he resumes his whining again. **"O, Lord, why have you brought trouble upon this people? Is this why you sent me? Ever since I went to Pharaoh to speak your name, he has brought trouble upon this people, and you have not rescued your people at all."** (Ex. 5: 22). I just love God's reply...

"Now you will see what I will do to Pharaoh: Because of my mighty hand he will let them go; because of my mighty hand he will drive them out of his country." (Ex. 6: 1). A bit later: **"And I will harden Pharaoh's heart and he will pursue them. But I will gain glory for myself through Pharaoh and all his army, and the Egyptians will know that I am the Lord!"** (Ex.7: 3). Aha! God will gain *glory* for himself! He is confessing that his glory is insufficient and that he needs to get more. It is apparent that it is important for him to prove to the Egyptians that he is top dog (er, I mean God).

So Moses and Aaron get back together before Pharaoh again and start with the snake trick. Moses throws his staff down and it becomes a serpent. Nobody is impressed. The court magicians do likewise. ... Actually, *that* has always impressed me! Here, Moses has to get special powers from an omnipotent god to pull off that stunt, and the Egyptians can do it without any help from God at all. Wow.

So Moses pulls the *ol' plague of blood* trick out of his hat. He stretches out his staff and the waters of the Nile River turn to blood. But not only that—all the ponds and reservoirs were turned into blood as well. Blood was everywhere, even in wooden buckets and stone jars. The fish all died and it was quite a mess. Two things follow that have always amused me. First of all, the Egyptians could match the snake trick, indicating that it was simply that—a trick, and not some mighty miracle. But get this: Because the Egyptians could not get fresh water from the river, they had to dig *nearby*. Well, then, the whole trick was a flop. If they could simply dig elsewhere for water then the trick was ineffective and pointless. Obviously it was, so on to the next one ... The famous plague of frogs!

The amphibian invasion follows. Those frogs got into everything! They got into every house, every room, every bed. What a scene! But just like with the other tricks, the magicians proved that they could call up frogs too! Clearly God was going to have to come up with something even more creative. How about gnats? So Moses waves his magic staff and the dust of the land of Egypt changed into gnats. But here's a twist ... Somehow the magicians couldn't duplicate the gnat trick. So what? Pharaoh, now quite bored with the whole thing, is still unimpressed and unmoved. (Remember God hardened his heart. He really has a hard heart.) So another plague? You bet! But this one exposes another obvious Biblical blooper; the plague of the livestock came next   and ... **all the livestock of the Egyptians died.** (Ex. 9: 6). Note the use of the word "all!" *Every* animal was dead.

Then, the following day, God threatens the plague of hail and tells Moses to warn Pharaoh, saying: **"You still set yourself against my people and will not let them go. Therefore, at this time tomorrow I will send the worst hailstorm that has ever fallen on Egypt, from the day it was founded till now. Give an order now to bring your livestock and everything you have in the field to a place of shelter, because the hail will fall on every man and animal that has not been brought in and is still out in the field, and they will die."** (Ex. 9: 17-19). Duh. Like, apparently God forgot that he had just killed all the livestock the day before, so telling Pharaoh to give an order to "bring in your livestock" is just a bit moot—don't you think? Oh well, the Bible is inerrant, so let's just move on.

The plagues of locusts and boils come next. They're kind of like the rest, but the plague of darkness that comes afterward is a total wonder to be sure. **So Moses stretched out his hand toward the sky, and total darkness covered**

Moses led the Hebrews out of captivity, but right into a howling desert.
The people ate manna, but what did the animals eat out there?
Inquiring minds want to know :-)

all Egypt for three days. No one could see anyone else or leave his place for three days. Yet all the Israelites had light in the places where they lived. (Ex. 10: 20-23). Who's kidding whom? Well, if that failed to convince anyone in Egypt, the final plague did the trick as it involved Pharaoh personally. It is referred to as the killing of the firstborn.

So Moses, in exasperation, informs Pharaoh thusly: **This is what the Lord says: "About midnight I will go throughout Egypt. Every firstborn son in Egypt will die, from the firstborn son of Pharaoh who sits on the throne, to the firstborn of the slave girl, who is at her hand mill, and all the firstborn of the cattle as well."** (Ex. 11: 4,5). Of course, all the cattle, firstborn or not, were dead already due to the plague of the livestock back in chapter nine. Remember? Oops.

Well, that one finally convinced hardhearted Pharaoh, as his first son died as well. Not only did he let the Hebrews go, but he actually kicked them out (just as God predicted). And, of course, on their way out, they plundered the Egyptians (just as God had predicted). And, believe me, they were ready to get the hell out of that place. In fact, according to Exodus 12:40, they had been there for exactly 430 years to the day! Of course, a quick glance back to Genesis 15:13 says it was 400 years even. Oh well, it's only a mere thirty-year discrepancy. Need I mention inerrancy again? LOL

The Bible is full of these wonderful numbers games. Here's one for you: **There were about six hundred thousand men on foot, besides women and children. Many other people went up with them, as well as both flocks and herds.** (Ex. 12: 37,38). Including the "other people" (read: slaves), at least a couple million souls headed out of Egypt en masse that day (weighted down no doubt with all that Egyptian plunder). I get a kick out of the note that they brought all their flocks and herds with them as well. The flocks—likely ducks, geese and chickens—make sense. Why leave them behind? But herds? I thought God killed all the animals back in chapter nine. Oh well, those were just Egyptian cattle—obviously ;-)

These numbers are significant, as this mob (with a population of a decent-sized state or small country) was heading out into a totally empty, howling wilderness called the Sinai Desert. OMG. Their adventures had just begun!

The Death Angel kills the first born of the Egyptians—people and animals
alike. Somebody forgot to mention that all the livestock had
been killed already anyway (firstborn or not)!

Wandering in the Wilderness

What the hell is it? ... manna from heaven!

We all know the story of the Hebrews crossing the Red Sea. After all, we all saw Charlton Heston, of NRA fame, lead the Jews out of bondage as Moses in *The Ten Commandments*. It really looked convincing. When you watch the Hollywood version, the music is very dramatic. It looks like this all happened in a few short minutes. The captives have their backs against the mighty sea with no place to go. Pharaoh's armies are approaching on the run. God appears as a swirling pillar of fire that is holding them at bay just long enough for the Israelites to scurry across posthaste to safety on the other side. The music gets louder and more exciting. You find yourself on the edge of your seat. Then the pillar of fire goes away and the Egyptian chariots charge ahead into the gap. Meanwhile, on the other side, the last Israelite scampers ashore and the entire weight of the ocean crashes back and drowns all the Egyptian soldiers. Most Evangelicals that I have ever talked to over the years just love that Hollywood portrayal. It really shows it like it was! ... But I have a somewhat different scene in my mind.

According to the Bible, it took all night for the wind to dry the land sufficiently for a crossing. I can buy that, I guess. But remember how many people we are talking about. There would have to have been two million or more escapees in all, including all the women, children and slaves, plus large droves of livestock —both flocks and herds. I still get hung up on the flocks and herds part. Herds were obviously cattle and horses, sheep and goats, and the like—maybe even some camels to boot. But flocks? Flocks of what? What else? Geese and chickens and ducks. Ducks? Now, you can't tell me they ran full tilt across that path in the sea. They could only move as fast as the slowest moving creature. And I ask you, how fast can a duck waddle?

Anyhow, after gathering themselves together again on the other side, they regrouped. With Egypt to their backs, they headed out into the wilderness of Shur (oh sure)!

For three days they traveled in the desert without finding water. When they came to Marah, they could not drink its water because it was bitter. So the people grumbled against Moses, saying, "What are we to drink?"

(Exodus 15: 22-24). I have always wondered if God planned this trip very well. With these millions of people and animals needing water, three days must have been sheer hell. I would have grumbled too. Then they came to a place in the bone dry wilderness that conveniently had been named already: Marah. According to the Bible maps, it is about one hundred miles south of where they had landed three days earlier. At this rate they would be doing around thirty-three miles a day! Assuming that they traveled eight hours a day—then set up camp, ate, slept, and then broke camp again during the other sixteen hours—they would have to be traveling at a speed of *ten miles an hour* or so. Hop in your car sometime and drive at ten miles an hour for a ways and then tell me whether you think those flocks of ducks and chickens could travel that fast—and for three days, and without water!

But, in any case, they managed to get to Marah and the water is bitter. Terrific. Now what? By this point they were all pissed off at Moses. What's a fella to do? **Then Moses cried out to the Lord, and the Lord showed him a piece of wood. He threw it into the water, and the water became sweet.** (Ex. 15: 25). How convenient! It was sure nice of the Lord to save the lot after starving them for three days en route. I am more concerned with the fact that God simply did not *provide* any water whatsoever along the way. The preachers and televangelists never seem to be bothered by this at all. Instead, they preach endlessly about the chunk-of-wood trick.

Myriad sermons are preached about this event—turning bitter water into sweet, with a chunk of wood. God was "testing" them, they explain. And likewise, when you encounter problems in your own life, just pray and God will provide you a piece of magic wood as well. It is a metaphor! Ah, I see.

This theme of "testing" recurs throughout the Bible, so be prepared. The omniscient God never seems to know whether or not his subjects really love him best, or are willing to serve him unswervingly no matter what. So these constant tests continue to the end of the book. At this point comes a famous verse that preachers love. It is a veiled threat.

"If you listen carefully to the voice of the Lord your God and do what is right in his eyes, if you keep all his decrees, I will not bring on you any of the diseases I brought on the Egyptians, for I am the Lord who heals you." (Ex. 15: 26). Let's pause for a sec and ask about this "voice of the Lord" concept.

We have found already that God spoke *directly* to Adam, Abraham, Noah, and Moses in an audible voice. And when he asked Cain, **"Where is your brother?"** or Jacob, **"What is your name?"** was that an earful too or not? There is a lot of debate about various passages of scripture throughout the Bible when God was communicating with mankind as to whether or not he was able to be heard with their ears, or was just "speaking to their hearts" (in a still small voice).

For years God had used these human conduits to get his message across to Earthlings. Now, all of a sudden, he is commanding *everybody* to listen carefully to the voice of the Lord. This presents somewhat of a problem, as I see it. If God is speaking audibly to millions of people, that would be rather cacophonous, wouldn't it? On the other hand, if God saves his audible voice for a select few but communicates with the masses through thought waves, how are we to ever know for sure when we hear Christians say "God told me," whether or not it was really God talking or just themselves hearing their heads rattle? (In my experience, it's usually the latter!)

But finally an explanation for the flood! **"And do what is right in God's eyes..."** explains why God killed every living creature on Earth, scattered them, confused their language, and rained fire and sulfur down on them from time to time. They were obviously *not* doing right in his eyes! As we have noted, up to now there has been no indication that God had ever set a standard by which anyone could know what is right and what is not right in his eyes. So, whatever behavior mankind was doing was subject to rightness or wrongness arbitrarily based on what God was thinking at the time.

But now we get a whiff of what is coming! **"If you pay attention to his commands and keep all his decrees ..."** Aha! Now we begin hearing of his *commands* and *decrees*! Up till now we have had no such commands and decrees, so how would anyone know whether or not he or she was complying with God's will? Up to now, God has been judging mankind's behavior by his own yardstick, and rewarding or punishing people without telling them what the rules were. I have already railed about how unfair that is. But now things are changing. And how! Here come the commands and decrees! And pretty soon we will overdose on them. Just wait and see! The narrative drones on as they all trek across the desert, whining all of the way: **"If only we had died by the**

Lord's hand in Egypt! There we sat around pots of meat and ate all the food we wanted, but you have brought us out into this desert to starve this entire assembly to death." (Ex. 16: 3).

God gets all upset with this constant griping and replies: Oh, alright! **"I will rain down bread from heaven for you. You will know that it was the Lord when he gives you meat in the evening and all the bread you want in the morning** ... Then a remarkable thing happens. **That evening quail came and covered the camp, and in the morning there was a layer of dew around the camp. When the dew was gone, thin flakes like frost on the ground appeared on the desert floor. When the Israelites saw it they said to each other, 'What is it?' For they did not know what it was. Moses said to them, "It is the bread that the Lord has given you to eat."** (Ex. 16: 4,8, & 15). So they had quail for dinner and *Frosted Flakes* for breakfast. :-)

The "Manna from Heaven" story is well known and universally believed by Bible enthusiasts. But let's ask a couple of logical questions. First of all, what is all this talk of *starvation* about? Okay, there was an obvious water problem. But with all their flocks and herds in tow, how could they possibly starve? But they wailed about how they should have stayed in Egypt around their pots of meat. The *King James Bible* uses the term "flesh pot." Lots of preachers bellow on and on from the pulpit about "the sinful flesh pots of Egypt," making it into a metaphor for riotous living. Like—oh sure—the slaves were out there sinning it up in the "dance halls," "movie houses," discotheques and gay bars of ancient Egypt. LOL.

But, fortunately for everybody, God did solve the hunger problem by sending all these quail for them to eat. Of course, he could have just saved himself the trouble and said: "Hey, eat your sheep, ducks and chickens, you morons!"

The manna is another story. This strange stuff that sounds a bit like corn flakes fell on the desert floor during the night; and the Israelites went out in the morning and picked it up and ate it. Cool. **Each morning everyone gathered as much as he needed, and when the sun grew hot, it melted away. Moses said to them, "No one is to keep any of it until morning." However some of them paid no attention to Moses; they kept part of it until morning, but**

it was full of maggots and began to smell. (Ex. 16: 20,21). Apparently the shelf life of manna was twenty-four hours, and that's it. But then they ran into this problem: the *Sabbath*, a day when no one is supposed to work. Picking up the manna, even if it's free, is still technically considered "work." So God solved that problem this way:

"Tomorrow is to be a day of rest, a holy Sabbath to the Lord. Save whatever is left and keep it until morning." So they saved it until morning and it did not stink or get maggots in it. (Kewl.) **Six days you are to gather it, but on the seventh day, the Sabbath, there will not be any.** (Ex. 16: 23). This really is amazing stuff, huh? **The people of Israel called the bread manna. It was white like coriander seed and tasted like wafers made with honey. So Moses said to Aaron, "Take a jar and put an omer of manna in it. Then place it before the Lord to be kept for the generations to come.** (Ex. 16: 32). I have always mused, wondering what ever happened to that jar full of manna, saved for future generations. I guess it just went the way of that magic sword flashing back and forth way back there in the Garden of Eden.

According to the Book of Exodus they ate manna for forty years—the entire time they were wandering in the wilderness before they finally reached the border of Canaan (the land that they would wrest from the local inhabitants who were there first). On a map it is a couple hundred miles tops. It sure took them a long time to get there. I think even the ducks could have made it in less time than that! But this forty-year sojourn wasn't at all boring. They had lots of interesting adventures along the way. One of my favorites is when they ran out of water ... this time in the Desert of Sin (just a name, with no connection to those sinful flesh pots back in Egypt). "What?" they wailed. "Out of water again?" (I would have thought to bring along that magic piece of driftwood from Marah.) Anyway ... God to the rescue. He tells Moses to strike a certain rock with his magic staff, which he no doubt brought with him from Egypt. Water gushes forth from the miraculous rock, thus slaking the thirst of millions of folks and their animals. Some rock!

During their years of wandering in the wilds of the Sinai Peninsula they took to living in tents. Clear back when Moses was arranging the plagues on Egypt, some of you were probably wondering what they were going to live in once they were expelled from the country. The Hebrew slaves in Egypt lived in houses. They were making bricks daily, like crazy, as you might recall, so when they made their grand escape from Egypt on a moment's notice, they somehow managed to get together enough tent material to accommodate these millions of people.

This is another good one ... At one point the bitching and complaining got so bad that God sent in an invasion of quail. Not just the regular evening feed, but sort of like the plague of frogs back in good ol' Egypt. I mean, they swarmed into the camp and everybody gorged themselves to excess. And guess what? They got *food poisoning*! Good grief. They died in droves and were buried in a place called The Grave of Greed. "Can you go visit that place today?" you ask. Nope, cuz no archaeologist has ever found it. Shucks.

Now, I am sure that you tourists are as impressed as I am about how these millions of people and animals managed to survive for forty years in the treeless, waterless wasteland of the Sinai. "What did the animals eat?" you ask. Hell if I know. That's why this is called the Biblical Mystery Tour. Lots of mysteries, huh? And there are many more to come. (Smile) But I promised to tell you about the commands and decrees, so let's move on. Here they come!

Part 4

Property
and
Propriety

The Slave is His Property

Rules and Regulations for Owners

One of the problems that travelers have on their Biblical journey is the order of things. God arranged the Bible in a most confusing fashion. The further we read, the more disjointed the narrative becomes. It is fairly easy to move from story to story, but it is also easy to get bogged down in all the rules, regulations, and ceremonies. The way to avoid that is to recognize that a great deal of the Bible is like a tossed salad. It is all jumbled together, line after line, verse after verse; and they often do not follow. It is better at this point to shift focus from trying to identify the chronology from story to story, and instead go from topic to topic.

For years I thought of the next collection of books of the Bible as a wasteland. I think most people do, as well. And you rarely hear preachers coming up with exciting sermons from Leviticus, Numbers, and Deuteronomy. Of course, there is a reason for this. They know what is in these books and prefer that no one discovers some of this really scary stuff, or asks them to explain.

Reading the Bible is a bit like driving from San Francisco to New York (and I have done it). No matter what, you have to drive across Nevada to get there. Nevada—like this part of the Bible—has all sorts of interesting things to discover, but you have to go well off the freeway to find them. Most readers are not motivated to do so—just hoping to skim their way through. Most preachers are not motivated to draw much attention to these books for reasons we will quickly discover. Like many a driver, they say, "I'll drive. You sleep. I'll wake you up if I see something interesting." For centuries priests and pastors have let their parishioners sleep through hundreds of pages of great material. That is not my intention on this tour. So let's take a trip off the beaten path!

Our story takes a new direction after the water-in-the-rock incident. Since leaving Egypt, the Israelites were primarily concerned with food and water. God managed to supply all that, and they seemed to be adapting to desert living. The Bible says that they were in that desert for forty years, and during that time a lot happened. First of all, God gave them the Ten Commandments, the first codified *rules* of behavior. I presume we are all relatively familiar with this story, so let's look beyond "You shall not murder. You shall not commit adultery. You shall not steal, etc." Okay?

Obviously, God was a little late in getting around to giving mankind some rules by which to evaluate his behavior. Clear back when God sent the flood that killed every living creature, it would have been nice at least to know why they were being killed. We were told they were wicked, but no one really knew what wickedness was, as it had not yet been defined. Now everything is changed. Instead of no rules, there are nothing but rules! That little list of rules that we call the Ten Commandments is just a preface to the myriad Biblical rules and regulations that follow. If you will look out your bus window to your right, notice ... The Bible says:

When the people saw the thunder and lightning and heard the trumpet and saw the mountain in smoke, they trembled with fear. They stayed at a distance and said to Moses, "Speak to us yourself and we will listen. But do not have God speak to us or we will die." (Exodus 20: 18,19). **Moses said to the people, "Do not be afraid. God has come to test you, so that the fear of God will be with you to keep you from sinning."** (Ex. 20: 20).

This is great. It says, "Don't be afraid. God has just come so that you *will* be afraid." Being afraid of God is good. It's a good thing. It will keep you from sinning! Sinning? Aha! A new concept. Sin. This is the first mention of it. Up to now we have heard of wickedness. It has been used as an adjective: The people of Earth were wicked. Now it is being used as a verb: to sin. If you are afraid of the big scary God, that is good because it will prevent you from doing something called sinning. As of yet, sinning is not defined. But don't worry. I assure you, it will be (in spades).

Immediately after giving the first Ten Commandments, the very next rule addresses property. And, of course, the most important piece of property one can own is a slave; so the very first commands and decrees thereafter deal with human servants and slaves. Even before we get out of Exodus, we are confronted with these rules. **"If you buy a Hebrew servant, he is to serve you for six years, but in the seventh year, he shall go free. If he comes alone**

The Bible says: **Anyone who strikes a man and kills him shall surely be put to death**. (Ex. 21:12). But of course it is okay to kill a mere slave. The penalty for that is a fine. Gotta love this book!

he is to go free alone. If his master gives him a wife and she bears him sons or daughters, the woman and her children shall belong to her master, and only the man shall go free." (Ex. 21: 2,3).

The roots of indentured servitude are to be found right here in the Bible, and the denigration of women continues as well. Notice that, in this case, the man can go free in seven years even as the woman is property forever. Of course, this only applies to Hebrew servants. Real slaves were not Jews, but "foreigners," and were considered property forever, in any case. More on this later. Moving on...

"If a man sells his daughter as a servant, she is not to go free as menservants do." (Ex. 21: 7). Women of the world, take note. Your position is being defined for you. A man can sell his daughter into servitude, but she is not able to be freed from that bondage as men can. If you don't call that sexism, what do you call it?

"If a man beats his male or female slave with a rod and the slave dies as a direct result, he must be punished, but he is not to be punished if the slave gets up after a day or two, since the slave is his property." (Ex. 21: 20,21). I have always thought of this verse with a great deal of embarrassment. I am embarrassed for God that this is among his commandments and decrees. I am embarrassed for the Jews that this is in their Book; for the Catholics who glossed over it for centuries; and especially for the Evangelical Protestants who would still defend it.

The Liberty Bible Commentary states: If a foreign slave was killed by a master, the judges would set his punishment. But if he continued a day or two before dying, the beating was not considered meant to kill, and the loss of the slave was punishment enough (LBC p. 155).

The outrageous thing that I see here is that the general command from the basic Ten Commandments, **You shall not kill**, obviously does not apply to everybody. It does not apply to slaves. If a man kills a slave, he is to be punished, although the punishment is not defined. But he is not to be killed himself. Not only that. If the slave happens to recover, then the owner is to receive no punishment whatsoever. After all, the slave is his property.

All that seems to fly in the face of the Commandment that we find just eight verses ahead of that, in Exodus 21:21, which clearly states: **Anyone who strikes a man and kills him shall surely be put to death.** (Ex. 21: 12). Dutifully toeing the Baptist line, the same commentary says of this verse: *To take the life of a murderer is not a violation of "Thou salt not kill" but is clearly commanded of God. Any nation who refuses to carry out the death penalty is inviting trouble from the Almighty* (LBC p.156). What a pile of bullshit! Obviously, the writer of the commentary (purportedly Jerry Falwell himself) is justifying capital punishment. Then, eight verses later, he justifies not meting out capital punishment to one who kills a mere slave, since that is not a human being at all, but just property. Am I the only one outraged by this? Twelve verses later we get another revelation. **If a man's bull gores a male or female slave, the owner must pay thirty shekels** (about 12 oz.) **of silver to the master of the slave, and the bull must be stoned.** (Ex. 21: 32). What? Here we are actually putting a price on human life! According to today's online financial report, the current price of silver is $20/oz. It comes out to about $240. Do the math.

The next bit of information about slavery comes from Leviticus chapter 25 where God clearly sanctions slavery. The Israelites were permitted to own slaves and they were required to interact with them and treat them with a certain protocol. These same Jews were not allowed to own other Jews as slaves, but only as indentured servants. Of course, female indentured servants could not be freed, so technically they were slaves, in fact. But then, they are women, and that's different! Right? We continue our reading:

"Your male and female slaves are to come from the nations around you; from them you may buy slaves. You may also buy some of the temporary residents living among you and members of their clans born in your country, and they will become your property. You can will them to your children as inherited property and can make them slaves for life, but you must not rule over your fellow Israelites ruthlessly." (Lev. 25: 44).

Before I give my commentary on this passage, let me quote from my cross-reference, the *Liberty Bible Commentary*, which touts itself as "Distinctively Baptist, Aggressively Fundamental and Historically Evangelical." Wow! Okay, here's Jerry Falwell posthumously speaking from the grave:

Israel was permitted to have slaves of the heathen. Their children would also be slaves perpetually. This should be viewed as a form of the just judgment of God upon the wicked and idolatrous practices of the heathen and differs from modern slavery, which was not commanded of God. (LBCp.241).

How does this differ from *modern* slavery? What exactly is the difference then? In fact, what is "modern slavery?" In nineteenth century America, both Roman Catholics and Protestants owned slaves. In both cases they justified it with these very passages. They even tried to enslave the Native Americans under the heading of "temporary residents" and "members of clans born in your country." They found the "Indians" did not make very good slaves. However, the "Negros" brought from Africa were more suitable. Nevertheless, it's all under the same Biblical decree. Many Christian commentaries I've read make brief statements glossing over huge and glaring issues like this and move on. But if it is something that they feel is important (e.g.: the remark about capital punishment previously mentioned), note how "aggressively fundamental" they can be.

I lived in Evangelical circles long enough to know that "born again" Christians think of themselves as a *type* of Israel. The really convenient thing about the modern Christian position on verses like these is that they get to ignore them. While pillorying the modern Jews for rejecting Jesus, they call up all the Old Testament verses that adjudicate their positions on various current issues, but deny those that are inconvenient to them. Modern Jews have all this Old Testament baggage to carry with them. The orthodox adhere to every single rule and law; the unorthodox pick and choose at the smorgasbord of do's and don'ts; the Catholics and Protestants alike disdain the Jews and consider all modern Jews born after Christ to be already condemned to hell, because there is salvation in no other than Christ. But they carry the same baggage. The difference is that the Jews carry it all on their backs and the Christians have luggage carts. Let me explain why.

Modern Bible readers and believers all claim to love and believe the Bible. All that the modern Jews have is the Old Testament. Among themselves, they contend endlessly about verses like these mentioned above, and like many more we will examine in the chapters ahead. They are hopelessly divided on the big issues as well as the small. Unfortunately for them, baggage from the Old Testament is very heavy. The orthodox point out the same question that the Fundamentalist Protestants and Catholics do: Namely, if you choose to reject, ignore, or gloss over *one* section or another of the Old Testament because it is incongruous with modern thinking, which verses do you ignore, which do you reject, which do you keep? In effect, *where do you draw the line?*

The Christians have a luggage cart. They can bring all the baggage of the Old Testament with them but appear not to really be carrying it. Their out is "We believe the law, we love the law (of the Old Testament), but Jesus came to set us free from the law!" In other words, the Old Testament is good. It is inerrant and to be read, quoted and preached. But any sticky or embarrassing area comes under the cliché "Jesus set us free from the law." The great thing about that kind of theology is that it allows fundamentalists to say things like "That slavery was different from modern slavery," and think that they can get away with it, while quoting all the verses they like about capital punishment and punishments for sins, etc.

They can't escape so easily, though. *The New Testament* clearly states: **Slaves, obey your earthly masters with respect and fear, and with sincerity of heart, just as you would obey Christ.** (Ephesians 6: 5). I love the part about fear. How convenient. I can I just hear Scarlet O'Hara reminding "Mammy" to obey her master with respect and fear. After all, it's in the Bible!

There are plenty of other references to slavery but we need not beat the subject to death (Get it?). The point is that the Bible sanctions slavery, and over the years, the Jews—and more recently the Christians—have used the Bible to indulge themselves by owning slaves. Modern fundamentalists deep down believe that slavery is really okay. They face the problem of modern public opinion against any form of slavery, so they waffle on the subject. Like witch burning, it is a subject that they hope will someday come back into vogue. Did I say witch burning? Now there's a perfect entree into a new region—one that is much harder for the Bible believers to shuffle under the rug! In recent history, American Christians have burned countless women accused of being witches. Let's continue along our journey and see what we can dig up. Our next topic? Women! That should interest about half of the planet's inhabitants.

As for the women...you may take these as plunder for yourselves. (Deut. 20:10)
The Biblical view of women: objects.

The Position of Women

As for the women ... you may take these as plunder for yourselves.

Every Mother's Day, churches across America dust off a certain section of Proverbs chapter 31, extolling the "virtuous woman." **Who can find a virtuous woman?** the Bible queries. Between verse ten and verse thirty-one we find the blueprint for what Bible believers see as the ideal of womanhood. Take a read for yourself, should you want to see all of it. But allow me to quote a few of the more typical lines: **She selects wool and flax and works with eager hands. She gets up while it is still dark; she provides food for her family and portions for her servant girls. She sets about her work vigorously; her arms are strong for her tasks. She watches over the affairs of her household and does not eat the bread of idleness** ... It goes on, but I think you get the drift. The systematic denigration of women by the Bible is a scandal more outrageous in our day even than the slavery issue. The reason I think so is because the secular, liberal, non-religious thinkers of the past few centuries have wrenched slavery out of the hands of the religious hardliners and have forced them to let go of it (if only on the surface). However, women are still second class citizens in the collective mentality of many of the world's religions—all those based on the Bible and the Quran.

Women made a great deal of progress in the 20th Century toward breaking the bonds of biblically sanctioned servitude. Nevertheless, Bible-believing males of every stripe continue to be programmed to think that the female gender is inferior, and it is continually reinforced throughout the Bible. Multitudes of modern women as well swallow the same line and knuckle under to male chauvinism. I have faith that women will join the ranks of former slaves someday and throw off this Biblical yoke. But, in the meantime, some women will still be willing or forced to accept this archaic and dehumanizing role.

Women got off on the wrong foot clear back in the garden. In addition to having been created as a helpmate for man, woman was deceived by the serpent and therefore technically responsible for all the curses God put upon Earth back when he drove them out of the garden. It has been all downhill from there. We note that women rarely are mentioned as major characters in the Bible. There are a few who get star status, but most of them are portrayed as temptresses, adulteresses, and sluts. Since we are still confining most of our reading to the first five books of the Bible (which are referred to as the *Pentateuch*) let's observe some passages that specifically detail how women should be treated in an ideal Bible-based world.

If a man's wife goes astray and is unfaithful to him ... and if feelings of jealousy come over her husband and he suspects his wife and she is impure—or if he is jealous and suspects her even though she is not impure—then he is to take his wife to the priest. (Note that he has only to suspect her of infidelity, and be jealous.) **Then the priest shall put the woman under oath and say to her, "If no other man has slept with you and you have not gone astray and become impure, may this bitter water that brings a curse not harm you. But if you have gone astray, may this water that brings a curse enter your body so that your abdomen swells and your thighs waste away."** (Nr. 5: 12-22).

I can't help myself here. I'm sure there are plenty of women willing to be unfaithful if it would mean getting some of that stuff that will make their thighs waste away. However, I am sure this is more serious a matter, really, as it is the root of centuries and centuries of similar practices which have killed and maimed untold numbers of innocent people. Here, drink this poison; if you die, you are guilty; if you are innocent, it will not harm you. Oh, too bad, you died. See, obviously you were guilty. Just a few hundred years ago, in our country, we were "testing" for various Biblical improprieties in similar fashion, as were our European brethren during their numerous "Inquisitions." We should never ever forget the lengths to which the religious Bible-believers will go if they are allowed to. The Inquisitions are a case in point, coming innocently from the root word meaning: to inquire, to be inquisitive, to seek to know. These inquiries into peoples' lives and behaviors wrought a reign of terror that will be unleashed again in our day if we let it.

Women are referred to as "plunder" in Deuteronomy chapter 20. This whole chapter is a must-read for anyone interested in ferreting out the true spirit of the Bible, and understanding the nature of Bible-believing people. But let me quote you a section of it for now—God speaking. Beginning with verse ten, we read: **When you march up to attack a city, make its people an offer of peace. If they accept and open their gates, all the people in it shall be subject to**

forced labor and shall work for you. If they refuse to make peace and they engage you in battle, lay siege to that city. When the Lord your God delivers it into your hand, put to the sword all the men in it. As for the women, the children, the livestock and everything else in the city, you may take these as plunder for yourselves. (Deut. 20: 10). What? Oh yes. But this is certainly not the only place in the Bible where God commands genocide, and we'll get to that ahead in the Book of Joshua. But the point I wish to make here is that women, children, and animals are all just thought of as "things."

Because women are things—like cattle and other property—there are occasions when men fight over them. Conveniently enough, the Bible has rules and regulations governing this as well. I have always loved this verse: **If two men are fighting and the wife of one of them comes to rescue her husband from his assailant, and she reaches out and seizes him by his private parts, you shall cut off her hand. Show her no pity.** (Deut. 25: 11,12). Oddly enough, I note that modern self-defense courses teach women to do the very thing for which the Bible prescribes the cutting off of a hand! Our modern society tsks at the horror of the Muslim custom of hand-cutting ... Yet, read it for yourself; the Bible sanctions this practice as well, and for such a terrible thing as trying to rescue her husband? Not likely. The crime deserving no pity here is that a woman would have the audacity to grab a man by the balls. Shocking, isn't it? The punishment I mean.

Another similar example is from that outrageous chapter, Exodus 21, which sets the stage for all sorts of ugly problems that remain to this day. Get this ... **If men who are fighting hit a pregnant woman and she gives birth prematurely but there is no serious injury, the offender must be fined whatever the woman's husband demands and the court allows. But if there is serious injury, you are to take life for life, eye for eye, tooth for tooth, hand for hand, foot for foot, burn for burn, wound for wound, bruise for bruise.** (Ex. 21: 22). Whoa!

Look carefully at this for a moment. There are two areas here that are not clearly defined but which deserve consideration. First of all, note that only the man fighting with the woman's husband faces possible punishment should the woman miscarry. If her husband were to hit her, what would his penalty be? No penalty! Since she's his property, he can hit her when he wants to. If there's serious injury caused by the other party then "life for life" kicks in. That is another way of saying *capital punishment*, a topic we will consider again, rest assured. But the question here is who is the injured party—the woman or the baby? Obviously it is unclear. Not to labor the inerrancy issue, but even Bible commentaries that I have read, point out that verses like this are unclear. It is important, however, to note how a verse as ambiguous as this can be used by those with a preconceived idea to substantiate their own points of view.

Note the commentary on this passage from the *Falwell Liberty Bible Commentary* (pp. 156, 157): *From the word order of the sentence, and since no further amplification is given, it would seem that the baby would be in view here. If so, this would strongly teach that abortion is a capital offense* (see verses 23-25).

The commentator (whether Jerry Falwell or a ghostwriter) admits that the verse is ambiguous, and, by using subjunctive terms like *would seem* and *would teach*, he indicates that he does not know at all to whom the verse is referring. Then, using catch phrases like *From the word order of the sentence*, he attempts to build an argument. Word order in which language—English or the original Hebrew? If he says English, I say that I fail to see how the word order in English indicates one way or the other. If he says Hebrew, then I say, how well does he speak and read Hebrew anyway? I have heard many preachers and wacko religious commentators in my day espousing their points of view based on the "original" languages argument—languages that they have no knowledge of whatsoever.

But, beyond this I see yet another anomaly: *If so, this would strongly teach that abortion is a capital offense.* What? What does this have to do with abortion? This is referring to accidental miscarriage brought about by third parties fighting, and has nothing whatsoever to do with the intentional act of abortion. It may well be true that a woman will miscarry if she is struck in a fight; but, to the writer of the commentary in question, I should like to point out that this is quite a different matter from clinical abortion, in the first place; and in the second place, it would not *strongly* teach anything at all. Besides, the whole issue of abortion is a modern one based on contemporary scientific and medical knowledge. Of course ancient techniques existed. Only a people with a strong preconceived idea in mind could stretch the implications of this ancient text to such an extent to serve their own ends.

What horrifies me here is the conclusion that abortion is a capital offense! Even though I don't see how fundamentalists can come to this conclusion from this particular verse, the fact that they do frightens me because it causes me to ask the next question ... Who should receive the death penalty for abortion? The perpetrator? The doctor? The woman? Who? I am sure there is a clever answer. Even though I have just pointed out that verses like this have nothing to do with abortion in the first place, the fact that they are used to justify a controversial point of view in a current debate shows how willing some Bible-believers are to take small bits and pieces of random text from the Bible, and—albeit, out of context—say: *This would strongly teach...* But, listeners to Christian talk radio lap it up.

Divorce is another case in point. If a man marries a woman who is displeasing to him because he finds something "indecent" about her, he can write her a certificate of divorce, give it to her, and send her away. Then, if she becomes the wife of another man, and he dislikes her too, he can do likewise. But if he dies, the first guy can't pick her back up again, because she has been "defiled." **That would be detestable in the eyes of the Lord.** (Deut. 24 : 1-4). What? Totally from the male point of view—if a guy finds his wife unpleasing to him, he can simply divorce her by writing her a *certificate*. (Like, assuming he can write, that is.) Okay.

Then, she can be picked up like a used car by another guy, no problem. However, if she displeases him as well, he can discard her like trash too. But the big deal here is that the Lord would be furious if the first guy decided to give their marriage another go, because—after all—the second man had "defiled" her. She is, at this point, basically damaged goods and is of no value at all after that. God is love. LOL.

Having lived in Evangelical circles for years, I have witnessed numerous "Christian" divorces. And, let me tell you, they are just as mean and ugly as any divorce that you may read of in the *National Enquirer*. Modern Christian women never submit to this Old Testament standard, but fight tooth and nail according to contemporary American legal jurisprudence. I wholeheartedly agree with them, but must point out the hypocrisy: Evangelicals constantly and loudly decry secular institutions; but the minute it suits them, they run full tilt to those very institutions for protection from the unfairness that their own Bible initiates! Go figure.

Women are also portrayed as sluts and "temptresses" throughout the Bible. We will examine the tale of Sampson and Delilah later, which is the best-known example of the "women are evil bitches" meme. Let me quote a lesser known but equally troubling section from Proverbs, which thoughtful people should easily recognize as pure male propaganda. **Like a gold ring in a pig's snout is a beautiful woman who shows no discretion.** (Pv. 11: 22). I have always wondered if this just applies to beautiful women, and not plain or ugly females as well ... Haha.

The Jewish male attitude toward female beauty is a reflection of their male god's anti-female orientation. From the very beginning, God has cast the woman in a subordinate role. Now he *warns* vulnerable young men about the wiles of the female race. This is so sick. Take a read:

My son, keep my words and store up my commandments within you. They will keep you from the adulteress. (An example follows.) **He was going down the street near her corner, then out came a woman to meet him dressed like a prostitute and with crafty intent. She took hold of him and kissed him and with a brazen face she said: "Come let us drink of love till morning; let us enjoy ourselves with love!" With persuasive words she led him astray; she seduced him with her smooth talk. All at once he followed her like an ox going to the slaughter little knowing it will cost him his life. Her house is a highway to the grave, leading down to the chambers of death.** (Pv. 7: 8-27).

There are numerous anti-female references in the scriptures, and some have really been exploited over the centuries. The most notable is: **Do not allow a sorceress to live.** (Ex. 22: 18). For ages, women have been burned for being "witches." It has always been hard to define what a witch actually is. It's been convenient to simply accuse someone of sorcery without any specific definition of the crime. The acid test would usually reveal that the woman in question was in fact a witch; she rarely survived the test of bitter water or whatever was contrived. In colonial New England, women were routinely accused of sorcery and maimed or killed by Bible believers who were just following the law of the Old Testament. I always feel a cold chill when I hear the "Traditional American Values" set of our day clambering for a return to good old time religion. Goodie, let's all go back to Salem and have some witch trials.

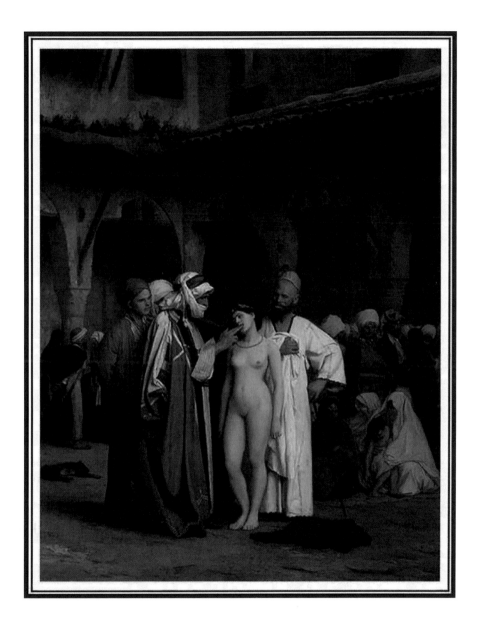

Like a gold ring in a pig's snout is a beautiful woman who shows no discretion. (Pv. 11:22). The biblical definition of women: whores, sluts, temptresses and witches. **Do not allow a sorceress to live.** (Ex. 22:18). Or, better yet, enslave them in a nice harem.

One more bone that I have to pick with the Fightin' Fundies ... It relates not only to women in general, and witches in particular, but to "foreign" woman most of all. Those are the worst. Remember, Yahweh is a stickler for ethnic purity and is constantly warning the Hebrews to lay off the foreign women. They are nothing but trouble :-(For years, certain of our southern states had laws forbidding interracial marriage. To this day, many white Protestant preachers will stand by the notion that marriage to a person of another race is forbidden by the scriptures. Of course, that is unfashionable to say from the pulpit, but you can't imagine the things you will hear coming out of the mouths of ministers over lunch privately after the sermon.

Let's look at an example ... Stop interbreeding! **"You have been unfaithful; you have married foreign women, adding to Israel's guilt. Now, make confession to the Lord, the God of your fathers, and do his will. Separate yourselves from the peoples around you and from your foreign wives."** (Ez. 10: 4). In this account in the Book of Ezra, they get rid of not only their foreign women, but the mixed-race children as well! God makes it abundantly clear that foreigners are poison. Judaism is an exclusive club; and modern Protestant Fundamentalist Christians see themselves as a "type" of Israel. When God addresses the Jews in the Old Testament, he is really talking to *them*! There are clear lines drawn between who is and who is not of the "tribe." I have read literature published by various Christian denominations in the last twenty years expressly teaching that "race-mixing" is forbidden. And, I might add, it's not just the Aryan Nation that publishes such crap.

In Numbers chapter 25 we read: **While Israel was staying in Shittim, the men began to indulge in sexual immorality with Moabite women, who invited them to sacrifice to their gods. And the Lord's anger burned against them.** (Nr. 25: 1). Obviously, he was much more pissed off that those women were inciting his boys to worship gods other than himself. Of course. How typical. Well, what was to be done? Get this: **The Lord said to Moses, "Take all the leaders of these people, kill them and expose them in broad daylight before the Lord, so that the Lord's anger will be turned away from Israel." So Moses said to Israel's judges, "Each of you must put to death those of your men who have joined in worshiping Baal of Peor."** (Nr. 25: 6-9). Whoa. Let's slow down here and not gloss over the "take all those guys out and kill them" part, okay? Having sex with immoral foreign women is one thing ... but worshiping their gods? Well, that's even worse! Kill them all!

During this time, the Israelites were undergoing one of God's plagues that he frequented upon his people for misdirected worship. So, how was the plague stopped? Well ... **Then an Israelite man brought to his family a Midianite woman. When the priest saw this he left the assembly, took a spear in his hand and followed the Israelite into the tent. He drove the spear through both of them—through the Israelite and into the woman's body. Then the plague against the Israelites was stopped; but those who died in the plague numbered 24,000.** (Nr. 25: 6-9). Interestingly enough, this plague was later referred to in the New Testament in the Book of First Corinthians 10:8. It says that 23,000 died in the plague. Well, the inerrant Bible was only off by 1,000 this time :-) Of course, there are no errors or contradictions, are there? Anyway, let's say that somewhere around 23,500 souls perished because of this one Midianite woman. Wow. Kinda leaves ya speechless, huh? Kind of a high price to get her, I'd say.

An entire book could be written on this subject alone, as this is just one example among so many. But we need to get back on the bus and head on. Suffice it to say that the God of the Jews and Christians has been on the outs with women since way back in the garden when he cursed her to severe pain in childbirth ... **"Your desire will be for your husband, and he will rule over you."** Remember? Well, that's pretty clear. But, ahead, in the New Testament, we will learn a new word, "submit," in the Book of Ephesians. But we'll get there! Moving right along...

The Lord will afflict you with the boils of Egypt and with tumors, festering sores and the itch, from which you cannot be cured! (Deut. 28:26-27)

Unsafe Sex

"When a woman has her regular flow of blood,
anyone who touches her will be unclean till evening ..."

Some years ago, when I was writing a newspaper column on religion, I caused a maelstrom of protest by printing excerpts from Leviticus chapter15. Everybody who read these direct quotations from the Holy Bible regarding bodily discharges and causes for "uncleanness," went into high freak. Of the many irate readers who were offended by this article, my favorite was the woman who wrote me at the newspaper declaring that these verses of scripture "should not be made public, but should be read in the privacy of one's own home."LOL.

It all starts out simply enough. **"When a man has a bodily discharge, the discharge is unclean."** (Leviticus 15: 2). This relates to all discharges except urinating, say my theological colleagues. I have no problem with this. Blood, puss, saliva, and semen are all considered rather unclean even in our modern society. The notion of ritual cleansing is introduced early on in the Bible and becomes a recurring theme throughout. The concept is that man is unclean and that through ceremonial cleansing he is able to face God.

God, sender of plagues, sealer of wombs, and curser of bad guys in general, cannot be approached unless the supplicant is ceremonially clean. This particular area of Leviticus lays out for us the things that put us in a state of uncleanness, and what we have to do to get it together again. **"Whoever touches a man who has had a discharge must wash his clothes and bathe with water, he will be unclean till evening. Everything the man sits on when riding will be unclean, and whoever touches any of the things that were under him will be unclean till evening; whoever picks up those things must wash his clothes and bathe with water, and he will be unclean till evening. A clay pot that the man touches must be broken, and any wooden article is to be rinsed with water."** (Lev. 15: 7-12). I am still okay with this—sort of. An ancient people beset with health problems could well do with some regulations about sanitation, due to their general lack of knowledge about hygiene—germs and all. Of course, an omniscient god might have been better advised to explain germs than to make up all the hocus-pocus that follows

... **"When a man has an emission of semen, he must bathe his whole body with water, and will be unclean till evening. Any clothing or leather that has semen on it must be washed with water, and it will be unclean till evening. When a man lies with a woman and there is an emission of semen, both must bathe with water, and they will be unclean till evening."** (Lev. 15: 16-18).

Now things become a bit trickier. Once women are in the picture, things get more complicated, given God's penchant for making things hard on women. **"When a woman has her regular flow of blood, the impurity of her monthly period will last seven days, and anyone who touches her will be unclean till evening. Anything she lies on will be unclean, and anything she sits on will be unclean. Whoever touches her bed must wash his clothes and bathe with water, and he will be unclean till evening. Whoever touches anything she sits on must wash his clothes and bathe with water, and he will be unclean till evening."** (Lev. 15: 19-23).

Menstruation is unclean. Menstruation is dirty. Menstruation is a female curse and whoever touches anything touched by a menstruating woman is unclean. What must one do to cleanse herself from such a mess? Get this ... **"When she is cleansed from her discharge, she must count off seven days, and after that she will be ceremonially clean. On the eighth day she must take two doves or two young pigeons and bring them to the priest. The priest is to sacrifice one for a sin offering and the other for a burnt offering. In this way he will make atonement for her before the Lord for the uncleanness of her discharge."** (Lev.15:28-30).

Give me a break—menstruation is considered unclean. I can understand how a primitive society could think this way. The problem I have is this ... How could an omniscient god allow this kind of nonsense to go on? A god who is all-knowing would surely know the mechanics of the human body and its functions. After all, he created it, didn't he? What's this about her counting off seven days, and on the eighth day having a priest sacrifice two pigeons on her behalf? One is a burnt offering (total waste of a good pigeon, I'd say), but the other is a sin offering! A what? A sin offering. This means that not only is menstruation dirty and unclean; it is also sinful. Sin and wickedness have been fairly interchangeable words in the Bible. I can see how these bodily discharges could be thought of as unclean. But sinful?

Just by living in our natural bodies we are sinning. I can't help myself here. But the requirement of bringing two young pigeons to the priest as a sacrifice is queer! Why must the pigeons be young? What's wrong with an old pigeon anyway? And tell me, how can you tell the difference? We all encounter pigeons on any average city street. But as pigeons go, I can't spot a *young* pigeon from an old one—can you?

Oh, as always, it just keeps getting better. **"If a man lies with her and her monthly flow touches him, he will be unclean for seven days; and the bed he lies on will be unclean."** (Lev. 15: 24). Okay. This is a bit ancient, but not totally outrageous. However, there is a problem a few chapters later when the death penalty is demanded for having sex with a menstruating woman. In Leviticus chapter 20, verse 18, to our horror, we read: **"If a man lies with a woman during her monthly period and has sexual relations with her, he has exposed the source of her flow, and she has also uncovered it. Both must be cut off from their people."** Do not miss the import of this. We've already explained that "cut off" means killed/banished. Call it what you will, but this is harsh, cruel, and unreasonable punishment. I love it when ministers quickly point out that just lying with a woman on her period is okay as long as you don't touch or have sex with her. But if you do, you're out of here. The debate in the United States rages on regarding the death penalty. But we have a whole chapter on that one ahead. Be prepared; it is nasty.

Obedience is a key word in the Old and New Testaments. God makes up all these absurd diabolical rules and expects mankind to obey them. We have thus far encountered some of these rules on our tour. However, there are hundreds more. But what happens if you don't obey them, or, perhaps, inadvertently fail to? Well, let's see what the result of disobedience is. We have only begun to explore the results of ignoring the rules. Let's check that out in Deuteronomy chapter 28, under the heading of "Curses for Disobedience." It starts out: **If you do not obey the Lord your God and do not carefully follow all his commandments and decrees I am giving you today, all of these curses will come upon you and overtake you.** (Deuteronomy 28: 15). Get ready ... here they come!

You will be cursed in the city and in the country. Your basket and your kneading trough will be cursed. The fruit of your womb will be cursed, and the crops of your land and the calves of your herds and the lambs of

your flocks. You will be cursed when you come in and cursed when you go out. (Deut. 28:16-19).

The Lord will plague you with diseases until he has destroyed you from the land. The Lord will strike you with wasting disease, with fever and inflammation, with scorching heat and drought, with blight and mildew, which will plague you until you perish. (Deut. 28: 21,22). I think I have had that plague of mildew in my bathroom once or twice. But I got over it.

Your carcass will be food for all the birds of the air and the beasts of the earth, and there will be no one to frighten them away. The Lord will afflict you with the boils of Egypt and with tumors, festering sores and the itch from which you cannot be cured. (Deut. 28: 26,27). Oh no, not the itch from which I cannot be cured! (Scabies.)

The Lord will afflict you with madness, blindness and confusion of the mind. (I think I have already been afflicted with the confusion of the mind part by reading all this.) But, please, not this ... **You will be pledged to be married to a woman, but another will take her and ravish her.** (Deut. 28: 30). (Ravish or ravage?) Oh well, I'm just reading what it says.

Your ox will be slaughtered before your eyes, but you will eat none of it. Your donkey will be forcibly taken from you and will not be returned. Your sheep will be given to your enemies, and no one will rescue them. Your sons and daughters will be given to another nation, and you will wear out your eyes watching for them day after day, powerless to lift a hand. (Deut. 28: 31). This is so awful, but true!

The Lord will afflict your knees and legs with painful boils that cannot be cured, spreading from the soles of your feet to the top of your head. (Deut. 28: 35). I really hate those boils, don't you? This is serious stuff. But wait, there's more...

All these curses will come upon you. They will pursue you and overtake you until you are destroyed, because you did not obey the Lord your God and observe the commands and decrees he gave you. He will put an iron yoke on your neck until he has destroyed you. (Deut. 28: 45). What a good, kind, friendly, loving God indeed.

The Lord will bring a nation against you from far away, from the ends of the earth ... They will leave you no grain, new wine or oil, nor any calves of your herds or lambs of your flocks until you are ruined. (Deut. 28: 49). I really appreciate a god who seeks my ruin.

Because of the suffering that your enemy will inflict on you during the siege, you will eat the fruit of the womb, the flesh of the sons and daughters the Lord your God has given you. (Deut. 28: 53). Wait wait wait! God is telling us that if we don't comply with his ridiculous rules and regulations, we are going to be subject to more of his heinous curses? What could be worse than eating our own children? Come on. Think about it. **Even the most gentle and sensitive man among you will have no compassion on his own brother or the wife he loves or his surviving children. And he will not give them any of the flesh of his children that he is eating. It will be all he has left because of the suffering your enemy will inflict on you.** (Deut. 28: 54).

It is really dangerous not complying with God's commands, like breaking the clay pots and sacrificing the two young pigeons, huh? If we do not go along with all of these commands, then we have to accept the above-mentioned punishments. These punishments are beyond the scope of modern man to comprehend or accept. The conflict is easy for some to dismiss, but for others, these decrees and commands and punishments are real. Most of us in the early 21st Century have chosen halfheartedly to reject all this as ancient history. However, many millions feel that these rules and resulting curses have *contemporary* applications. When we read this stuff we can easily just laugh it off as barbarism revisited. The problem for us in the 21st Century is that there are still millions among us who totally subscribe to this ancient creed. They will never repudiate it. They will always fall back on this well-worn cliché ... "Christ came to set us free from the law." But if you then ask them if that means the eating of our own children is invalid, they will say NO. It is not actually invalid; it is out-of-date. It had its day. It had its purpose. To which I reply, "What could *that* purpose possibly be?"

Modern preachers, pastors, televangelists, and priests are all used to their congregations not questioning them. Like, since when are the sheep allowed to question their shepherd? A famous cliché that so often glides effortlessly across modern pulpits goes like this: "You can't pick and choose at God's table. The Bible is not a smorgasbord—a buffet where you can take whatever you want and leave the rest." In other words, you have to take it all or suffer eternal damnation in hell. Very Evangelical.

Millions of modern Americans and other Christians worldwide would defend Deuteronomy 28 to the death to avoid even the appearance of picking and choosing at God's table. They read these verses about boils and festering sores, and would wish them upon those of us who do not believe them or comply with their updated version of what they think all this really means. Of course they *know* what it means. Too bad they actually don't know at all.

So many modern believers thump their Bibles instead of reading them. Have you ever noticed that fundamentalist Protestant and Catholic ministers, and priests, *and* politicians are always screaming and yelling against the "sinners" in our midst? If they would read instead of railing, they might notice that all these rules, regulations, decrees, and commandments apply not to the nonbelievers or sinners, but to *them*. Not once does the omnipotent God of the Old Testament command the Hebrews to go out and tell those terrible Amalekites, Ammorites, and Moabites to stop sinning and follow the Lord's decrees and commandments (or else). No. He says to his people: *You* stop sinning (or else)!

Well, as we move along, I wouldn't be much of a tour guide if I left you without sharing one of my favorite Bible verses (curses) of all times. Dig this ... **Then the Lord will scatter you among all nations. You will live in suspense, filled with dread both night and day, never sure of your life. In the morning you will say, "If only it were evening!" and in the evening, "If only it were morning!"— because of the terror that will fill your hearts and the sights that your eyes will see.** Now get this ... **The Lord will send you back in ships to Egypt on a journey I said you should never make again. There you will offer yourselves for sale to your enemies as male and female slaves, but no one will buy you.** (Deut. 28:64-68).

What could be worse? No one will buy me. Now that's a real curse!

"All who would not seek the Lord, the God of Israel, were to be put
to death, whether small or great, man or woman."
(II Chronicles 15:13). Believe or die! How very Sharia!

Put to Death

I will cut him off from his people; he must be put to death.

One of the most outstanding features of the Bible is its brutality. It has been claimed that television and movies have anesthetized us to violence and bloodshed. To some degree, I am sure this is so. But long before the electric media numbed us to splattering guts and tearing flesh, Bible readers could read passages about stoning and similar fatal mutilations without flinching. In the Bible there are so many crimes and infractions that call for the death penalty, I will be hard-pressed to narrow it down to the few that I think we should note along the way on our tour.

From our reading so far, it is obvious that Yahweh places primary importance on us worshiping him. All other human endeavor is secondary. The lives of the early Jews centered around their religion, as did the lives of other races of ancient human beings. Religion—and religious ceremonies—were the focus of the lives of the ancients. Singing, dancing around the campfire, telling tales of great glories of the past, or sacrificing (grains, animals, or humans) all have had a rather universal application to tribal peoples, whether they be the ancient Jews, the Mayans, the Aborigines, or the Sioux.

Ancient primitive peoples seemed to evolve along similar lines to each other, developing from nature/fertility cultures into spiritual/ethical ones; and the need for more formalized rules of behavior became more apparent. By the time the Jews were getting into the spiritual/ethical mode, many other cultures were already far more highly evolved. The Egyptian and Chinese cultures, for example, had long before been formalized; the entire subcontinent of India had been settled; and the cultures along the Fertile Crescent were well-established. Many ancient cultures had already progressed to what is called a priestly/legal religious system. They had been around longer and their laws tended to be more civilized and human-centered. That was not the case at this point in the Bible.

"Anyone who strikes a man and kills him shall be put to death." (Exodus 21: 12). There are certain key chapters in the Pentateuch that concentrate on capital punishment, so we will take a close look at these. There are, however—scattered throughout scripture—more references to stoning, being cut off, and

and death by sharp objects; so we'll check them out as well. The 21st chapter of Exodus opens the door for formalized capital punishment. Premeditated murder is addressed in verse 14: **"If a man schemes and kills another man deliberately, take him away from my altar and put him to death."** Most states in the US still have laws calling for this. But that is about where it stops. From here on, we're on our own.

But before I begin listing the other infractions for which one must be killed, I think it is important to explain that there is a great deal of debate in conservative Protestant circles these days regarding this subject. The debate centers not around whether capital punishment in itself is indeed right or wrong, current or outmoded, but whether or not the inerrant Bible's demand for death—for what we now would not even consider a crime— should be upheld.

The inerrancy set is stuck with a particular problem as it relates to sexual, moral, and relationship issues. On the one hand, they go to this section of the Bible to get their straight-laced moral values; but, on the other, they find horrendous punishments for noncompliance. A particular group, called the *reconstructionists*, maintain that in order to be a true Christian one must take the entire Bible literally and act upon it thusly. (This is the Christian version of the much dreaded Muslim Sharia Law.) The traditional literalists agree that the Bible should be read and believed literally, but hedge about following through with its every specific diabolical demand.

Much ado is seen in the press these days about domestic violence. The Bible says if a person attacks his father or mother, he must be put to death. There may be some in our society who would agree with this—but few, I think. **"Anyone who curses his father or mother must be put to death."** (Ex. 21: 17). Wow! This is not full-scale attacking, but just cursing—like backtalk or sassing of one's elders. Dangerous stuff, kids. Pay attention.

Exodus chapter 35 is our next stop. **"For six days, work is to be done, but the seventh day shall be your holy day, a Sabbath of rest to the Lord. Whoever does any work on it must be put to death."** (Ex. 35: 2). Well, well, well. It seems to me that—whether the Jews and Seventh-day Adventists are correct or the Catholics and Protestants are, regarding the actual day of the Sabbath—anyone who has worked a seven-day stretch should be on death row, in any case. I have often wondered if police officers, fire fighters, doctors, and nurses who have to work on Saturday or Sunday from time to time are at all aware that they are doomed according to Sharia—I mean, Biblical law.

Moving right along. Leviticus chapter 20 is rich material indeed on this unnerving topic. I recommend you read the whole chapter sometime at your leisure. But allow me to draw attention to a few of my favorites: **"I will set my face against the person who turns to mediums and spiritists ... I will cut him off from his people."** (Leviticus 20: 6). **"A man or woman who is a medium or spiritist among you must be put to death. You are to stone them; their blood will be on their own heads."** (Lev. 20: 27).

I can't let this one go by without a comment. For centuries these verses have been applied to spiritualists, astrologers, mediums, witches, and all manner of non-church-related psychics. Countless men and women have been stoned, stabbed, or burned at the stake for practicing divination, astrology, and sorcery. Now, when our own leaders (Read: Ronald and Nancy Reagan) consulted astrologers before travel or even cabinet meetings, where were Billy Graham, Jerry Falwell or Pat Robertson? Why were they not then—as not now—calling for the gas chamber for modern politicians who dabble in the "dark arts?" After all, the inerrant Bible is quite specific. Ah yes, "Jesus came to set us free from the law." But did he? Does he presently? Let's see ...

"If a man commits adultery with another man's wife—the wife of his neighbor—both the adulterer and the adulteress must be put to death." (Ex. 20: 10). Several of our states still have laws prohibiting adultery. In recent cases, many jilted spouses have appealed to the courts to enforce these anti-adultery laws. It has been quite a sideshow in light of all the adultery going on around the country. Jesus had an encounter with an adulteress about to be put to death under this law from Exodus 20. Do you recall this famous event? Just before the mob was about to dash her brains out with rocks, Jesus says: **"If any one of you is without sin, let him be the first to throw a stone at her."** (John 8: 7). The Christians always point to this verse as an indication that Jesus was excusing mankind from the Old Testament (Sharia) law. I don't see it that way at all. When we get to the New Testament we shall look at plenty more examples of capital punishment (which is still quite well in place) along with the rest of the ancient laws.

Before we get out of this chapter, let's look at a few more examples. **"If a man lies with a woman during her monthly period and has sexual relations with her, he has exposed exposed the source of her flow, and she has also uncovered it. Both of them must be cut off from their people."** (Lev. 20: 18). Well, most modern Christians just ignore a decree like this one. After all, what could it really hurt? And besides, who would really know anyway? It's really kind of silly and harmless. But then comes the real *biggie*. I saved it for the last of the "sex equals death" collection. Why? Because this one the Evangelicals of our time really believe in! I call it "The Fundie's Favorite" ...

"If a man lies with a man as one lies with a woman, both of them have done what is detestable. They must be put to death." (Lev. 20: 13). Yea! Finally something that has true modern applications. As a gay man, I have heard this verse of scripture hurled at me more often than any other by far from irate Bible-thumpers and wild-eyed televangelists. They love this verse. It adjudicates all their prejudices and biases. The word "bigot" is defined in Webster's as a person who is intolerant of others unlike themselves.

I recall encountering (at the Portland Gay Parade some years ago) a particularly obnoxious Christian with a little trailer parked beside the parade route, flying banners proclaiming this very verse. I couldn't help myself. I went over to engage him. When he put down his bullhorn I simply asked him how he planned to kill all of us. "Are you planning to bring back the ovens?" I asked. He looked puzzled, then picked up his bullhorn and began ranting once more (only louder).

Deuteronomy is fertile ground for more material on executions for various "crimes." Not all infractions requiring the death penalty are sexual in nature. Let's look at some more capital crimes for which the Bible calls for execution. Stoning is advocated for drunkards and profligates. A profligate is defined in the dictionary as an extremely wasteful or extravagant person. OMG, Zha Zha, Leona, Tammy Faye—look out! Oh well, perhaps you can have diamond-studded electrodes on your electric chair.

Drunkenness is no small matter, but are we to take Mrs. Robinson out and shoot her? Isn't it kind of ironic that AA meetings conclude with The Lord's Prayer? A supplication to the very deity that commands death for the disease of alcoholism. Hmmm. Under the general banner of "marriage violations" in

Deuteronomy chapter 22, we find a couple of eye-opening verses. **If a man takes a wife and, after lying with her, dislikes her and slanders her and gives her a bad name, saying "I married this woman but when I approached her, I did not find proof of her virginity," then the girl's father and mother shall bring proof that she was a virgin.** ...If it can be proved that she was indeed a virgin, by the parents displaying a cloth before the elders, the man must be fined. On the other hand ... **If, however, the charge is true, and no proof of the girl's virginity can be found, she shall be brought to the door of her father's house and there the men of her town shall stone her to death.** (Deut. 22: 21). Whew! That ought to slow down those teenage trysts in the back seats of Chevys if nothing will, huh?

Further on, in that same chapter, a modern and most timely subject is discussed: rape. **If a man happens to meet in a town a virgin pledged to be married and he sleeps with her, you shall take both of them to the gate of that town and stone them to death—the girl because she was in a town and did not scream for help, and the man because he violated another man's wife.** (Deut. 22: 23,24). But wait, there's more (I love this) ...

If a man happens to meet a virgin who is not pledged to be married and rapes her and they are discovered, he shall pay the girl's father fifty shekels of silver (about 2 1/2 lbs.). **He must marry the girl, for he has violated her. He can never divorce her as long as he lives.** (Deut. 22: 28,29). Now let me get this straight. The death penalty is required for drunkenness, extravagance, sodomy, spiritism, sorcery, adultery, sleeping with a woman on her period, and working on Sunday ... but not for rape? What? No. The punishment for rape is a fine (of under fifty bucks). But that's not the *real* punishment! The real punishment is that the guy has to marry the girl, and has to stay married to her for the rest of his life. He cannot divorce her. He is stuck with her. I just wonder if anybody would ever bother to ask the "girl" if she wanted to be joined to her rapist in holy matrimony for the rest of *her* life.

Capital punishment for military disobedience or insubordination has been around since armies were first formed eons ago. We'll get to the famous story of Joshua and the mighty army of Israel coming up. Joshua, God's supreme allied commander in the battle for Jericho and other military targets, had mega-powers given directly to him by God Almighty, who decreed: **Whoever**

rebels against your word and does not obey your words, whatever you command them, will be put to death. (Joshua 1:18). Neat and tidy. Joshua was not the only commander with such discretionary powers over human life. King David, whom we shall meet later, defeated the Moabites (Remember the story of Lot and his daughters in the cave?). Creative fellow that he was, he lowered slaughter to a game. **He made them lie down on the ground and measured them off with a length of cord. Every two lengths of them were put to death, and the third was allowed to live.** (II Samuel 8: 2). How generous.

In early Puritan America, church attendance was mandatory, worship obligatory, and belief undisputed. They were really just following the example of the Old Testament Israelites. Belief was likewise mandatory—or else. **All who would not seek the Lord, the God of Israel, were to be put to death, whether small or great, man or woman.** (II Chronicles 15: 13). Believe or die.

In our modern world this may sound a bit harsh. Nevertheless, many of our Muslim planetary coinhabitants do *require* both belief and worship. You can't just quit being a Muslim, under pain of death. I wonder if our Christian fundamentalist friends, neighbors, and family would force *us* to believe and worship as they do—if they could. Would they actually enforce the worship of their god? My guess is that the answer to that question is simple. Yup.

Well, I hope you were enlightened by that topical stop along our tour. Our next stop is one of the Bible's most enduring themes. Get ready for ... war!

God has a simple plan for waging war: Genocide.

War and the Bible

Do not leave alive anything thatbreathes.

No subject in scripture is more pronounced than war, killing, and fighting. Typical of a tribal warrior society, the Israelites, who had fled Egypt, encountered one battle after another during the duration of their sojourn. The point here is that—as the story goes—God blasted them out of their enslavement in order to fulfill the promise to Abraham, Isaac, and Jacob to repopulate the land that was then inhabited by the Canaanites and many other contending tribes.

This grand scheme was not without its detractors. In fact, the people who were so heroically delivered from Egypt, griped and complained bitterly about their forty-year trek through the Sinai Desert. Moses, Aaron, and then Joshua had to put up with their constant bitching. In Numbers 21 we read how God dealt with their complaining.

They traveled from Mount Hor along the route to the Red Sea (that I think they were already supposed to have crossed) **to go around Edom. But the people grew impatient on the way, they spoke against God and against Moses, and said, "Why have you brought us up out of Egypt to die in the desert? There is no bread! There is no water! And we detest this miserable food!"** (Nr. 21:4,5).

Then the Lord sent venomous snakes among them; they bit the people and many Israelites died. The people came to Moses and said, "We sinned when we spoke against the Lord and against you. Pray that the Lord will take the snakes away from us." So Moses prayed for the people. (Nr. 21: 6,7).

The Lord said to Moses, "Make a snake and put it on a pole; anyone who is bitten can look to it and live." (Nr. 21: 8). Make a snake? Didn't I hear something about forbidding graven images? In fact, God forbade the Jews to make *any* images whatsoever. Representational art is not at all part of the Jewish purview (nor the Muslim, for that matter). Here it seems that God is contradicting his own commandment. Back in Exodus, when the Israelites made a golden calf, God went into a tailspin.

Now he is ordering them to create an image as a cure for snakebite. Is that ever consistency! But there is more to this story. Later God sanctions the destruction of that very image. For those of us who have read ahead, we note in II Kings (700 years later): **He** (King Hezekiah) **broke into pieces the bronze snake that Moses had made, for up to that time the Israelites had been burning incense to it.** (II Kings 18: 4). Curious, huh? But moving right along on our tour

Having already encountered a tribe called the Amalekites, and having totally routed them, they moved on to Moab. You remember the Moabites? In Genesis chapter 19, Lot's elder daughter, who got pregnant by her father, bore him a son named Moab. He spawned the Moabites who were now being attacked by the wandering Israelites. Lot was Abraham's nephew, so these people were related! Since the Moabites could trace their lineage back to Abraham, why was God so willing to condemn them? They were not too distant cousins. Hmmm.

En route they encountered the Amorites ... whom they slaughtered. And Og, the King of Bashan, and his army were likewise summarily dispatched, leaving no survivors. The Moabites heard of this and were scared out of their wits. They said of the Israelites: **This horde is going to lick up everything around us, as an ox licks up the grass of the field.** (Nr. 22: 4). Whereupon the King of Moab, a certain Balak, sent for a fellow named Balaam to put a curse on the approaching Israelites. I have always loved the story of what happened en route. Balaam is riding his donkey to meet Balak. An angel of the Lord stands in the middle of the road with a drawn sword to oppose him. When the donkey saw the angel, it bolted into a field, whereupon Balaam beat it, forcing it back onto the road. They encounter the same angel again and the donkey pressed up against a wall along the side of the road, crushing Balaam's foot. So he beat the animal again. Then the angel moved ahead and stood in a narrow place where they were hemmed in. The donkey saw the angel and laid down on the road. Now, this animal is definitely freaked out. Balaam begins beating the poor thing to a pulp. So get this! The donkey turns around and says, **"What have I done to make you beat me these three times?"** Balaam answered the donkey, **"You have made a fool of me! If I had a sword in my hand, I would kill you right now." The donkey said to Balaam, "Am not I your own donkey, which you have always ridden, to this day? Have I been in the habit of doing this to you?"** (Nr. 22: 28-30).

I have heard many sermons referring to this incident. This is a favorite with Bible believers. They have no trouble whatsoever swallowing the talking donkey part at all. In fact, they say it proves that God can indeed use anyone or anything—no matter how humble—to communicate with us. Balaam finally saw the angel himself and went on to discourse with it. I guess after all the amazing things we have already encountered in scripture so far, a talking ass is not at all strange. I have always wondered if the teeth, tongue, and lips of a mule could ever really create human sounds. Oh well, I guess if Mr. Ed can do it, Balaam's ass can too. The only difference is that no one actually believes that Mr. Ed is doing the talking, but millions of people in our modern world of science and discovery still maintain that the animal actually was articulate enough to talk directly to good ol' Balaam. Think about it.

The Bible is bloody reading. Hundreds of pages that follow are dedicated to war. Having already destroyed a few tribes that got in the way, God pushes the Israelites further where they encounter several other tribes, notably, the Hittites, Perizzites, Jebbusites, and Canaanites. In Deuteronomy chapter 20 we begin to encounter God's command for his people to commit genocide.

"When you go out to war against your enemies and see horses and chariots and an army greater than yours, do not be afraid of them, because the Lord your God, who brought you out of Egypt, will be with you. For the Lord your God is the one who goes with you to fight for you against your enemies to give you victory." (Deuteronomy 20: 1-4).

This verse is a favorite of Evangelicals today. As a "type" of Israel, they feel that they are divine warriors of God, invading and conquering enemy territory. God commanded Israel to move into and conquer land occupied by these other tribes. He commanded that every man, woman, child, and animal be killed. Why? Because they worshiped gods other than him! OMG, imagine that! Modern Christians see life as a battle. Like Israel, saved out of bondage in Egypt, they are saved from the "bondage of sin" and saved for a purpose—to go forth and conquer enemy-held territory for God. Their enemies are many, but they all have one thing in common; they do not worship Yahweh, the one true god. And for this crime they must be destroyed. Unfortunately for our modern Israelites (Christian fundamentalists), they are forbidden by human law from killing us sinners physically; although they would love to. Instead, they kill us through other means such as the courts, the ballot box, and the media. These sociopolitical hybrids still love reading of the great battles of the Old Testament. It gets them all whipped up against their perceived enemies, such as unbelief, immorality, wickedness, godlessness, and homosexuality. They define their enemies in these abstract terms, whereas the Jews—who fought their way into the "Holy Land"—fought against real armies in real battles where thousands died on both sides.

You'll love this. Whenever the subject of war is broached in the Old Testament, God spends an inordinate amount of time and energy to instruct the Jews in the art of warfare. And despite the high-sounding notions of massive armies colliding in battle, there are other more mundane issues that God feels compelled to explain in the pages of the divinely inspired Holy Bible. Such a topic as field sanitation simply has to be addressed. Actually, I do suppose these potty rules make for happy campers even today.

Designate a place outside the camp where you can go to relieve yourself. As part of your equipment have something to dig with, and when you relieve yourself, dig a hole and cover up your excrement. (Now get this ...) **For the Lord your God moves about in your camp to protect you and to deliver your enemies to you. Your camp must be holy, so that he will not see among you anything indecent and turn away from you.** (Deut. 23: 12-14). I don't mean to raise the "does God have a literal body?" issue again, but—simply to point out the obvious—God moves around your bivouac area at night and doesn't want to step in a pile of shit. Duh.

The notion of warfare is woven into the entire fabric of the Bible. The problem for modern believers is to separate what is literal from what is symbolic. As in the case of slavery and the position of women, the problem that they face regarding war is how far is far enough, and how far is too far? They are hopelessly divided on this issue. Let us read on . . .

In the cities of the nations the Lord your God is giving you as an inheritance, do not leave alive anything that breathes. Completely destroy them. The Hittites, Amorites, Canaanites, Perizzites, Hivites and Jebusites—as the Lord commanded you. Otherwise they will teach you to follow all the detestable things they do in worshiping their gods, and you will sin against the Lord your God. (Deut. 20: 16-18).

**In the cities of the nations the lord your God is giving you ... do not leave alive
anything that breathes. Completely destroy them.** (Deut. 20: 16-18).
No wonder we call them the "Fightin' Fundies." War is in their DNA.

This command was not symbolic. It is not to be taken as symbolic, even to this day. It is clearly a command to commit genocide. By the time we get to this point, and have already been shocked by all manner of things from the flood to the pillar of salt, it is easy to get weary and even a bit numb. For those who do not believe the Bible, it is just one more outrage. But, in an effort to refocus, we have to realize that millions of Christians feel no such outrage. After all, they reason, God promised that land to Abraham, Isaac, and Jacob, and their offspring as an inheritance. It belonged to them, and he went to great lengths to get them out of bondage to make good on his promise to give it to them.

There were already other people living in the land that was to become theirs and these people had to be displaced. The fact that God ordered the Israelites to *kill everything that breathes*, does not faze them. I have never heard a sermon calling into question God's commandment to commit genocide. After all, they reason, those peoples *deserved* to die. Why? Because they were doing detestable things by worshiping their "false gods."

I have always wondered which is more detestable—worshiping false gods or killing everything that breathes. If I could isolate one particular topic along our route through the Bible that gives us all a reason to beware, this has to be it. God's attitude toward his own followers is reflected in his many curses upon them, as we have already seen (particularly in the last chapter). However, his attitude toward the people who do not worship him properly is even more horrifying. Just kill them all!

The sweet little old lady in Sunday school, when asked to read aloud from Deuteronomy 20, will gladly do so without flinching. The entire congregation can hear passages like these and not bat an eye. Like reading the account of the Genesis flood, the idea of God committing wholesale murder, or commanding it, does not register a complaint. Bible believers of every stripe read words of death and destruction with about as much thoughtfulness as reading a grocery list. "Parental guidance" movies and television are far tamer stuff than this, yet Christian children are reared on a constant diet of slaughter, murder, and mutilation. I have often pondered how insensitive modern pew-sitters are to mass murder and destruction. They relate to the murderers and not the victims. But let them get going about the "detestable" practices of those being slaughtered ... That's a different story for sure.

God drowned countless millions in the Genesis flood, killed the firstborn of everyone in all of Egypt, and commanded total annihilation of all the inhabitants of the lands promised to Abraham. Modern televangelists and their stooge donors consider this their due—they deserved what they got. After all, in each case—they argue—the people who were destroyed were wicked. Their wickedness is ill-defined at best, but because they were not worshiping Yahweh in the proper way, they deserved death; and the mode of dispatch is somewhat immaterial.

I think it is also important to point out that in each of these cases, the real reason for their demise is not that they are actually committing some indescribable crimes. Their crime was not worshiping Yahweh. But, of course, why would they know how to worship the Jewish god properly anyway? Who would have taught them? Answer: nobody. It is a total catch-22, like God killing all the wicked inhabitants of the Earth in the flood without informing them and warning them of their wickedness. These poor saps were simply targets for elimination, without even a chance to change their ways. The real problem here is that the Old Testament is a total Jewish treatise. The entire focus is on the Jews. And whatever other peoples of the world were doing was of no consequence to them or their big buddy in the sky; they were simply obstacles that needed to be removed. Frankly, neither God nor his chosen people gave a damn about the people they slaughtered. As far as they all were concerned, those blockheads could just go out, eat onion sandwiches, suck eggs, and die, bastards, die!

If all mankind was spawned from those two in the garden, as we have read, then all men are indeed brothers. But at a certain point God begins playing favorites. He promised Abraham that his descendants would be favored above other men and women on Earth, and now we see by extension the result of that favoritism. The favored are commanded to murder the non-favored. We read about the Hittites, Perizzites, and Jebusites as if they were cockroaches that needed to be exterminated. Their humanity is never addressed. They were simply breathing obstacles. And, besides, God never liked them anyway. Later, when we get to the New Testament, we will hear pious Christians claim that God loves *all* men regardless of race, gender, ethnicity, or sexual orientation. Well, let me warn you, at that point the divine attitude toward the poor Jebusites just might stick in our craw.

Thus we come to the end of the first five books of the Bible. The Pentateuch, in my opinion, is the richest section of scripture. The fundamentalists insist that it was written exclusively by Moses. Its richness is that it contains all the particulars we need to know in order to understand the rest of the "Good Book." Few casual readers ever get this far ... congratulations! So, as we plunge forward, I hope you are still with me. There is a lot of new territory to cover and we need to get going. But one last thing about Moses (I think you will get a chuckle).

At this point Moses is dying. He climbs up Mt. Nebo and God shows him the "Promised Land." Then, miraculously, he *writes* his own obituary. He pens the account of his own death and burial! Here goes: **Then Moses climbed Mt. Nebo from the plains of Moab. To the top of Pisgah, across from Jericho. There the Lord showed him the whole land—from Gilead to Dan, all of Naphtali, the territory of Ephraim and Manasseh, all the land of Judah as far as the western sea, the Negev and the whole region from the Valley of Jericho, the City of Palms, as far as Zoar. Then the Lord said to him, "This is the land I promised an oath to Abraham, Isaac and Jacob when I said: 'I will give it to your descendants.' I have let you see it with your eyes, but you will not cross over into it."**

And Moses, the servant of the Lord, died here in Moab, as the Lord had said. He buried him in Moab, in the valley opposite Beth Peor, but to this day no one knows where his grave is. Moses was a hundred twenty years old when he died, yet his eyes were not weak nor his strength gone. The Israelites grieved for Moses in the plains of Moab thirty days, until the time of weeping and mourning was over. (Deut. 34: 1-8).

Does any of that make sense to you? Not likely. I checked, and Jerry Falwell's *Liberty Bible Commentary* does not even touch upon this obvious impossibility. If Moses wrote the whole Pentateuch, then who wrote Deuteronomy chapter 34? My guess is that sometime in the first or second century C.E. (AD), some monk was frustrated with this obvious problem. Like lots of places in the early Bible, scribes helped God out by editing a bit here and there to make the story work. LOL

The natural transition that brings us into the middle of the Bible begins with Moses laying hands on Joshua and transferring to him the leadership position. The final verses of Deuteronomy say that no prophet since Moses has ever been as intimate with God as he was. For that reason nobody since then has ever been able to do all those tricky miracles like he did back in Egypt. I actually find this to be untrue. I will admit that I was impressed with the plagues, the blood, the frogs, the boils, and all. But Joshua pulls off a miracle right at the beginning of his tenure that leaves all that in the shade. You'll see what I mean. Let's march on with him to Jericho!

Part 5

Priests
and
Palaces

Joshua commands the Sun: Ooo, that's so gay!

Joshua

"O sun, stand still over Gibeon, O moon, over the valley of Aijalon."

Joshua never needed to take a back seat to anyone. In chapter one, after the death of Moses, God charged him to be strong and courageous. **"I will give you every place where you set your foot, as I promised Moses."** (Joshua 1: 3). God gets Joshua all wound up. Joshua is a natural leader and military commander. He organizes his troops to prepare to invade the area on the opposite side of the Jordan River, where Moses was not allowed to go. **"Get your supplies ready,"** he charges his officers. **"Three days from now you will cross the Jordan here to go in and take possession of the land the Lord your God is giving you for your own."** (Josh. 1: 10).

Joshua was a clever leader, and in chapter two he sends out two spies to Jericho to check out the scene—the territory that they plan to conquer shortly. The spies must have liked what they saw, as they found a whorehouse and immediately checked in. This chapter has been an embarrassment to Bible believers for centuries. Numerous attempts have been made to explain why they ended up in a bordello and what they were doing there. Naturally there is always a lot of editorializing, but just reading it as is, it says: **So they went and entered the house of a prostitute named Rahab and stayed there.** (Josh. 2: 1). All the Bible commentaries that I have read assure us that they "didn't do anything" with Rahab. Oh sure. Of course, the Bible doesn't say that they didn't do anything—if you know what I mean. We are supposed to just *assume* that those nice Jewish boys didn't do anything at all while in the brothel. But I have my doubts. Don't you? LOL.

Whether or not they were doing it with Rahab or her girls is a no-biggie. Something gave them away. Don't quote me, but I wonder if *circumcision might* have had something to do with it. Anyway, somebody tattled to the king of Jericho that these two Jewish spies were at the local house of ill repute. Whereupon he sends a message to Rahab to give them up. But Rahab has an uncanny survival instinct. She has heard of the Genocide. **"We have heard how the Lord dried up the water of the Red (Reed) Sea for you when you came out of Egypt, and what you did to Sihon and Og, the two kings of the Amorites east of the Jordan, whom you completely destroyed."** (Josh. 2: 10). Their reputation for mass God-sanctioned murder preceded them.

Rahab cleverly bargains with the spies, hiding them and lying on their behalf in exchange for a promise that when the Israelites sweep into the city and kill everybody, she and her business will survive under the new administration. The spies escape with her help and tell her to tie a red cord in her window, so the advancing troops will know to spare the house from the destruction that will inevitably follow.

Preachers gloss over the whole notion that all this takes place in a whorehouse, and that a lying pagan prostitute saved them. Instead, they concentrate on the *symbol* of the red cord! So typical. Like the blood on the doorposts in Egypt, this is—they say—a precursor to the blood of Jesus that allows destruction to pass us by. For fundamentalists, symbols always seem to take precedence when substance should be avoided, or if the obvious is too uncomfortable for them.

The destruction of Jericho is a story known to us all. Somehow even the most unsophisticated reader knows that "the walls came a tumblin' down." Well, as usual, there is more to the story than meets the eye (or ear). In chapter five we read that the Lord dried up the Jordan River so that the armies of Israel could pass through on dry land. After the Red (Reed) Sea story, this is a bit anticlimactic. In fact, it looks like another copycat story, based on the original but garbled over the centuries. Joshua 3:7 says that they already crossed the Jordan, and in the next chapter (4:10-11) it states the opposite—that they did *not* cross.

Either way, there is an old axiom that I have always loved. "Beware of old men who nod wisely and speak foolishly." In my mind, I see this white-haired old duffer trying to retell the story of Joshua for his grandkids (after a few brewskis perhaps). "Now let's see ... the children of Israel crossed the Red Sea on dry land—er, eh—or was that the Jordan River? Hmm, let's see ... Well, one way or the other, the point is that they crossed somewhere on *dry* land."

Anyhow, the story moves forward thusly: **Now when all the Amorite kings west of the Jordan and all the Canaanite kings along the seacoast heard how the Lord had dried up the Jordan before the Israelites until they had crossed over, their hearts sank and they no longer had the courage to face the Israelites.** (Josh. 2: 10,11). Heavy stuff, huh?

In any case, they managed to get across the Jordan. I've been there a few times, and it isn't much of a river anyway, so don't be too impressed. The next stop: Jericho. This is a walled city. All the cities were walled, so that is also a no-big-deal. A direct frontal assault on a walled city would require all sorts of equipment, and would be costly in terms of personnel and material. So, God told them to march around the city for six days, blow their horns, and make a bunch of noise. On the seventh day they were to shout and the walls would collapse. They would then rush into the city—kill everybody—and victory would be theirs! They did as ordered.

We all know this story. I have no problem with the tale as such. I have even read how when they shouted, it coincided with an earthquake and that was what in fact flattened the walls of Jericho. I don't really know how it happened, but God managed to get the job done. Over the centuries of retelling, I am sure there was some license applied. The issue for me is, once again, the wholesale slaughter of the inhabitants of the city. Why do we let religious self-righteous Bible thumpers get away with sanctioning genocide? The preachers love to paint verbal pictures for us of mighty armies of Israel marching around the city walls with their ark, their banners, and their ram's horns, and all. They love the symbolism of the armies of God surrounding the already defeated forces of evil cowering behind walls of clay and brick. A zillion sermons have been preached about how the wicked people of Jericho hid in paralyzed fear behind their walls while the already victorious forces of God marched triumphantly around them. Then on the seventh day Joshua's men shouted and the walls collapsed. Yea!

Then, true to form, the genocide began. They killed every inhabitant of the city—including the sinful animals. There was total ethnic cleansing—except for Rahab and her girls. **When the trumpets sounded, the people shouted, and at the sound of the trumpet, when the people gave a loud shout, the wall collapsed; so every man charged in, and they took the city. They devoted the city to the Lord and destroyed with the sword every living thing in it—men and women, young and old, cattle, sheep and donkeys.** (Josh. 6: 20). Stop and let that sink in.

Doesn't this bother you just a bit? Is this all so distant, remote, and unreal so as to be of no importance? True—if this tale has any point, in fact, whatsoever—it is not unlike hundreds of other tales of murder and mayhem. However, the presence of the omnipotent, omniscient God is somehow supposed to legitimize the slaughter. We are just supposed to accept this as totally cool and justified. After all, we teach little children in Sunday school that all those people (and their animals) deserved to die due to their wickedness. I call that child abuse.

One Christian apologist whom I have read frequently over the years justifies the massacre in Jericho like this: *"The people of the city were hopelessly infected with the cancer of moral depravity."* (Archer, p.158). Wow. They did not know to worship Yahweh, so they were depraved and deserved to die. I have always wondered if the death in the capture of Jericho means less than the deaths in Warsaw in 1939, Shanghai in 1949, or My Lai in 1969. It is carnage no matter when it happened.

One other thing I notice here: **All the silver and gold articles of bronze and iron are sacred to the Lord and must go into his treasury.** (Josh. 6: 19). What in the world does God need with gold, silver, and bronze stuff? Think about it. This is the God who supposedly spoke the Universe into being. He created the galaxies, the nebulae, quarks, and black holes. He is as big as the Universe itself, and simultaneously present in every nook and cranny of the entire interstellar realm in its infinite scope. Yet he needs a few trinkets of gold, silver, bronze, and iron for his "treasury?" Please.

Then they burned the whole city and everything in it, but they put the silver and gold and the articles of bronze and iron into the treasury of the Lord's house. (Josh. 6: 24). The Lord's house? The Lord has a house? Not to nitpick here, but what is this about the Lord's house? Are not we dealing with an omnipresent being here? One who commands the firmament? Now we read that he has a house full of groovy cups and bowls of gold, silver, bronze, and iron. *Iron?* Is that sort of like cast iron skillets, frying pans, and other useful kitchen accouterments? What the heck does God Almighty need with iron fry pans anyway? If he wants a steak why would he need to cook it? Why not just speak it into existence? Good grief!

Anyhow, they finished off Jericho, spared Rahab, and annihilated everybody else. Then Joshua pronounced this solemn oath: **"Cursed before the Lord is the man who undertakes to rebuild this city, Jericho. At the cost of his firstborn son will he lay its foundations; at the cost of his youngest will**

he set up its gates." (Josh. 6: 26). Don't look now, but long after Joshua departed the planet along with his curse, Jericho was indeed rebuilt—and is still standing today! I've been *there* too.

Shortly thereafter God noticed that some of the plunder was missing. Obviously, he was paying attention. Somebody had ripped off some of those cool gold and silver articles from the treasury and God was royally pissed. So much so in fact that it was affecting the new war—the campaign against the town of Ai. Joshua was in a total tizzy. The battle for Ai was going very wrong. So, Joshua throws himself down on the ground and grovels before the Lord. "Why is Ai beating the shit out of us?" he asks God—weeping and wailing.

So God tells him that somebody has stolen some of his bling. The battle, then underway, will flop unless the missing doodads are returned to the storehouse. God roars out: **He who is caught with the devoted things shall be destroyed by fire, along with all that belongs to him. He has violated the covenant of the Lord and has done a disgraceful thing in Israel.** (Josh. 1: 15). Aha! The reason that things are not going well in Ai is that somebody has had his fingers in the till. They caught the culprit—a certain Achan, son of Carmi, son of Zimri, son of Zerah of the tribe of Judah—who saw in the plunder a beautiful robe from Babylon, 200 shekels of sliver, and a wedge of gold weighing fifty shekels. Yo! So, he just had to have it all. He ripped them off and buried them under his tent. When Joshua grilled him, he confessed. Then Joshua screamed, yelling at him: **"Why have you brought this disaster on us? The Lord will bring disaster on you today."** (Josh. 7: 25). Whereupon they stoned him and his family, and cremated them, thus fulfilling God's curse of fire. God was incensed that someone took a robe that belonged to him! And it was just the right size! But once they threw rocks at Achan and his family, killing them all, everything was okay. Ai was destroyed and Israel was ready for its next victim.

Joshua burned Ai and made it a permanent heap of ruins, a desolate place to this day. He hung the king of Ai on a tree and left him there until evening. At sunset, Joshua ordered them to take the body from the tree and throw it down at the entrance of the city gate. And they raised a large pile of rocks over it, which remains to this day. (Josh. 8: 28). Really? To *this* day? Where is it? Hmmm.

Whether or not that pile of rocks actually remains to this day is immaterial as far as I am concerned, because the most remarkable event recorded anywhere in the Bible happens next. I cannot express strongly enough that Bible "scholars" and other believers who hold this account to be accurate are forced to defend the validity of this jaw-dropping event. Israel sets out in a massive battle against the combined forces of the King of Jerusalem, Hebron, Jarmuth, Lachish, and Eglon. This is no ordinary battle.

On the day the Lord gave the Amorites over to Israel, Joshua said to the Lord in the presence of Israel: "O sun, stand still over Gibeon, O moon, over the valley of Aijalon." So the sun stood still, and the moon stopped, till the nation avenged itself on its enemies, as it is written in the book of Jashar. The sun stopped in the middle of the sky and delayed going down about a full day. There has never been a day like it before or since, a day when the Lord listened to a man. Surely the Lord was fighting for Israel! (Josh. 10: 12-14).

Talk about an understatement! **"There has never been a day like it before or since."** Holy shit, I'll say! As I said before, this is way bigger than anything Moses ever pulled off with his magic rod. This just leaves all those plagues on Egypt in the shade, huh? Take note: If the Bible is inerrant, then the Sun and Moon did indeed halt in their orbits. A host of scientific questions follow. The utter imponderability of this mondo-cosmic extravaganza should dissuade even the most ardent Bible believer. But it does not!

So strong is the need of Christians—both Catholic and Protestant (and cults) — to believe that their scripture is divinely inspired and true and accurate in every detail of science, that the very suspension of reason is often called for. Of all the baggage that believers are required to carry, I think that this one is the heaviest and bulkiest of all.

Some time ago I was lurking on a particularly stupid fundamentalist website. All of the participants were ranting on and on about how the Bible is flawless in all areas of history, culture, and science. I couldn't help myself. I dove in with the abovementioned story of the Sun and Moon standing still. It was like smacking a hornet's nest with a stick. The Fundies attacked me in full force. One particular woman from somewhere in Texas called me a moron. "Obviously the Sun and Moon didn't really stand still," she lectured. "The *Earth* stood still, thus making it appear as if it were the Sun and Moon." Whereupon she called me an atheist, a communist, a socialist, and everything else she could think of to put me in my place. Gotta just see the love of Christ shining through, huh?

One Sunday morning some years ago I was sitting in a church listening to a particularly obnoxious southern fried preacher rant and rave about the *inerrancy* of the Bible. I don't think he knew that word, but he called it "authority." The scripture is perfect and complete and accurate on its own. It does not need explanation, interpretation, or justification. It is simply so. On this authority he was able to build some argument relating to a current political issue. The argument makes perfect sense if the authority of the scripture is unchallenged and taken for granted. However, if certain parts of the Bible are questionable, where is the line drawn? Well, it never is drawn. There never is a line.

Literalists know that in order to use the portions of scripture that adjudicate their preconceived ideas, they must accept it *all* as true and valid. (All or nothing at all.) I still remember the very words he used because I wrote them down. "I don't try to understand everything in the Bible; I don't try to interpret it. I just read it and *believe* it!" Whoa.

Samson is God's own Rambo. He wrought death and destruction wherever he went.
Yet, modern believers consider him a hero of the faith!

Samson

With a donkey's jawbone I have killed a thousand men.

This is one of those Bible stories we all sort of remember—but not quite. It is always included in those books of Bible stories for children that you can buy at religious (Christian) book stores. Yet, the story of Samson is not one that Bible believers should tout too much. Samson was quite a failure even though God had great plans for him.

The story begins in the Book of Judges chapter 13. **Again the Israelites did evil in the eyes of the Lord, so the Lord delivered them into the hands of the Philistines for forty years.** (Judges 13: 1). This happens again and again in the Old Testament. Whenever the Jews were captured or thwarted somehow, it was because they "did evil in the eyes of the Lord." Much like assigning blame for earthquakes and floods in other ancient cultures, the Israelites always had a reason for their woes.

We hear a lot about the Philistines in the Bible. The current term with which we all are more familiar is: *Palestinians.* Anyway, these folks have been around a long time, and they were there before the Jews arrived from Egypt. Intermittently throughout the Old Testament, they beat up on the Jews and were beaten up by the Jews. It has not been a happy relationship over the years. So, during one of the periods when the Philistines were on top, a certain man named Manoah had a wife who was sterile. With a copycat story to that of Abram and Sarai—this couple was visited by an angel who told them that she was going to conceive and have a son. In this case he was to become a Nazarite, one set apart to God from birth. His mission was to begin the deliverance of Israel from the occupation of the Philistines.

The Nazarites were those who were set apart to serve God. They took a vow that was threefold. They were not to drink wine or "strong drink," not to touch dead bodies, and not to cut their hair. That all makes sense, huh? See the connection? Duh. I never have.

No razor may be used on his head, the angel instructs the woman—who in typical Biblical sexist fashion is not even named—**because the boy is to be**

A Nazarite, set apart to God from birth, and he will begin the deliverance of Israel from the hands of the Philistines. (Jud. 13: 5). **The woman gave birth to a boy and named him Samson. He grew and the Lord blessed him, and the spirit of the Lord began to stir him while he was in Mahaneh Dan, between Zorah and Eshtaol.** (Jud. 13: 24). Wherever in the hell that is!

Samson was your typical "only child." He was spoiled rotten. In chapter 14 he is a young man and takes one look at a Philistine beauty and says to his dad and mom: **"I have seen a Philistine woman in Timnah; now get her for me as my wife."** Demanding little snot, isn't he? His parents are appalled. **"Isn't there an acceptable woman among your relatives or among all our people? Must you go to the uncircumcised Philistines to get a wife?"** they wail. (Jud. 14: 3).

To make a long senseless story short, Samson's parents acquiesced and got the Philistine woman for him. En route to the wedding, Samson was attacked by a lion. (Since lions are native to Africa and not the Middle East, I have to presume that those medieval monks and scribes were editing again.) Anyway, **the spirit of the Lord came upon him in power so that he tore the lion apart with his bare hands as he might have torn a young goat.** (Jud. 14: 6). Quite frankly, either would seem difficult to tear apart with one's bare hands, but, after all, the spirit of the Lord "came upon him in power." Wow.

Later he encountered that same lion's carcass, which was full of bees by then. He ate the honey and concocted a riddle for the Philistines. His new Philistine wife coerced him into divulging the answer to the riddle. Then the Philistines duped him by guessing the riddle and humiliating him. He was furious. He was so angry, in fact, that he gave his new wife away to a friend. Later, when he wanted her back, her father pointed out to Samson that she now belonged to the friend. He suggested that Samson take her younger sister instead. OMG, was Samson ever pissed off again! (I told you he was a spoiled brat.).

So what does he do? **So he went out and caught three hundred foxes and tied them tail to tail in pairs. He then fastened a torch to every pair of tails, lit the torches and let the foxes loose in the standing grain of the Philistines.**

He burned up the shocks and standing grain, together with the vineyards and olive groves. (Jud. 15: 4,5).

Whoa. Let's take a break here. Let's not simply accept this (as our fundamentalist friends do) without thinking about it more carefully. Doesn't this just strain credibility a bit? 300 foxes? Try to imagine *anyone* undertaking to locate, trap, and contain 300 wild animals in that desert country. How much time and effort would be involved in such a process? I can't imagine a hothead like Samson ever taking the time and energy to invest in such a project. A typical true Alpha male with an ADHD personality, he was impulsive to a fault and had a massive ego and a temper to match. Why not just torch the fields himself? Why waste all that time and effort on the fox story? It is generally just stupid. In fact, I see this story as another example of some old goobers retelling a story and adding their own embellishments. Well, you have to admit, it does make the story more interesting.

It goes on. Tit for tat, the Philistines kill his wife and father as revenge for the field burnings. Didn't his wife now belong to his friend? Oh well, Samson was in a rip-roaring rage. Definitely not keen on anger management, he vowed to get back at them. Surprise. **"Since you've acted like this, I won't stop until I get my revenge on you."** (Jud. 15: 7). He won't stop. The feud intensifies. To prevent an all-out war, the Jews actually give him up to the Philistines, who imprison him. Since the Jews are occupied at this time, they don't need a slaughter on their hands. But Samson isn't about to take this lying down. He breaks out. **The spirit of the Lord came upon him in power. The ropes on his arms became like charred flax, and the bindings dropped from his hands. Finding a fresh jawbone of a donkey, he grabbed it and struck down a thousand men.** (Jud. 15:14).

I have often wondered while sitting through sermons on the topic of Samson—one of the true heroes of fundamentalist Christians—if that jawbone might have belonged to Balaam's donkey. You remember the ass that could talk? Actually, it sounds to me like another garbled story told by old men who speak foolishly around the fire at night—in their cups.

Whether or not it is really possible to kill 1,000 (presumably armed) men with a bone is anyone's guess. Not to labor the issue again, but when Christians hear sermons of Samson personally committing mass killing, they wriggle with glee in their church pews. Sort of like that 1960s expression about "killing Commies for Christ," they adore Samson. God came upon him "in power" and gave him superhuman strength to kill. He was a total killing machine. Samson is a Biblical Rambo. But Rambo is more sensible and even compassionate. Samson, on the other hand, is mean-spirited and downright cruel. He has killed countless Philistines and remains a rogue. So what do the Jews do? They elect him president for twenty years! Go figure. But think about it. If modern right wing Christians could nominate a candidate like Samson, they definitely would in a New York minute. (Make that a Texas minute!) LOL.

Well, finally the mean bastard met his match. Her name was Delilah. Remember the story? It starts out like this: **One day Samson went to Gaza, where he saw a prostitute. He went in to spend the night with her.** (Jud. 16: 1). Even the most fundamental Bible commentaries admit he was arrogant and stupid for going there in the first place, and for getting involved with her in the second. As a Nazarite, he was one of God's special people, assigned to deliver his people from bondage, and he was wasting his time consorting with whores. Like the two spies sent out by Joshua, Samson was detected. Why do I think again that circumcision and brothels have some part in this? Anyway, he gets away, but just for the moment.

Sometime later, he fell in love with a woman in the Valley of Sorek whose name was Delilah. The rulers of the Philistines went to her and said: "See if you can lure him into showing you the secret of his great strength and how we can overpower him so we may tie him up and subdue him." (Jud. 16: 4,5). In the end, as you may recall, she got him to admit that his long hair was the source of his great strength. The Philistines captured him, shaved his head, and gouged out his eyes. He was a prisoner and a laughing stock to boot.

But in prison his hair grew back. One day they brought him out to entertain them. He knew his time was ripe. He grabbed the two central pillars of their temple and pulled it down, killing himself and thousands of Philistines in the process. **Thus he killed many more when he died than while he lived.** (Jud. 16: 30). Talk about a suicide bomber!

That's the end of Samson's story ...except for one small detail. Like, who reported his demise? Since he killed himself and the odd 1,000 Philistines, who was there to tell the tale? I suppose it comes down to the old white-haired men again. Maybe they heard the story from some quarter, or maybe they just made it up. But this story has staying power, being one of the Fundies' favorites. Like six-year-old boys cheering for Rambo, modern churchmen and women love the part when he kills himself and takes all those nasty Philistines with him.

Modern Christians—both Protestants and Catholics—wrench themselves apoplectic when the word "suicide" is even mentioned in passing. "It is a mortal sin!" Woo Woo Woo. Yet they all love Samson's suicide, as it appeals to their baser nature—their love of revenge. And this isn't the last we are going to hear of this topic. There's way more on our tour. If you loved Samson's revenge, wait till we get into the New Testament! But we still have a lot of real fun stuff right ahead. Let's meet Samuel!

God sent plagues on the Philistines. When they recanted, he made them pay a ransom. Five gold tumors and five gold rats!

Samuel

And he smote the men of the city, both small and great,
and they had emerods in their secret parts!

Samuel's story begins with the typical Old Testament sealed womb theme. His mother, Hannah, was a great devoted wife—one of two—whose womb was sealed. Obviously you are getting the picture that this is quite a curse. She is even more disgraced because Pininnah, her rival—bitch that she was—kept rubbing Hannah's nose in the fact that she was infertile. It is no wonder that for centuries a woman's value was determined by her fertility, as the Bible continually emphasizes a woman's baby-making facility as the basis for her existence, purpose, and worth.

Once when they had finished eating and drinking in Shiloh, Hannah stood up. Now Eli the priest was sitting on a chair by the doorpost of the Lord's temple. In bitterness of soul Hannah wept much and prayed to the Lord. And she made a vow, saying, "O Lord Almighty, if you will only look upon your servant's misery and remember me, and not forget your servant but give her a son, then I will give him to the Lord for all the days of his life, and no razor will ever be used on his head." (I Samuel 1: 11).

I love this part. Eli, this great prophet of the Lord, is trying to deal with this wailing woman. He thinks that she is just *drunk* and says: **"How long will you keep getting drunk? Get rid of your wine!"** (I Sam. 1: 14). Whereupon she replies: **"Not so, my Lord. I am a woman who is deeply troubled. I have not been drinking wine or beer; I was pouring out my soul to the Lord. Do not take your servant for a wicked woman; I have been praying here out of my great anguish and grief."** (I Sam. 1: 15, 16).

Eli replies, **"Go in peace, and may the God of Israel grant you what you have asked of him."** (I Sam. 1: 17). **Sometime later, her womb was opened by God, and she had a son** (of course), **and his name was Samuel. The boy Samuel ministered before the Lord under Eli. In those days the word of the Lord was rare; there were not many visions.** (I Sam. 3: 1). This has always amused me. It seems that from time to time God gets all involved in the affairs of men, and at others he gets bored with it all. This was obviously one of those times. There were not many visions—sort of like today, or the past 2,000 plus years, in fact. God seems to be sleeping. He just doesn't do those really neat things like he used to back there with Noah and the flood and Moses in Egypt and all that. I am still holding out for another performance of making the Sun stand still myself. If that happened, I would surely believe all this stuff and more! What comes next is totally boss.

God ordains Samuel as a prophet—a sort of intermediary between God and the people. In various battles ahead, Samuel becomes a key figure. The Israelites lose a big battle early on in his administration and they are wringing their hands in despair. They conclude that they lost because they did not have the "Ark of the Covenant" with them. You remember the *Raiders of the Lost Ark* ... right? Well, *that's* the ark we are talking about here—not to be confused with Noah's ark, which was a wooden ocean liner full of wildlife and farm animals (livestock). Anyway, they retrieve the ark and march off to battle and lose! What? ... Not only did they lose 30,000 troops, but they lost the ark as well! OMG. What, no magic?

What a mess! The ark is captured and when the news finally reaches Eli, he keels over and dies! But, as usual, that's not all. His daughter-in-law, pregnant and in labor, hears the news and gives birth prematurely. They called the child "Ichabod" (precursor to Ichabod Crane I guess) because that name means "The glory has departed." I'll say.

Well, like the Nazis in Steven Spielberg's film, the people who captured and possessed the ark—the Philistines—were cursed. No one can forget the fabulous graphics of melting faces and dismembered bodies of the captors of the ark in the film version. They were really cursed and got what was coming to them. But the curse upon the Philistines was likewise quite painful *and* annoying! **"The Lord's hand was heavy upon the people of Ashdod and its vicinity; he brought devastation upon them and afflicted them with tumors."** (I Sam. 5: 9). I love the King James Bible's translation of this verse ... **And he smote the men of the city, both small and great, and they had emerods in their secret parts!** (I Sam. 5: 9). OMG, emerods! (Nowadays we just call them *hemorrhoids*) ... Where's the Prep H when you need it? LOL. After all that, nobody wanted the ark around, nor anything to do with it. They wanted to shuffle it off to somebody else instead of sending it back. In chapter 6 we read that the Philistines got tired of all the disgusting corruption that the ark brought with it, and decided to return it to the Jews no   matter what.

As is typical, they learned that it wouldn't be so easy. Neither Yahweh nor the Jews would take it back without bargaining with the hapless Philistines. Samuel demanded that they pay a "guilt offering" to God! I love what they were required to produce. Get this. Their fine was: **Five gold tumors and five gold rats, according to the number of Philistine rulers, because the same plague has struck both you and your rulers. Make models of the tumors and of the rats that are destroying the country, and pay honor to Israel's God. Perhaps he will lift his hand from you and your gods and your land.** (I Sam. 6: 4).

Keep in mind that God has already decreed *not* to make any representational images. Nevertheless, he demands that the Philistines do *just that* and make images of hemorrhoids and rats in order to satisfy him. This is the god who created the Universe, all mankind, the wild animals, and livestock—then killed them all in a flood, delivered the Israelites from Egypt, and made the Sun stand still. But he is interested in five gold tumors and rat images? I don't get it. Never did. Do you?

I guess the Philistines didn't buy into the "guilt offering" idea. So they dragged the ark around from place to place, but to no avail. Finally, they wailed**: "Send the ark of the god of Israel away; let it go back to its own place, or it will kill us and our people. For death had filled the city with panic; God's hand was very heavy upon it. Those who did not die were afflicted with tumors, and the outcry of the city went up to heaven."** (I Sam. 5: 11,12).

Isn't all this talk of rats and tumors reminiscent of the tales of Moses in Egypt? Doesn't this sort of remind you of the plagues visited upon Pharaoh and the people of his realm? Likewise, here there are plagues unleashed upon innocent people. They were already in the land before the Jews got there, but they had to be displaced (ethnically cleansed).

Finally, the Philistines just put the ark on a cart and sent it back to the Israelites, because they didn't need the aggravation. The jubilant Israelites rejoiced in receiving the gold tumors and rats. They were vindicated. Hip hip hurray!

As far as I am concerned, they were duped. In the meantime, **"God struck down some of the men of Beth Shemesh, putting seventy of them to death because they had looked into the ark of the Lord."** (I Sam. 6: 19). Oh. Imagine that. They looked into the ark of the Lord. What a mistake. They deserved death. Right. Even Indiana Jones knew enough to keep his eyes closed!

Meanwhile, change is afoot. Israel wants a king. Up till now they had had a charismatic leader of one kind or another. Suddenly, they look around them and realize that they are the only nation without a bona fide king. The judges who more or less kept things afloat after Moses and Joshua, just wouldn't do anymore. Samuel, the sort-of-leader at the time, got fed up with all this whining and sniveling for a king; so he designated Saul, a born loser (with an ego), as the king.

If Samson was the Rambo of the Bible, Saul was George W. Bush. Saul bumbled into power but once he got there he kind of liked it. Samuel knew that God's plan was for Israel to have no ruler as such, cuz God himself was supposed to be their real king. But they wanted a king, so God played a dirty trick on them. He gave them a king alright: *Saul*! Oh dandy.

Samuel fades from the scene with a most remarkable soliloquy: **"Be sure to fear the Lord and serve him faithfully with all your heart; consider what great things he has done for you. Yet if you persist in doing evil, both you and your king will be swept away."** (I Sam. 12: 24, 25). So the Israelites got what they wanted in the end—a king! But God got the last laugh. He gave them Saul—a story worth telling! Let's move on.

Where do we get this notion of a subterranean domain of the dead? Try (I Samuel 28).
"Why have you disturbed me by bringing me up?" Samuel asks Saul.

Saul

The clod that would be king.

The asses of Kish were lost! (I Samuel 9:3). Well, kish my asses! OMG, what could be worse? Who knows? But, anyway, Kish is the father of the antihero of this chapter, a dimwit named Saul, who is assigned to go out and find the straying ungulates. He can't find them. Discouraged, he takes the advice of an underling, and in the district of Zuph consults a "seer." Like a gypsy with a crystal ball—or a medium—a seer is defined thusly in the Bible: **Formerly in Israel, if a man went to inquire of God, he would say, "come, let us go to the seer" because the prophet of today used to be called a seer.** (I Sam. 9: 9). Anyway, Samuel (of the last chapter) meets Saul when he shows up looking for the lost livestock. Saul wants Samuel to tell him where the animals can be found. Instead, Samuel tells Saul that he is about to become king of Israel! Wow. Saul acts like Miss America ... Who me? Unworthy as I am? Oh no ... you must be mistaken. Surely this honor is too great. Where's the crown?

So Saul begins his reign. Unqualified as he is, he has beginner's luck and defeats the Philistines at an obscure battle right off the bat. Immediately he goes on a PR campaign. **"Let the Hebrews hear!"** So all Israel heard the news: **"Saul has attacked the Philistine outpost, and now Israel has become a stench to the Philistines."** (I Sam. 13: 3,4). Actually, I am sure they were already such a stench. But, be that as it may, I just love what comes next.

The Philistines assembled to fight Israel, with three thousand chariots, six thousand charioteers, and soldiers as numerous as the sand on the seashore. They went up and camped at Micmash. (I Sam. 13: 5). Isn't that something you eat with grits? Or maybe a kind of moonshine? Whatever. But, suffice it to say, Saul's men were scared shitless. They hid in caves and thickets, and among the rocks, pits, and cisterns. Finally, they began scattering. Saul made a burnt offering to the Lord. But for some reason God wasn't taking offerings that day. Then Samuel arrived on the scene—hopping mad—and said: **"You acted foolishly."** (I Sam. 13: 13,14). **"You have not kept the command the Lord your God gave you; if you had, he would have established your kingdom over Israel for all time. But now your kingdom will not endure; the Lord has sought out a man after his own heart and appointed him**

leader of his people, because you have not kept the Lord's command." (I Sam. 13:15,16).

This is tough talk. Something must be missing in the translation. Exactly how did poor Saul screw up? It is unclear. God is mad. Samuel is mad. And Saul is out on his ear. Sort of like the story of Abraham in reverse; God never did like Saul in the first place. Whereas, God chose Abraham and coddled him, letting him get away with anything, poor Saul couldn't even get to first base with God. Samuel informs him that Saul is a failure, and it is all downhill from there.

Saul was staying on the outskirts of Gilbeah under a pomegranate tree in Midron. With him were about 600 men, among whom was Ahijah, who was wearing an ephod. (I Sam. 14: 3). I have always wondered what an ephod should be worn with—a tuxedo or a turtleneck. Unfortunately, it never says.

The real crunch comes in chapter fifteen. Samuel informs Saul that God is pissed at the Amalekites for what they did to Israel en route from Egypt. The time is at hand to settle an old score, and Saul is designated to do God's bidding. **Now, go, attack the Amalekites and destroy everything that belongs to them. Do not spare them; put to death men and women, and children and infants, cattle and sheep, camels and donkeys.** (I Sam. 15: 2,3).

Not meaning to labor a point, but is infanticide not called for here by the Almighty God himself? When I hear those of the righteous religious right in America and elsewhere tout their moral outrage over such issues as abortion (which they consider murder), a little bell goes off in my mind, and I remember verses like this. "Do not spare them ... kill them all." Let's have a recap...

The Evangelicals of our day and time accept the Bible as inerrant. They accept the message of the Bible as well as the spirit of it. They reject no part of it. To them it is the guiding light of their lives, and if allowed, they would force all of us to bow our knee to it as well. When we encounter verses of scripture like this one, we are perplexed. How can a righteous loving god—a wonderful father-god—instruct his own to slaughter innocent children and infants? Yet he does!

Now, we have already caught wind of the fact that God does not like the Amalekites. But even Saul is squeamish about slaughtering babies. The pro-lifers of our day wail and rail against the "killing" of what they call "innocent fetuses." They cry crocodile tears for the "snowflake babies" and yet don't give a damn about the slaughter of those Amalekite infants. Oh, but that was then ... as the stupid argument goes. God would *never* condone such killing in this day and age. Well, I always think, why did he do it *back then*? What other commandments from "back then" are nowadays out of fashion? What other Old Testament commands are today invalid, inappropriate, out-of-date as well? You may as well not ask, as they have no answers.

Saul really screwed up, and I have heard many many sermons outlining how and why he did. God commanded him to eliminate the Amalekites. It was clear that he was charged to obliterate them right down to their animals. When the Nazi Party tried to do this to the Jews everybody recoiled in horror. Yet the god of the Jews commanded *them* to do the same thing to the Amalekites, and we just ignore it. Why? Well, whoever the Amalekites were, they are no more, so it is ancient history. And we are not particularly mindful of history unless it serves our present day interests. For example ...

The religious right-wingers of our day harken back to the Old Testament constantly without repudiating a word of it. In their minds, it's as valid today as ever. If you call them on the carpet for sections like this they will sing and dance around it, excusing it but never denying it. If you ask, "Did your god command the execution of all the Amalekite peoples?" they will say "*Yes*, but they *deserved* it!" Sort of like killing all life forms in the flood, frying the inhabitants of Sodom, or slaughtering the folks in Jericho. They all deserved it. Remember?

But Saul is remembered not so much for committing genocide, as for *not* committing it (in a way). True, he followed God's order to kill every man, woman, child, and baby; but he kept back some of the livestock! Oops. Not good. He retained some of the "better" animals, ostensibly for sacrifices to God. Likely story. God knew right away that he had kept them for himself. Greedy bastard. Of course, God got right in on this and called him to task for it. God was kind of perplexed. The omnipotent, omnipresent, omniscient God realized that he had made a mistake assigning Saul to be king of Israel. He was just not working out.

"I am grieved that I have made Saul king, because he has turned away from me and has not carried out my instructions." (I Sam. 15: 10). God is angry because Saul failed to kill *all* of the livestock along with the people. He just killed the people (and the inferior beasts) while keeping the best for himself. So God begins formulating plan B.

Samuel confronts Saul with his ineptitude. He tells him that God himself is furious that he did not finish the job and that, as a result, Saul is going to be replaced. But God is not tipping his hand. He does not make it clear yet who the new king is meant to be. During all this hubbub, Samuel dies. He just checks out for good and never sees Saul again ... *alive!*

Shortly thereafter, Saul is afflicted by an evil spirit from the Lord. So much for the notion that the Lord is the giver of only *good* gifts to his Earthly children. **Now the spirit of the Lord had departed from Saul, and an evil spirit from the Lord tormented him.** (I Sam. 16: 14). I guess any god that would send plagues of frogs and boils on innocent Egyptians, could just as easily cast an evil spirit on poor ol' Saul.

It seems the only relief Saul had was listening to the harp played by a certain friend of his son, Jonathan. (Great story. Next chapter. You'll love it.) Meanwhile, he continued to fight various battles on behalf of Israel. But, like a drunk on a downward spiral, Saul gets more and more out of touch with God and more and more involved in stuff that God really dislikes. It culminates in chapter twenty-eight when he is still fighting the Philistines again. He is not doing well at all. The Philistines are assembled at Shenem.

When Saul saw the Philistine army, he was afraid; terror filled his heart. He inquired of the Lord, but the Lord did not answer him by dreams or Urim or prophets. (I Sam. 28: 6). By dreams, Urim, or prophets? Nothing seemed to work, huh? God has already written Saul off, but he keeps on fighting anyway. He is totally demoralized by the Philistine army. He asks God what to do but hears nothing back. He inquired of the Lord, but the Lord did not answer him by dreams, Urim, or prophets.

God obviously has communicated with men via dreams from the beginning. Heck, even Abimalech and Pharaoh had dreams. But Urim? What in the world is that? Actually, it is a kind of sacred gambling device of the ancient Hebrews

—sort of like we would use dice or cards today to foretell events and give advice, answering questions. And if you want to know more about that, don't ask me; ask a Mormon friend. They love that shit. And, while you are at it, ask them about "Thummim" as well :-)

First Samuel chapter 28 is a very interesting one indeed. Ranking just below the Sun standing still, the plague of flies, and the flaming sword flashing back and forth at the garden, this one is mind-boggling. Saul doesn't have a clue what to do about the Philistines. He's in it deep and it isn't getting better, so he contravenes the law of God and consults a *witch*! Wow, that's heavy stuff. Leviticus 20:27 expressly states that witches are to be put to death, and I am sure our good Christian (Puritan) forefathers in Salem took this verse to heart as Saul should have done. But he didn't. Well, there weren't too many witches left around Shunem, so he had to go elsewhere to find one. He had to go all the way to Endor. Modern Christians often breathlessly refer to the "Witch of Endor." But I always just think of Agnes Moorhead as Samantha's mom, Endora. Remember? Clever, huh?

Saul meets Endora in disguise. **"Who shall I bring up for you?"** she asks. (I Sam. 28: 11). **"Samuel,"** he replies. Then she recognizes him and is frightened out of her wits. But he calms her down and assures her that he won't kill her if she brings Samuel back from the dead for him. **The king said to her, "Don't be afraid. What do you see?" The woman said, "I see a spirit coming up out of the ground."** (I Sam. 28: 13). **"What does he look like?"** he asked. **"An old man wearing a robe is coming up,"** she said. **Then Saul knew that it was Samuel, and he bowed down and prostrated himself with his face to the ground.** (I Sam. 28:14).

Then the ghost of Samuel talks to Saul! **"Why have you disturbed me by bringing me up?"** he asks testily. His spirit talks directly to Saul at this point and converses with him. **"I am in great distress."** Saul blubbers. **"The Philistines are fighting against me, and God has turned away from me. He no longer answers me, either by prophets or dreams. So I have called on you to tell me what to do."** (I Sam. 28: 15).

Samuel, in death, is just as condescending to Saul as he was in real life. **"Why do you consult me, now that the Lord has done what he predicted through me? The Lord has torn the kingdom out of your hands and given it to one**

of your neighbors—to David. Because you did not obey the Lord or carry out his fierce wrath against the Amalekites, the Lord has done this to you today." (I Sam. 28:16-18).

If the Bible is truly inerrant then the existence of a subterranean "spirit world" is proven by the Witch of Endor! All those grim and grizzly images of spirits rising up from the ground, that we associate with the Greek concept of Hades and modern horror movies, are true in Biblical fact. Medieval art is chock-full of gloomy ghostly images of the dead being stored in the Earth. Do modern men and women living in the early 21st century actually believe this notion? You bet they do. But even if we accept for a moment the existence of a spirit world located inside the Earth—beneath the roots of trees and all—why would a god who condemned this very practice of calling up the dead, allow Endora to bring Samuel up for Saul in the first place? And why would God even bother to use Samuel to explain to Saul why God was ignoring him?

The whole story is morbid and disgusting in the first place, but the most disturbing thing of all is that the actual reason for it all is that Saul failed to commit total extermination of the Amalekites. God just never forgave him for that. Then, like a bad politician, Saul just wouldn't go away. He didn't disappear gracefully, but hung on despite the rise of God's real *favorite*, David. Talk about pets! This one is a star!

David and Jonathan's homosexual love affair nearly cost them their lives.
**"Your love for me was wonderful, more wonderful
than that of women."** (II Sam. 1:26)

David

A man after God's own heart!

The story of David is a long and interesting one. It all begins with an odd line by the old prophet, Samuel. Remember him? The guy who Saul and Endora dragged up from the dead. **He who is the glory of Israel does not lie or change his mind; for he is not a man, that he should change his mind.** (I Samuel 15: 29). Here the Bible says that God does not change his mind. But a few verses later he does just that. Lamenting having chosen Saul as king, God sets up Samuel to go out and fetch David, who is divinely chosen to replace Saul. David was a boy at the time but a talented one. He was a musician and could really play the harp like a pro. Saul took to him right away.

We all remember David as a lad with a slingshot who clobbered Goliath, the Philistine, and chopped off his head. In fact, that feat alone made him famous around those parts early on. But as he got older, his status as a great warrior became increasingly obvious to everybody—including King Saul.

It is true that most people are more or less governed by either the right or left hemispheres of their brains. The verbal/artistic types are what are often called right-brained, and the analytical/technical people are governed for the most part by their left brain. It is rare indeed to find a person who is equally gifted on both sides. These unique human beings usually succeed in just about anything they try. David was the perfect example of this rare phenomenon. He was both an artist (singer, dancer, player of musical instruments and composer of music, poetry and literature) and also—as the ruler of a growing nation—a brilliant, if brutal, military tactician, commander and gifted leader all-around. His story is well worth a pause for retelling along our tour route.

There is a lot of discussion in art schools about whether David was homosexual. And I will have to say that the first time I saw his likeness as imagined by Michelangelo in Florence, I definitely could have believed it. But most art, history, and even military experts more or less conclude that he was bisexual. He genuinely had massive sexual passions for men and women. We will look into some examples in this chapter—on this leg of our tour.

After his KO of Goliath, David—like many modern boy wonders—was catapulted into the limelight early on and managed to not only stay there; but his fame fortune and "glory" just kept increasing as the years went on. He started on a roll and never quit. Sure, he had his issues, and did some real dastardly things that really pissed God off. But a little groveling here and there, and a few sonnets or psalms later, and the Lord would forgive him and elevate him even higher. Of all God's "pets" David was way close to the top of the list. He could get away with murder. And he did. He was a man after God's own heart. And did it ever show!

Saul was the King and he liked David (who liked his son, Jonathan). As we have seen, Saul was kind of a flop as king, but he wasn't very good at being a military commander either. Sure, he had some luck in battle from time to time, but he never seemed to get the hang of it. On the other hand, every time he would send David out to war, David succeeded swimmingly. The Israelites even sang a song that extolled David's prowess in uniform—but it really rankled Saul.

"Saul has slain thousands, and David his tens of thousands," went the chorus, which upset Saul like crazy. (I Sam. 18: 7). Then inevitably: **Saul was afraid of David, because the Lord was with David but had left Saul. So he sent David away from him and gave him command over a thousand men, and David led the troops in their campaigns. In everything he did he had great success, because the Lord was with him. When Saul saw how successful he was, he was afraid of him. But all Israel and Judah loved David, because he led them in their campaigns.** (I Sam. 18: 12).

Then, so predictably, Saul's daughter, Michal, fell for David. So, Saul decided that he would use this situation against David. *Good luck.* Anyway, David plays Miss America and demurs. "Oh, I am way too humble to aspire to be the son-in-law of the king" ... (and all that). But Saul says: Oh, come on. All you have to do is some little something to prove that you are worthy. Don't worry, surely this is not out of your price range. All you have to do is this ... (gotta love this assignment). Go out and get and bring back to me a hundred Philistine foreskins. Piece of cake.

When the attendants told David these things, he was pleased to become the king's son-in-law. So, before the allotted time elapsed, David and his

David just loved to dance buck naked in public (in the spirit)! LOL.
His wife was pissed about it, so God stopped up her womb. So there!

son went out and killed two hundred Philistines. **He brought their foreskins and presented the full number to the king so that he might become the king's son-in-law. Then Saul gave him his daughter Michal in marriage.** (I Sam. 18: 26,27). So David actually ended up donating twice as much as was called for, but hey, he really wanted Michal. Certain things in the Bible tickle my funny bone, and a pile of bloody foreskins is just one of those images. LOL

Things didn't work out quite as well as Saul had planned. God loved David. Israel loved David. And Michal loved David. **Saul became still more afraid of him, and he remained his enemy the rest of his days.** (I Sam. 18: 29). It seemed that only Saul did not love David. Everybody else certainly did—especially Saul's son, Jonathan. And that was definitely a love that dared not speak its name. Hmmm.

The feeling was mutual. They had quite an affair. **And Jonathan made a covenant with David because he loved him as himself. Jonathan took off the robe he was wearing and gave it to David, along with his tunic, and even his sword, and bow and his belt.** (I Sam. 18: 3,4). (He really took it all off, huh?) When Jonathan caught wind that his father intended to kill David, he was demoralized. They got together and kissed and wept together before splitting up. Their love affair did not end at this parting, however, as they both carried a torch for one another for the rest of their lives. David even wrote a soliloquy for Jonathan when he was killed in battle: **I grieve for you, Jonathan my brother; you were very dear to me. Your love for me was wonderful, more wonderful than that of women.** (II Sam. 1: 26). Obviously he had a point of *comparison* :-)

David was very eclectic. He was bisexual; a musician, a poet, a singer, a warrior, and a great dancer. I love the part where David gets carried away, dancing "in the spirit." Unlike such dancing that you can see in almost any Pentecostal megachurch these days, David put quite a spin on it. He was buck naked. He put on quite a show. His wife, Michal, was pissed. She was furious! **"How the king of Israel has distinguished himself today, disrobing in the sight of the slave girls of his servants as any vulgar fellow would!"** (II Sam. 6: 20). I would have bought a ticket to that performance :-)

But David doesn't take any guff from Michal. **"It was before the Lord, who chose me, rather than your father or anyone from his house, when he** appointed me ruler over the Lord's people Israel—I will celebrate before the Lord. I will become even more undignified than this and I will be humiliated in my own eyes. But by these slave girls you spoke of, I will be held in honor." (II Sam. 6: 22). Telling her to shut up, he lets her know that he will dance whenever, wherever, and however he damn well pleases. He really puts her in her place. After all, she is just a woman. And besides, he *already* has two other wives at this point anyway ... so what does he need her for? He just didn't need the aggravation. And (get this)... God seconded it by sealing up her womb. (This is *so* Yahweh). **And Michal daughter of Saul had no children to the day of her death.** (II Sam. 6: 23). So there.

There is no doubt that David lived a charmed life. Not only was he multi-talented, strong, handsome, healthy, and loved by everybody. He already had three wives and a boyfriend/lover. And who knows what was going on with those aforementioned slave girls with whom he promised to become even more undignified. And between battles and orgies, David wrote songs and poems, played his harp and was king of Israel. It is no wonder that he is so revered even to this day. He was a real dream boat.

But was he satisfied? Heck no! Most of us have heard this story but it is well worth looking at again. David observed a hot little number bathing one night and just had to sample the merchandise. So he sent a servant to find out about her. Come to find out, she's already spoken for. Well, that wouldn't have to stop the king of Israel, would it?

Anyway, the guy came back with the news: The man said, "Isn't that Bathsheba, the daughter of Eliam and the wife of Uriah the Hittite?" Then David sent messengers to get her. She came to him and he slept with her. (Of course, she purified herself afterward from her uncleanness). **Then she went back home. The woman conceived and sent word to David, saying, "I am pregnant."** (II Sam. 3-5). Oh, great. Just dandy.

Uh oh, the fair-haired boy of Israel knocked up the wife of another man! Oops. That could be pretty messy. So, to solve the problem, he assigned Uriah to the front line of battle where he was sure to get killed. He did. How convenient! His wife, Bathsheba, then became David's next wife and she gave birth to their lovechild. **But the thing David had done displeased the Lord.** (II Sam. 11: 27). No kidding.

So God informs David that the gravy train is over. This is what the Lord says: **"Out of your own household I am going to bring calamity upon you. Before your very eyes I will take your wives and give them to one who   is close to you, and he will lie with your wives in broad daylight. You did it in secret, but I will do this thing in broad daylight before all Israel."** (II Sam. 12: 11,12).

David snivels and grovels around on the floor whining. **"I have sinned against the Lord!"** (II Sam. 12: 13), whereupon—predictably—God *forgives* him. But as a hand slap, the newborn dies. David is bummed but he gets over it. Obviously, God retracted his threat to give David's wives to someone else, as well, because **shortly thereafter David comforted his wife Bathsheba, and he went to her and lay with her. She gave birth to a son, and they named him Solomon.** (II Sam. 12: 24). His story is next. You'll love it!

The story of David's wars grinds on and on for many chapters. Israel, as a nation, was on a roll. It was on a growth curve and was, step by step, conquering the various "countries" or surrounding kingdoms. One after another, the Israelites absorbed all the territory surrounding them, under David's leadership.

David's tenure as king of Israel went smoothly for the most part, but as time went on and the battles were never-ending, David became less and less like the youth that we all read about—herding sheep and killing giants. In fact, even the "David kills Goliath" tale that we have all heard since childhood, has a copycat story that even poor Ol' Jerry Falwell can't fake. Apparently there was yet another of countless battles that David instigated against the ubiquitous Philistines; this one at a place with a cool name: Gob. (Gotta love it, huh?)

According to this account, a fellow named Elhanan killed Goliath. **In the course of time, there was another battle with the Philistines, at Gob. At that time, Elhanan son of Jaare-Oregim the Bethlememite killed Goliath the Gittite.** (II Sam. 21: 19). I couldn't resist. I had to see what the *Liberty Bible Commentary* says about this. As usual they glossed over things that defy explanation, by indicating that there must have been two Goliaths, the Gittite of Gath and the one that the boy David killed. So convenient. But I am going to spare you 112 chapters, giving our tour a skip over the books first and second Kings and first and second Chronicles. Talk about depressing! War, war, war.

Some non-fundamentalist Bible scholars have pointed out that in David's forty-year reign, as he got older and more entrenched in power, he was more like a Tony Soprano-type character. He was really more like a mafia godfather than a benevolent king. I think we can all recall from our reading so far that David had unlimited power over all the lives around him. He became a despot. Kind of a bummer ending for the young lad with his harp and slingshot, huh? But his legacy lived on ... Let's see : -)

Solomon wows the Queen of Sheba, but the glory of Israel was short-lived.
Solomon screwed up, and next thing you know, God is dumping on
everybody again. He couldn't stand Solomon's foreign wives.

Solomon

His wisdom was greater than all the men of the East!

Solomon was just like his dad, David—only more so. A chip off the ol' block. He was a brilliant leader as well, but was also a talented administrator. During David's reign as king of Israel, he expanded the borders of his kingdom substantially; so when he died, Solomon slid right into his shoes and began running the show as only a career politician could do.

The big thing that Solomon had going for him was that after hundreds of years of wandering around in the wilderness, and then fighting endless wars for seeming ages, Israel was at relative peace for the first time; and Solomon saw that it might be time to try to establish something of a more permanent nature. It had been nearly 500 years since the Israelites had come out of Egypt. And during most of that time they were fairly nomadic and unsettled. The main reason for this is primarily due to their physical and geographic location in the Middle East. Kind of like Poland, their borders were not well-fixed and were constantly changing. Well, David fixed that by wiping out all those pesky tribes like the Amalekites and the Ammorites. He didn't quite finish off the Philistines, though, and we are still reading about that ongoing struggle in today's newspapers and on the net.

But, whereas David just loved to march out and conquer neighboring peoples by massive slaughter as we have seen, Solomon was a diplomat. He liked to make the deal. And it was kind of cool how he managed to turn political negotiations into personal benefits. It was the custom of the time (and well into fairly modern times) that when two parties, tribes, or nations called a truce and signed a peace treaty, one king would give one of his daughters to his counterpart on the other side. This was great for Solomon as he began collecting wives!

Much to the chagrin of modern fundamentalist blowhard preachers and politicians, "one man—one woman equals marriage" is not only ridiculous, it is untrue and not biblical. The biblical model for marriage could be best summed up thusly: *One man and as many women as he could afford.* And Solomon could afford quite a few. Oh, come on—more than a few. He had the sexual appetite for a *lot* of women. Modern preachers and wing-nut Southern politicians rant and rave, kick and scream, and tear out their hair over marriage equality (also known as gay marriage). They roar from pulpits around the country and at every "town hall" opportunity to tell us that they *know* that one man—one woman is indeed God's plan. Well, I always say that they should try *reading* their Bibles instead of just thumping them as they all are so wont to do. Just look to David (with seventeen wives) for starters. But then there is Solomon. As near as anyone can figure, he had around 700! Yo!

There are a few key words that are always associated with Solomon: wise, rich, and driven. I would also include a fourth adjective: *horny*. Anyway, let's start with wise. **Solomon's wisdom was greater than the wisdom of all the men of the East, and greater than all the wisdom of Egypt. He was wiser than any other man, including Ethan the Ezrahite—wiser than Heman, Calcol and Darda, the sons of Mahol.** (I Kings 4: 31). His fame spread far and wide. And it is always comforting to know that he was smarter than Heman. LOL

We all know the story about the two women bickering over the baby. In a major show of wisdom, Solomon offered a simple solution: simply cut the child in half. Wow, totally wise, huh? But as the story goes, the real mother, unwilling to see her child sawn in half, gives up and lets the child go to the other woman; whereupon Solomon discerns that the child should be given to the good mother. I always wondered, sitting through this story in church, if Solomon really would have followed through with the bifurcation. Actually, I don't really know, but I'll bet David would have done it for sure.

Well, Solomon's riches came to him thanks in part to David's conquests and his own negotiating skills. As Israel was on top of its game at this point, the vassal states around it sent a little thing called "tribute." **King Solomon was greater in riches and wisdom than all the other kings of the earth. The whole world sought audience with Solomon to hear the wisdom God had put in his heart. Year after year, everyone who came brought a gift—articles of silver and gold, robes, weapons and spices, and horses and mules. Solomon accumulated chariots and twelve thousand horses, which he kept in the chariot cities and also with him in Jerusalem.** (I Kings 10: 23-26). This guy was definitely on a roll, huh?

Not to get too picky here, but in my humble opinion (and after a net search)... Let's halt our tour for just a moment to consider this outlandish biblical claim that, "Not only was Solomon smarter than everybody else in the world," but that "the whole world" managed to find its way to Solomon's court bearing gifts. This sounds to me like another example of the authors of this tome having little—if any—understanding of the "world" as we know it. Do you remember the flood story that we read several chapters ago? The biblical account states that the flood waters covered the entire planet. As we pointed out at the time, likely the Mount of Olives was the highest peak that anybody in the ancient Near East had ever seen. So the Judean hills were all covered in water. That in itself is total foolishness as we saw back then, but it simply indicates that these people—including their scribes—had no concept of the very existence of the Himalayas, the Alps or the Andes.

So what does this have to do with Solomon? Well, the Bible states that *all* the kings of the Earth came to pay tribute to him. Total bullshit. Not only was Egypt way older and more developed and sophisticated at the time of Solomon, but so were India and China! A simple glance at Wikipedia indicates that the reign of Solomon was a grand total of thirty-eight years ... 970 to 931 BC. Concurrent with that time, the Zhou Dynasty in China alone reigned over a territory like a hundred times the size of Israel, and for 850 plus years! (Over twenty times as long). Do you really think the Chinese emperors actually trudged across the Gobi Desert, crossed the Hindu Kush—and other geographic and political obstacles—to bring cash and women to the king of a little country barely ninety miles wide? I don't *think* so.

Well, maybe the monarchs of ancient China didn't really pay Solomon a visit but we all know about someone who did. The famous "Queen of Sheba" managed to make her way up from Africa to check out the rumors of Solomon's massive wealth, power, and status. She just had to see for herself. Well, the Bible indicates that she was indeed wowed and knocked off her feet by the king: **"I did not believe these things until I came and saw with my own eyes. Indeed, not even half was told me; in wisdom and wealth you have far exceeded the report I heard."** (I Kings 10: 6). She really lays it on thick with the flattery. But what I was always impressed by was her gift: four and a half tons of gold according to several Bible commentaries that I've read (plus our good friend, Wikipedia). Wow, that's a lot of gold! And at today's price of that commodity ($1,225/oz.) That is like giving him 200 million bucks in today's currency. Well, you have to admit that she was really impressed, to donate a sum like that. Of course, my next question is: Where the hell did she get cash like that—especially coming from Ethiopia, one of the poorest places on Earth? Come on, isn't somebody adding a few zeroes somewhere along the line? LOL

Well, even though the account of the visit of the queen and her overwhelmingly generous gift, is only ten verses long in First Kings chapter 10, there has always been a whole lot of speculation whether or not Solomon and the queen "did it." Let me point out—like many other examples that I have indicated along our tour route, it doesn't *say*. But you can't believe the sermons and commentaries I have read over the years absolutely assuring us that their relationship was purely platonic. They were just good friends, pals, buds. After all, all those racist Southern preachers over the years couldn't imagine their hero, Solomon the Wise, shacking up with a *black* woman from the wilds of East Africa! Impossible. Unthinkable. Well, I'll leave that up to your imagination, given Solomon's taste for "foreign" women.

Speaking of foreign women, Solomon had a collection of exotic beauties from "all over the world." Or so we are told. But herein lies his fatal flaw. Now, don't miss this: **King Solomon, however, loved many foreign women besides Pharaoh's daughter—Moabites, Samsonite, Edomites, Sidonians, and Hittites. They were from nations about which the Lord had told the Israelites, "You must not intermarry with them, because they will surely turn your hearts after their gods."**

Nevertheless, Solomon held fast to them in love. He had seven hundred wives of royal birth and three hundred concubines, and his wives led him astray. As Solomon grew old, his wives turned his heart after other gods, and his heart was not fully devoted to the Lord, his God, as the heart of David his father had been. (I Kings 11: 3-7). **He followed Ashtoreth the goddess of the Sidonians, and Molech the detestable god of the Ammonites. So Solomon did evil in the eyes of the Lord; he did not follow the Lord completely, as David his father had done.** (I Kings 11: 6).

Oddly enough, I don't recall David following the Lord "completely" either. But, in any case, Solomon—in all his wisdom—did the one thing that Yahweh will simply not tolerate. He got involved with other peoples' gods. Bad news.

The Lord became angry with Solomon because his heart had turned away from the Lord, the God of Israel, who had appeared to him twice. Although he had forbidden Solomon to follow other gods, Solomon did not keep the Lord's command. So the Lord said to Solomon, "Since this is your attitude and you have not kept my covenant and my decrees, which I commanded you, I will most certainly tear the kingdom away from you and give it to one of your subordinates. (I Kings 11: 9-11).

But for the sake of David, your father, I will not do it during your lifetime. I will tear it out of the hand of your son. (I Kings 11: 12). And he did. Remember when Noah cursed his grandson instead of his son (the one who covered his nakedness)? Same story. God lets Solomon slide even though he is majorly pissed at him. But because he loved David so much he gives his son Solomon a pass and tears the kingdom out of the hands of his son, Rehoboam. What's that all about? Duh. As usual, there's more.

But we can't finish up this section of our tour without mentioning something of paramount importance to both our Jewish and Christian friends and neighbors. It is really Solomon's signature accomplishment. It is called the building of the "Temple." I'll just give you a "once over lightly" glance at this subject, as we will revisit it both later in the Old Testament and again way later in the New.

Since the Jews escaped Egypt like over 500 years earlier, they trashed around the desert for years, dragging the "Ark of the Covenant"—of Indiana Jones fame—around with them. As we have seen, it is a real big medicine. It is also a pain in the butt from time to time. It has quite a history as we have seen. It does wonderful magic tricks and helps the Jews win battles, but gets lost and/or stolen now and then with dire consequences. But a trophy like that simply can't be left out in the rain, can it? So the wandering Israelites built a special kind of tent to house the thing. It is called the *tabernacle*. I guess that's where the Mormons got the name for their famous choir. Anyway, the original tabernacle wasn't all that impressive. But they dragged that thing around for years. That is, until David and Solomon came along.

As we have noted, by this time in our story, Israel was on top of their world, and that old drag-around tent just wouldn't do. God wanted a really cool place to live. He charged Solomon to build a real honest-to-God worship center—like the Crystal Cathedral or Notre Dame. And Solomon did it. Now, this place is referred to in both Jewish and Christian settings as The First Temple or Solomon's Temple. It was a real *wow* kind of place and was full of all kinds of groovy accouterments. And although I cannot speak for the Jews or the Christians—especially the Fundamentalists—I can go on and on for ages about what all the temple trappings meant. Don't worry, we will deal with that in more detail when we get to the *second* temple, as the first was destroyed by King Nebuchadnezzar of Babylon. We will tell his story when we get to the Book of Daniel. It's a great yarn. But I hasten to add that most scholars consider the first temple a total myth, as no archeological evidence exists even hinting of its presence. But I recommend you don't tell your Protestant friends of your doubts unless you want to have a fight on your hands.

Anyway, the glory of Solomon and Israel at its zenith was short-lived. After Solomon's death things went downhill fast. The succession of kings and prophets and miscellaneous characters that follow fades into a blur of plots, subplots, intrigues, revolts, famines and plagues, sieges and murders, slaughters and deliverances, and a hodgepodge that grinds on and on and on. Israel under Solomon's son Rehoboam and his whelps, begins to disintegrate and fall apart. The kingdom is split in two—north and south. And the collapse and destruction of the kingdom goes on and on for years. I have likened the "historical" books of the Chronicles as like driving across the Great Plains— miles and miles all looking the same. Kind of like driving through North and South Dakota. If you didn't notice the signs, you wouldn't notice the difference.

But *now* we get a break from the monotony of our cross-country drive and can look at several chapters that are a really welcome and refreshing break from all the wars, battles and court intrigues. I told you that David and Solomon's stories didn't end here. Welcome to the "poetic" books of the Bible. After our long encounter with the "historic" books, this is going to seem like "heaven" (just kidding).

Part 6

Poetry
Passions
and
Praise

Satan knows full well that Job is God's obedient servant because he is in fat city.
**"Stretch out your hand and strike everything he has, and he will
surely curse you to your face."** (Job 1: 12)

Job

I know that my redeemer liveth!

This next section of the Bible is comprised of five books that are referred to as the *Poetic Books*, since they are not dealing with chronological events, as in section two, but matters of a more esoteric nature. Up to this point we have been driving through some very rough territory. Religionists refer to all that we have covered so far as "history," although I am quite sure that there are lots of historians who would shudder to call it that.

Beginning with Job, we encounter a wholly different and refreshingly welcome change. It is totally unlike the stories we have been reading—murder, mayhem and slaughter. It has a rather allegorical beginning in a setting outside the Earth somewhere. Like the Greek gods who lived in a mythical otherworld called Olympus, Yahweh apparently had his own Olympus where he received angels as they came to present themselves to him.

I sort of get the impression that his place at Mt. Sinai—complete with the burning bush—was sort of like a vacation condo for him compared to his place "above the sky." (Remember the colander?) We have already read that on several occasions he "came down" to Earth to walk in the garden, talk with people, or check out various reports of sin and debauchery. So we can assume that this place, sometimes referred to as "heaven" by various religious persuasions, was "up" there someplace in relationship to the Earth—"beyond the blue."

One day the angels came to present themselves before the Lord, and Satan also came with them. The Lord said to Satan, "Where have you come from?" Satan answered the Lord, "From roaming through the earth and going back and forth in it." (Job 1: 6,7). I have heard a gazillion sermons preached about this encounter. Even though I don't see any indication of any particular animosity between God and Satan (at this point), the theologians assure us that it was there. The omniscient god who is supposed to be all-knowing, had to ask Satan where he had been. Whether he actually did *not* know, or *chose* not to know, did know, or was just jerking Satan around ... he asks anyway and Satan tells him that he has been down roaming around, back and forth on the Earth.

Preachers get all wound up over this. They say that Satan's answer is flippant, rude, and disrespectful. It implies, they say, that he just feels like the Earth is his domain, and, further, that he can come and go back and forth on it as he pleases. It is these few verses of Job Chapter One that they use to paint such a hideous portrait of Satan. God didn't seem the least bit nonplussed that he had been down there "roaming around." It sounds to me like he was just curious to know where Satan had been, and when he found out that Satan had been touring the Earth, God asked him a casual question about his travels.

Sort of like, "Oh, so you have been in France! ... Did you happen to see the Eiffel Tower while you were there?" Then God asks, **"Have you considered my servant Job? There is no one on earth like him; he is blameless and upright, a man who fears God and shuns evil."** (Job 1: 8). While you were down there did you happen to meet Job? You know him—that righteous fellow from the land of Uz? (That's Uz, not Oz). FYI.

But before we go ahead with his answer I have a question. We are taught that Satan was in the garden with Adam and Eve, in the form of a serpent. After deceiving them and causing them to sin by eating the forbidden fruit, he was cursed. Let's recall that curse, okay? **So the Lord said to the serpent, "Because you have done this, cursed are you above all the livestock and all the wild animals! You will crawl on your belly and you will eat the dust all the days of your life."** (Genesis 3: 14). Now, if this curse was valid in Genesis, eons before Job, how is it that Satan is roaming—not slithering on his belly—around the Earth? And since the curse was for all the days of his life, how long was that life anyway? In other words, is he *still* alive? Way more on that later.

Bible commentaries date Job's life as somewhat contemporary with Isaac or Jacob. The original serpent presumably could not have lived up to the time of Isaac even if it had survived the flood that killed everything with breath in its nostrils. So either this is a different character, or Satan was able to free himself from the snake body at will and roam around on the Earth at his pleasure, rendering God's curse back in the garden a sheer folly.

Anyway, Satan somehow appears in heaven with God and is still in a position to question him, the curse notwithstanding. **"Does Job fear God for nothing?"** Satan asks in sly reply. **"Have you not put a hedge around him and his household and everything he has? You have blessed the work of his hands, so that his flocks and herds are spread throughout the land."** (Job 1: 9, 10). Job is a wealthy guy with thousands of cattle, sheep, camels and slaves, etc. "Take all that stuff away and see how blameless, upright and righteous he really is," Satan challenges. **"Stretch out your hand and strike everything he has, and he will surely curse you to your face."** (Job 1:12).

"You're on!" God accepts the challenge. Whereupon Job is stripped of his lands and possessions. His many children are all killed, and he breaks out in festering sores. (You remember the boils and itches that cannot be cured?) That kind!

Job is indeed in a mess. Like the Greek gods who toyed with the lives of Earthlings, God and Satan are having an argument and using Job to see which of them is right. Of course, it should be obvious. An omniscient god would *already* know the answer—the outcome of the wager. But in this case, he either really doesn't know, or chooses not to, or he is just baiting Satan. Hmmm. I wonder which it is.

Job has three friends who come around when they hear of his plight. Chapter after chapter after chapter here is dedicated to these three blowhards and their dialogue with Job. He is devastated. He cannot understand how someone as righteous and upright as he should be suffering all this torment. He looks introspectively and tries to see if there is anything he has done to bring about this horrible suffering. He cannot find any sin or wickedness in himself, so he is totally befuzzled.

He curses his life; he curses the day he was born; he weeps and wails, whines and snivels, but still cannot understand why the godly should suffer. I told you this book was esoteric. Considering such a theme requires a lot of time, energy, and discussion. It just keeps going. For *thirty-five chapters* the same basic question is analyzed from every point of view. The friends sort of keep coming back to the supposition that Job must have *done* something to "cause" these unfortunate conditions, but he insists that he is innocent.

Capsulizing these thirty-five chapters is fairly easy as their import has been debated over the centuries, and plenty of theologians have scrutinized them to point out various areas of note. Suffering, of course, is the key theme and question. *Why* is there suffering anyway? And particularly, why do the righteous suffer? A great deal of time and energy is spent here to refute the conventional wisdom of the three friends. Their mantra is: Job offended God somehow, and now he is paying for it.

Like during the plagues that swept throughout Europe during the Dark ages, everyone just assumed the same thing. The people were sinful, wicked and evil. They did wrong in the eyes of the Lord. They screwed up and God was sending down the Black Death to punish them. Oh, what a little modern science could have done to save a third of the European population that died in ignorance, trying vainly to appease an angry god who was pissed at them. (Or so they thought.) Anyhow, I'll save you the thirty chapters of boring repetitive reading and get to the last few chapters, which bear the actual message and meaning of the Book of Job. But be prepared. It is a shocker.

After all the bullshit from the three philosophers, God finally makes the scene and let's go on poor old worn-out Job. God's tirade lasts for four chapters. Ready, here we go ... God gets all wound up and blows Job right off his feet. The message is clear. God is God. God is sovereign and arbitrary. He can do whatever the hell he wants, whenever he wants, however he wants, and to whomever he wants! It is none of Job's damn business why God fucked up his life. God gets to do whatever he wants because he is God and he doesn't owe an explanation to anybody—any time.

He rants and raves. He hoots and howls. He snorts and blows. And when he has finished with Job, the poor jerk is reduced to a quivering mass of Jell-O, wrenching himself every which way for even asking to understand. But I just scratch my head in wonder. How difficult is it really to figure out what Yahweh is like? Just look at his track record. Presumably Job and his friends could have done likewise. Surely we all have done so already on our tour. God sets up stupid and ridiculous rules like "don't touch my special tree" ... then curses those who do, sends fires, and floods, frogs, and boils down on people who don't even know what's going on. And still demands that everybody love him and slaughter animals on his altar—and do so without questioning. Then, if like Job, we comply with all that, he can still destroy our lives on a bet or a whim if he wants and there is nothing that can be said or done about it.

God got seriously pissed that Job has the cajones to even ask a simple question ... Why?

I think Yahweh would fit right in on Mt. Olympus. The message of Job is that God is *sovereign*, and sovereignty means arbitrary. It does not mean *fair*! God is certainly not fair, as we have seen over and over on our journey.

We could just leave it at that, but the last four chapters are so totally over the top, I simply have to point them out to you. What kind of a tour guide would I be if I didn't show you some of the real cool stuff tucked away in the pages of the Bible? Okay, it took the writer of the Book of Job thirty chapters or so to finally make the point that God is totally unfair. But those of us living in the early 21st century can get more out of this book than just that.

Still mad that Job had the cojones to even *question* him or ask for understanding, God is not done with him yet. He puffs himself up and begins shouting down at poor Job—justifying himself. This is good.

"Where were you when I laid the earth's foundations? Tell me if you understand! Who shut up the sea behind doors when it burst forth from the womb? (Beats me.) **Have you ever given orders to the morning, or shown the dawn its place, that it might take the earth by the edges and shake the wicked out of it?** (Not recently.) **Have you entered the storehouses of the snow or seen the storehouses of the hail?** (Answer to the question on p.1 of Creation: What's above the sky? The storehouse of rain, snow, and ice :-) **From whose womb comes the ice? Who gives birth to the frost from the heavens when the waters become hard as stone, when the surface of the deep is frozen? Do you send the lightning bolts on their way? Do they report to you 'Here we are?'"** (Surely you jest—talking lightning. Cool.)

"Do you give the horse its strength or clothe his neck with a flowing mane? Does the eagle soar at your command, and build its nest on high? Can you pull in the leviathan with a fishhook or tie down his tongue with a rope? Can you put a cord through his nose or pierce his jaw with a hook? No one is fierce enough to rouse him. Who then is able to stand against me? Who has a claim against me that I must pay? Everything under heaven belongs to me. Who dares open the doors of his mouth, ringed with his fearsome teeth? His back has rows of shields tightly sealed together; they are joined

fast to one another; they cling together and cannot be parted. His sneezing throws out flashes of light; his eyes are like the rays of dawn. Firebrands stream from his mouth; sparks of fire shoot out! Smoke pours from his nostrils as from a boiling pot over a fire of reeds. His breath sets coals ablaze, and flames dart from his mouth. Nothing on earth is his equal—a creature without fear. He looks down on all that are haughty; he is king over all that are proud." (Job 40 & 41). What the hell is God talking about here? The only thing I can think of that even remotely fits this description got its ass whipped by Sigourney Weaver in *Aliens*! Not to beg the issue one more time, but run that section by your minister, priest or rabbi and see if you are satisfied with the explanation. (I doubt you will be.) LOL

Okay, God had made his point. He is a mean machine. Job throws himself down and tearfully wails: **I despise myself and repent in dust and ashes.** (Job 42: 6). Finally God is satisfied that Job is sufficiently humiliated and degraded. So God restores his fields and fortunes, his family and friends, and his gold and silver. **And he also had several sons and three daughters. His first daughter he named Jemima** (who made it big in pancakes, I've heard). **The second Kezieh and the third Keren-Happuch**. (With a name like that you've got to be good.) (Job 42: 13,14).

So the Book of Job has a Hollywood ending. **After this, Job lived a hundred forty years; he saw his children and their children to the fourth generation. And so he died, old and full of years.** (Job 42: 16,17).

The only thing missing is God telling Satan, "See, I told you so!"

Let everything that has breath (in its nostrils) **praise the Lord.** (Ps. 150)

Psalms

I lift up my eyes to the hills...

Psalms is located in the geographical center of the Bible. It covers a great deal of territory and is rarely ever read in any particular order. The way our tour should approach Psalms is different from the linear approach we have used throughout most of our journey. Like parts of Leviticus, Numbers, and Deuteronomy, the Psalms are more topical in nature than historic or narrative.

Think of the Psalms, if you will, as a large tossed salad. Just looking at it you can easily see that it is indeed a mishmash. It is a jumble of various parts. There are tomatoes and onions, peppers and shallots, lots of lettuce, and some croutons on top. Unlike a soup, which is uniform, a salad remains the sum of its parts. The tomatoes remain tomatoes and the onions are still onions. The nice thing I like about a salad is that you can pick out the parts you don't like and sort of push them to the side of your plate. The Psalms are just like that!

Psalms are poems that were originally set to music, we are told. There are several recurring themes. I should emphasize the word "recurring," as they go on and on again and again and again. I have never really seen the need for hundreds of lines of song being included in scripture actually. The only thing I have ever seen the Psalms really used for is to make a point or to prove something. Whenever you want to win an argument using the Bible as a "prooftext," it is a safe bet that somewhere in Psalms there is an appropriate verse of Scripture to substantiate your preconceived idea.

The first theme comes from the very first Psalm. Many people are familiar with this one. I guess because it is first, and after reading it, they conclude that the rest is much like it. (And they would be right.) **Blessed is the man who does not walk in the counsel of the wicked or stand in the way of sinners or sit in the seat of mockers. But his delight is in the law of the Lord and on His law he meditates day and night. He is like a tree planted by streams of water, which yields its fruit in season and whose leaf does not wither. Whatever he does prospers.** (Psalms 1: 1-3). Okay, that's the theme.

"Blessed is the man." That's it. This basic mantra is like the lettuce in the salad. It is the predominant ingredient and meme that runs throughout the length of this collection. Religious people of every stripe love the Psalms because they extol the virtues of righteousness and the great way God is going to treat the righteous people as a result of their goodness.

The most well-known psalm of all—the twenty-third—is a case in point. I'll bet you can quote it. **The Lord is my shepherd, I shall lack nothing. He makes me to lie down in green pastures, he leads me beside quiet waters, and he restores my soul.** (Ps. 23: 1-2). How pastoral! No wonder these words are so often read in times of crisis. They are calming, soothing and reassuring. **Surely goodness and love will follow me all the days of my life, and I will dwell in the house of the Lord forever.** (Ps. 23: 6). I'll buy that :-)

The blessings of righteous behavior are enumerated throughout the Psalms. These well-worn passages, drilled into the minds of Jewish and Christian young people over the years, offer a guideline for living. How often have I heard the clergy dust off these ancient verses to point their flocks to the "paths of righteousness?" The rewards for right behavior are extolled. **I lift up my eyes to the hills—where does my help come from? My help comes from the Lord, the maker of heaven and earth.** (Wonderful) **He will not let your foot slip—he who watches over you will not slumber or sleep.** (He may, however, occasionally *rest*, as on the seventh day—remember?) LOL.

The Lord watches over you—the Lord is your shade at your right hand; the sun will not harm you by day, nor the moon by night. The Lord will keep you from all harm—he will watch over your life; the Lord will watch over your coming and going both now and forevermore. (Ps. 121: 1-8). The righteous can expect help and protection from a constantly vigilant god who keeps a 24/7 watch over them, lest they slip or get sunburned—or worse: moonburned. Can't have that...OMG!

On the other hand, the wicked are promised all manner of horrible things. **The arrogant cannot stand in your presence; you hate all who do wrong. You destroy those who tell lies; bloodthirsty and deceitful men the Lord abhors.** (Ps. 5: 5,6). Many of these psalms, like those great curses we ran across a while back, are very assuring to the "righteous" that the baddies are going to get theirs! **Why do you boast of evil, you mighty man?**

Why do you boast all day long, you who are a disgrace in the eyes of God? **Your tongue plots destruction; it is like a sharpened razor, you who practice deceit. You love evil rather than good, falsehood rather than speaking the truth. You love every harmful word. O you deceitful tongue! Surely God will bring you down to everlasting ruin. He will snatch you up and tear you from your tent; he will uproot you from the land of the living.** (Ps. 52: 1-5). You may recall from all those earlier great curses like boils, scabies (the itch from which you can't be cured), and eating your children, that God was addressing his *own* people who do not toe the line. But the curses in the Psalms are directed to a more general audience. References to the wicked, foolish, arrogant and deceitful could apply to just about any of us! Oh my!

Psalm fifty-three is very well known and seemingly illustrates God's attitude toward the Jews and non-Jews alike. For example: **The fool has said in his heart, "There is no God." They are corrupt, and their ways are vile; there is no one who does good. Everyone has turned away, they have together become corrupt; there is no one who does good, not even one.** (Ps. 53: 1-3). Notice this phrase: *"No one does good."* This notion that no one (not even one) is righteous and that all have gone astray becomes a recurring theme and later becomes one of the foundations of Christian theology in the New Testament. But here in the Psalms it is just one more element of the salad.

The "righteous" tend to like these verses that condemn the unrighteous, but right next to verses that uplift the good guys and vilify the baddies are verses in direct contradiction. For example, Psalms chapter 10 goes on and on about the prosperity of the unrighteous. Like Job, who likewise was distraught about God letting the wicked prosper, the "poet" (or whoever wrote this gibberish) was appalled. I love this verse: **Break the arm of the wicked and evil man; call him to account for his wickedness that would not be found out!** (Ps. 10: 15). Come on, God. Break a bone or two—crack a skull. Don't let those evil guys get away with-it!

In his arrogance the wicked man hunts down the weak, who are caught in the schemes he devises. He boasts of the cravings of his heart; he blesses the greedy and reviles the Lord. In his pride the wicked does not seek him; he is haughty and your laws are far from him; he sneers at all

his enemies. He says to himself, "Nothing will shake me; I'll be happy and never have trouble." (Ps. 10: 1-6). This jealousy of the righteous when they see the undeserving doing well really ticks them off. It is a longstanding gripe and this isn't the last we are going to hear of it; but you get the picture.

An even more vexing problem for the righteous is their *own* suffering. Not only is it unfair to them for God to let the evildoers slide and do well; but how come *they*—the King's kids—have to eat shit? Like bitter onions in a salad, some of the verses here and elsewhere stand without seemingly appropriate answers. As in the case of Job, God can simply say to them "tough titty." Deal with it. I am God and I am sovereign. Get over it. Then again, like picking out the bitter onions, modern Bible-believers pick and choose the Psalms, proclaiming the ones that they like and ignoring or pushing the rest off their plates.

Be it fair or unfair—be it right or wrong, apparent or vague—the worst result of unrighteousness is, in the end, the same result as righteousness ... namely, death! Bummer, huh? Everybody good or bad ends up dying. Throughout the crazy quilt of the Book of Psalms we continue to encounter the notion that death is the final reward for both the righteous and the irreligious bastards. In the case of the unrighteous, the story seems to be: Go ahead, scoff at God. Ignore him. Get rich and be arrogant. But in the end you are all going to die! So there. But the song for the right-minded, well-behaved and compliant seems to be the same: Go ahead, sing praises to God even if you suffer. After all, surely goodness and mercy shall follow you all the days of your life :-) Then you die. ...In either case, death is the grand finale of life no matter whether a man acts uprightly or is a scoundrel. Therefore, if the result of life is death then it has always seemed obvious to me that a life of wealth and indulgence is way more fun than poverty and suffering. So it begs the question: Why serve God? Good question, huh? We'll get back to this dilemma in a few chapters, so moving right along on the t o u r ...

Don't get me wrong. Although this worldview is kind of bleak, we are about to catch wind of change. Up to now the only real curse that could make a man cringe was to curse his children and grandchildren. As in the case of Noah cursing his grandson's sons into slavery, that was like the worst thing anybody could come up with (other than the seven-year itch and all those cool bodily curses, of course). But upon death even those went away. But as time went on, and the Jews organized themselves more and more into a "nation" and not a motley collection of tribes, thinking men like David, Solomon and the Psalm writer(s) began to face these more philosophical problems. We know that the Egyptians and other ancient peoples had a concept of an afterlife; but the Jews never seemed to. Well, they had a half-assed concept called Sheol—a place of the *departed*. Remember Saul and Endora calling Samuel "up" from his rest? He was just departed—sleeping. He was not enjoying himself or suffering.

He was just plain old dead. Like Adam, he died. Noah died. Moses died. The story grinds on, but like a dash of garlic salt or some new spice thrown into the salad to titillate the palate, a hint of an afterlife begins to emerge. And as you will see, this concept really perks the story up substantially :-)

Notice the new element that begins creeping into the narrative when we come to the forty-ninth Psalm. Perhaps there is more of a reason to shun evil, wealth, and arrogance after all. Maybe righteousness might have some reward—somewhere, some time. This is like a road sign on our journey. Pay attention. Check this out:

Hear this, all you peoples; listen all who live in this world, both low and high, rich and poor alike; my mouth will speak words of wisdom; utterances from my heart will give understanding. Why should I fear when evil days come, when wicked deceivers surround me—those who trust in their wealth and boast of their great riches? No man can redeem the life of another or give to God a ransom for him—the ransom for a life is costly, no payment is ever enough—that he would live on forever and not see decay. Note: Remember the word "ransom" here. It is one of the keys to understanding what is coming. It is still miles away at this point, but there is a glimmer of hope on the horizon. Catch this hint…

For all can see that wise men die; the foolish and the senseless alike perish and leave their wealth to others. But man, despite his riches, does not endure; he is like the beasts that perish. Like sheep they are destined for the grave, and death will feed on them. (Ps. 49: 1- 14). Total *woe*. But the very next verse changes that to wow! Ready? Here it comes—right at you:

But God will redeem my soul from the grave; he will surely take me to himself. (Ps. 49:15). Heavy stuff, huh? I'll say; but it doesn't just turn into kittens and moonbeams right away. Let's go on. Here's some literature you are sure to enjoy! Proverbs.

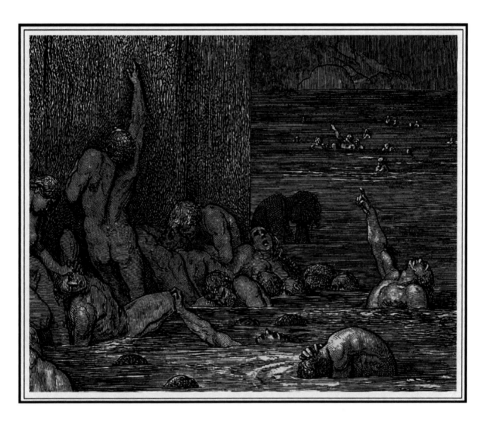

Proverbs is a wealth of good advice. **Give Beer to those who are perishing, wine to those who are in anguish...** (Pv. 31: 67)

Proverbs

An honest answer is like a kiss on the lips.

The next stop on our path is a well-worn source of wisdom (occasionally). The proverbs are neat little gems. They are pithy, succinct and fun. Like the Psalms, they are ideal for proving a point. There are thirty-one chapters and hundreds of verses—mostly conceptual in nature. That means that they can stand alone as an idea, a concept. Just about anything can be proven by quoting from the Proverbs. It helps if both the quoter and quotee agree and believe them, but even if they both do, it is often said: "Well, sure, it says *that*, but it also says this *(just the opposite)*! So I am still r i g h t!" (Sigh)

If the Psalms are a tossed salad, the Proverbs are a jar of jelly beans. I say that because they are all rather uniform. They sort of look alike, sound alike, and have a similar meter and tone. And like jelly beans, you have difficulty distinguishing one from another. We all tend to choose the colored beans that appeal to our visual nature; but if you ask a friend to close his or her eyes and sample the various colored beans, they really can't tell the difference, as it is just a matter of different food coloring. In my experience, the only ones that really stand out are the black ones because they are made of licorice, and lots of people don't care for that distinct flavor and tend to leave those at the bottom of the jar after all the red, green, and orange ones are gone. Likewise, the Proverbs come in several amusing colors. Most go down okay but a few get left every time.

The Proverbs are often touted as "pearls of wisdom" ... and some are. But, as we will see on this part of our tour, some are clearly not! And reading these ditties in any organized order is pointless, as they are not arranged by a mortal man, a committee or a computer—but by Almighty God himself. LOL. Nevertheless, despite the total lack of organization, there are certain themes or topics that can be recognized. Most relate to behavior. And their structure is kind of like this: Line A and line B. Line A usually starts out like this: If you do this... Then: (line B) ... the result will be such and such. Or... (Line A) If you *don't* do this... Then: (line B) ... something *else* will result. Pretty simple, huh? The subjects deal with a wide range of human interest themes. Eating and drinking, sex, money, women, lying, cheating, stealing, and gossiping spring to mind. So let's look at a few well-known and oft-quoted proverbs, shall we?

It is not good to eat too much honey. (Proverbs 25: 27). I think that is reasonable, don't you? Sure. I mean the sugar alone could rot your teeth out.

And then there's the ever popular: **When you sit to dine with a ruler, note well what is before you, and put a knife to your throat if you are given to gluttony. Do not crave his delicacies, for that food is deceptive.** (Pv. 23: 1-3). I could make a joke or two here, but then so could anybody. Haha.

Following on the gluttony theme… You gotta love this one…

As a dog returns to its vomit, so a fool repeats his folly. As a door turns on its hinges, so a sluggard turns on his bed. The sluggard buries his hand in the dish; he is too lazy to bring it back to his mouth. (Pv. 26: 11-15). Even *modern* Bible translations like the NIV (that we are using on our tour) use words like sluggard. My thesaurus can improve on that. I prefer "torpid" and/or "indolent." In any case, lazy fat gluttons are like dogs. The Bible says so. Evangelicals and fundamentalists are not at all careful about following these suggestions from Proverbs, as they are—in my experience—more obese than the average US Citizen. Due to the fact that they cannot drink alcohol, their only entertainment is eating!

But speaking of alcohol, the Proverbs have plenty to say about that too! And how! Ready? Here we go!

Who has woe? Who has sorrow? Who has strife? Who has complaints? Who has needless bruises? Who has bloodshot eyes? Those who linger over wine, who go to sample bowls of mixed wine. (Pv. 23: 29,30). Our heavy-duty Bible believing friends and relatives love these verses, as they justify fierce prohibitionist positions on alcohol consumption. Actually, this isn't bad advice. Like too much eating, too much drinking is surely not a good idea. I do think AA should put this verse somewhere in their literature. It is great—don't you think? Now this is really poetic…

Do not gaze at wine when it is red, when it sparkles in the cup, when it goes down smoothly! In the end it bites like a snake and poisons like a viper. Your eyes will see strange sights and your mind imagine confusing

things. You will be like one sleeping on the high seas, lying on top of the rigging. (Pv. 23: 32-34). It seems that somebody is definitely speaking from experience here!

Raising children is another recurring theme throughout Proverbs. Who has not heard the famous: **Train up a child in the way he should go and when he is old he will not depart from it.** (Pv. 22: 6). I don't think anyone on the tour would strenuously disagree with this. It is kind of vanilla childrearing 101.

However, the Bible can fly in the face of some modern methods when it comes to recommendations of actual child *beating*. Having been in this position, I know how conflicted any parent can be regarding the disciplining of small children. They can drive you crazy, right? But consider this: **He who spares the rod hates his son, but he who loves him is careful to discipline him.** (Pv. 13: 24). I don't want to get too off-track on our tour, debating methods of bringing up kids. But let's leave it at this: the Bible is definitely pro-spanking.

Another great proverbial theme is *thrift* and *diligence*. Oddly enough, this might be a perfectly good place to insert the fact that the ancient Jews were not the only authors of proverbs promoting various virtues. In fact, Biblical proverbs can often appear downright heavy-handed and rather thuggish compared those of the Chinese, the Greeks, the Indians (of India) and Native Americans— to avoid confusion. But teaching certain concepts seem universal in one form or another. Saving for a "rainy day" is enshrined around the world. It just makes common sense. But the biblical model leaves a lot to be desired. It is ludicrous. And don't tell me you haven't heard it.

Go to the ant, you sluggard; consider its ways and be wise! It has no commander, no overseer or ruler, yet it stores its provisions in summer and gathers its food at harvest. (Pv. 6: 6). Oh, come on. We were all raised on the famous "ant and the grasshopper" story. It really goes down well if you are five or six years old. But for a modern thinking person, a reevaluation should be in order. The scientific fact is that ants are not wise at all, but totally stupid. The individual ant is a mindless unit consisting of a few neurons that without the rest of the hill is totally incapable of any independent action whatsoever.

It was Mark Twain who first pointed out the total ineptitude of this insect species in his short vignette entitled *The Fraudulent Ant*. I read it for the first time in seventh grade and was amazed. He was right! Twain laughs at the antics of an individual ant. It runs hither and yon, constantly changing direction and often carrying burdens ten times its own weight, unable to figure out where the ant hill really is. For God, in all his universe-creating splendor, to advise man to observe the *Pachycondyla Verenea* (worker ant) as a source of wisdom, is sheer folly. I am not championing the cause of the grasshopper, mind you, but of the two, I am not sure that the ant is any wiser. Ants, black and red, are primitive lifeforms with an important place in the ecosystem, but are hardly role models for men and women of the emerging 21st century, now are they?

Let's change the subject slightly. Let's talk about sex (again). The Bible, as we all know by now, is a totally male-oriented treatise. In each case here in Proverbs, there is advice given from one male to another. Women are simply the objects of discussion (and warnings). Here is a case in point from an overcooked chapter of the Proverbs: **My son, keep my words and store up my commands within you. Keep my commands and you will live; guard my teachings as the apple of your eye. Bind them on your fingers; write them on the tablet of your heart. Say to wisdom, "You are my sister," and call understanding your kinsman; they will keep you from the adulteress, from a wayward wife with her seductive words.** (Pv. 7: 1-5).

My son, give me your heart and let your eyes keep to my ways, for a prostitute is a deep pit and a wayward wife is a narrow well. Like a bandit she lies in wait, and multiplies the unfaithful among men. (Pv. 23: 26-28). There are tons more like these, but why keep this up? Surely you get the picture. Oh well, maybe just one shorter proverb about the evils of the female sex. This is good. **A quarrelsome wife is like a constant dripping on a rainy day: restraining her is like restraining the wind or grasping oil with the hand.** (Pv. 27: 15,16). Notice how women have to be restrained. After all, they are annoying and stupid. Foolishness and stupidity are also common themes. Women are considered foolish and dumb by nature; but of course some men are foolish. Maybe just not as foolish as dames! (My father's vintage word.)

Like snow in summer or rain in harvest, honor is not fitting for a fool. A whip for a horse, a halter for a donkey, and a rod for the back of fools! (Pv. 26: 1-3). Beatings again. This time for simply being a "fool." Too bad the Almighty, who prescribes whipping or caning for fools, forgets to tell us just what a fool is, or who. For centuries some people with certain kinds of mental illnesses have been referred to as *fools*. The Bible doesn't cut them much slack. Just beat them—knock some sense into them. Slap the ADD right out of them. **Like a madman shooting firebrands or deadly arrows is a man who deceives his neighbor and says, "I was only joking!"** (Pv. 26: 19). You know, it's no wonder our Puritan forefathers were so dour. To them joking was no *laughing* matter.

Wealth, poverty, generosity, and stinginess are also common proverbial themes. **Do not eat the food of a stingy man, do not crave his delicacies; for he is the kind of man who is always thinking about the cost. "Eat and drink," he says to you, but his heart is not with you. You will vomit up the little you have eaten and will have wasted your compliments.** (Pv. 23: 6-8). What? Give me a break.

One man pretends to be rich, yet he has nothing; and another pretends to be poor, yet has great wealth. (Pv. 13: 7). **Do not wear yourself out to get rich; have the wisdom to show restraint. Cast but a glance at riches, and they are gone, for they will surely sprout wings and fly off to the sky like an eagle.** (Pv. 23: 4,5). We won't dwell on the subject of wealth and poverty here, as a really great chapter on the subject is coming up shortly, and that is a discussion you're sure to like.

Proverbs indeed has something for everybody. Our Fundie friends and family members who like to thump their Bibles simply pick and choose the proverbs they like and ignore the rest. And so many of the rest are like totally stupid and inane. When was the last time you heard a televangelist preach from Proverbs chapter 30?

Four things on earth are small, yet they are extremely wise; ants are creatures of little strength, yet they store up their food in the summer; conies (relatives of the guinea pig) **are creatures of little power, yet they make their home in the crags; locusts have no king, yet they advance together**

in ranks; a lizard can be caught with the hand, yet it is found in kings' palaces. So what?

There are three things that are stately in their stride, four that move with stately bearing; a lion, mighty among beasts, who retreats before nothing; a strutting rooster, a he-goat, and a king with his army around him. (Pv. 30: 25-28). I am so glad that the creator of the Universe points out to us the wisdom of the guinea pig and the stately stride of the rooster and he-goat :-)

But to wrap up, I must confess that not all of the proverbs are pure bullshit. There are actually a few that make some sense. I have always found amid the clutter a few real funnies. If you have played the fool and exalted yourself, or if you have planned evil, clap your hand over your mouth! For as churning the milk produces butter, and as twisting the nose produces blood, so stirring up anger produces strife. (Pv. 30: 32,33). I should say so.

So as we depart Proverbs, let me leave you with my favorite. Now this is real wisdom. Give beer to those who are perishing, wine to those who are in anguish; let them drink and forget their poverty and remember their misery no more. (Pv. 31: 6,7). I'll drink to that!

Solomon, much touted for his wisdom, calls it all a "crock" in his cynical
treatise called Ecclesiastes. Life's a bitch and then you die!

Ecclesiastes

Everything is meaningless.

I have always liked Ecclesiastes. I still get a kick out of reading it. So this part of our tour will be fun for me. It is claimed to have been written by our friend King Solomon (remember ... the guy with 700 wives?). It could have been written by him—or not. It is a cynical look at life that flies in the face of Proverbs, which ostensibly was also his creation. However, whereas in the Proverbs much ado is made of wisdom, in Ecclesiastes it is totally deprecated. Take this, for example:

Then I turned my thoughts to consider wisdom, and also madness and folly. What more can the king's successor do than what has already been done? I saw that wisdom is better than folly, just as light is better than darkness. The wise man has eyes in his head, while the fool walks in the darkness; but I came to realize that the same fate overtakes them both. (Ecclesiastes 2: 12-14).

When you read Ecclesiastes you see how schizophrenic it is; another literary hodgepodge, it reads like Proverbs in reverse. It is said that Solomon must have written the Proverbs during his prime when he was extolling the virtues of wisdom and right living, and having loads of sex; and Ecclesiastes in his old age when he had become a cynical old curmudgeon, pooh-poohing all of that as meaningless.

Doesn't it make you wonder how it is that there are so many questions and disputes as to the authority and authorship of various books in the Bible? The Fundamentalists hold fast to the inerrancy theory—that the Bible is perfect, complete and literal, as God dictated it right into the ears of guys like Moses, David and dear Solomon. Yet they dicker endlessly with each other about the authorship of books like Ecclesiastes.

Of course, they have a convenient way of explaining away such problems. The Bible, according to literalists, is inspired by God himself. In short, God is the author; so it is of little actual consequence who really took down the dictation. No man thought these "thoughts" or wrote these words all by himself anyway. They were inspired by God—and men simply wrote them down. This works well for books like the Psalms, Proverbs, and Ecclesiastes because they were written at a time when the Jews were more or less established and were involving themselves in scholastic endeavors. Once the Jews ceased to be a collection of nomadic wanderers and full-time warriors, they were able to devote themselves to thinking, writing, music, construction projects, and other hallmarks of civilization. The problem is that for eons before this, they were (as we have seen) a rather barbaric bunch. And so much of what we have already read is myth and hand-me-down history— all very unreliable. So where exactly is the divine inspiration? Events happen and are recounted by each successive generation. We have already seen how easily the stories can be embellished, augmented, or confused. Ecclesiastes is definitely another head-scratcher.

The same preacher who uses **Wisdom is more precious than rubies, and nothing you desire can compare with her** (Proverbs 8: 11) one week, to extol the virtues of wisdom, will say this of wisdom one week later: **What then do I gain by being wise? I said in my heart, this too is meaningless. For the wise man, like the fool, will not be long remembered; in days to come both will be forgotten. Like the fool, the wise man too must die.** (Ecc. 2: 15,16). One section of the Bible says that wisdom is better than rubies, and another says it is useless and vain. These are as contradictory as the verses on killing that we have encountered along our way so far. And there's m o r e !

Quick review. Remember back in Exodus when we read from the Ten Commandments—so oft-quoted: **"Thou shall not kill."** But here in Ecclesiastes we find another famous verse that most of us could likely quote verbatim: **There is a time for everything, and a season for every activity under heaven; a time to be born and a time to die, a time to plant and a time to uproot, a time to kill and a time to heal** ... (Ecc. 3: 1-3). Huh?

Long before the Byrds made this passage famous to rock and roll fans in the 1960s, it was often quoted as a justification for killing in wartime. Obviously, from what we have read already, this was unnecessary. We have seen plenty of places where killing is sanctioned—even *commanded*. Remember Jericho? Those who live by the Bible and have to defend endless killing, maintain that the commandment against killing in Exodus applies only to premeditated murder. And it might be pointed out that it meant that only Jews killing other Jews was prohibited. However, killing of the Amalekites, the Midianites, and the Philistines—well, that's okay.

I have a feeling that as long as the Bible and other religious guidebooks maintain that killing is alright, men will continue to kill each other throughout the world. If the holy writings of the world's great religions would repudiate war and all killing instead of encouraging it, there would be far less slaughter in our world today. I guess with a god who would himself kill everything with breath in its nostrils by drowning them, and command the slaughter of all the inhabitants of the "Promised Land" and atomize Sodom for its wicked ways … that should not raise an eyebrow. Obviously, there is indeed a time to kill!

Ecclesiastes also decries labor and achievement as meaningless. Just as in other cases, where Proverbs sanctifies hard work and diligence, Ecclesiastes trashes it, calling it worthless. Read this: **My heart took delight in all my work, and this was the reward for all my labor. Yet when I surveyed all that my hands had done and what I had toiled to achieve, everything was meaningless, a chasing after the wind; nothing was gained under the sun.** (Ecc. 2: 10,11). Bummer, huh?

Your average Bible-believer does not have as much trouble with this contradiction as I do because they define "labor" in their own particular way. Most Christians consider work or labor as of no value unless it is directed toward a religious purpose. According to them, work is a necessary evil visited upon mankind as a result of the "fall in the garden." Remember that famous curse? God cursed man to work and earn his eats by the sweat of his brow. Well, since we are all condemned under that general curse, we all have to do labor. True, some have to do more labor than others, and some don't do much at all; but nobody is advocating sloth in lieu of working, as that is our lot in this life. Thank you, Adam and Eve. We are required to care for our families—our children and all—so work is necessary. But this kind of work is purely functional. It is needed to sustain our lives and that of our own. But real and meaningful work is eternal. It is the type that serves God.

Christians have an expression that goes like this: "When everything has come to pass, only work for Christ will last." Work we do for ourselves and our families is okay, but it is transient in nature. It is important to sustain our lives, but it is in vain and is folly to strive for more than we need for that purpose. In other words, seeking material gain or prosperity is folly and will be of no value when we are dead, and certainly not in the afterlife. Ecclesiastes bears this out. I have always resented the smug attitude of evangelical Bible- believers as they look down their noses at any altruism other than their own. After all, if anything is done in the name of humanity, kindness, or goodness but is separate from having religious (Christian) purpose, it is useless.

Hand in hand with labor are the fruits thereof—namely wealth. Ecclesiastes clearly states that the accumulation of wealth is pointless. **Whoever has money never has money enough; whoever loves wealth is never satisfied with his income. This too is meaningless. As goods increase, so do those who consume them. And what benefit are they to the owner except to feast his eyes on them?** (Ecc. 5: 10,11). For years the Fundies have quoted this verse and have gone out of their way to do the opposite. The Jews became notorious over the centuries for accumulating wealth despite this admonition. The Catholic Church pays lip service to vows of poverty, and piles up more and more wealth. The Vatican Museum is a tribute to bloated luxury. I wonder how many poor starving Catholics in Latin America or Africa could be fed with the proceeds from the sale of all those ridiculous golden jewel-encrusted chalices in that travesty in Rome.

And the Protestants? Hah! All that show of the early New England colonists living simple humble lives before the Lord has long given way to what is now referred to as the "prosperity doctrine." One of the reasons for the incredible growth of the evangelical churches—and especially the Pentecostals—is that they totally ignore verses like the above ... in favor of others that promise all manner of goodies to believers.

Preaching poverty has never been popular. The Bible enshrines it in one verse and wealth in another—on the same page! Get this: **The sleep of the laborer is sweet, whether he eats little or much, but the abundance of a rich man permits him no sleep.** (Ecc. 5: 12). Yeah, right. But then, seven verses later, we read: **Moreover, when God gives any man wealth and possessions, and enables him to enjoy them, to accept his lot and be happy in his work, it is a gift from God. He seldom reflects on the days of his life, because God keeps him occupied with gladness of heart.** (Ecc. 5: 19). Well, good grief. Which is it?

Personally I adhere to the latter. It would be better if God would just give everybody wealth and be done with poverty all together. He could do it. After all, he is omnipotent, right? For centuries the church has been telling the poor that they are blessed and that their sleep is sweet even if they have to go to bed hungry. And, by comparison, the wealthy are tossing and turning in constant worry about maintaining their lifestyles. Are you buying this? A lot of pithy modern proverbs that IMO rival anything in the Good Book, are of unknown authorship. But when I first heard this gem it was quoted by that beloved philosopher, Whoopie Goldberg, who said it so well: "I've been rich and I've been poor. And of the two, *rich* is better."

Karl Marx was put off by religion because it promoted the uneven distribution of wealth. Religions in general tend to say: "Now, all you poor people, don't sweat it. Sure you are miserable. Sure you are hungry and needy, but *Don't worry. Be happy!* Think of that unfortunate rich man who can't even get a good night's sleep. Besides, think of all those treasures you are going to get to enjoy in heaven!" Goody.

The uneven distribution of material wealth sticks in my craw, and that of most "liberals," but the uneven distribution of talents, abilities and life gifts really burns my shorts. Throughout the Bible, God treats people differently, blessing some and cursing others. Think back to Saul and David. It is cool if you are born smart, rich or good-looking, athletic, healthy, and can play the piano or the marimba. But not everybody is dealt a fair hand. Look around. Some are simply born with congenital diseases, are athletic klutzes, or are slow in school. Surely the clever and talented are predisposed to rise to the top, gain wealth, and live better than the poor who have to toil and suffer.

I am always upset when I hear Christian believers dismiss the suffering of the poor as God's will. I know how they come to that conclusion. After all, God takes credit for afflicting some with misery, and blesses others from birth. But it is still that issue of sovereignty that nags at me. Since God is so sovereign and can do whatever he wants, what is the purpose for doing anything at all—as your fate is sealed? A whole religious movement is founded on this notion. It is called Calvinism and is based on the idea that, indeed, some persons are simply born wrong. They are unlucky. Too bad. Did they do something bad in their last lifetime? Were they just born in a bad place or to bad parents? Is there a reason? Likely not. That's just fate. *Sayang naman* (shit happens).

Now Christians claim loudly that they don't believe in fate. But they do. The Bible is a very fatalistic book. Nothing matters. Everything is meaningless and in vain. No matter what we do, in the end we will all end up dead. Period. **All share a common destiny—the righteous and the wicked, the good and the bad, the clean and the unclean, those who offer sacrifices and those who do not.** (Ecc. 9: 2). In contrast to the very idea that in this life of woe we can actually change something, the writer is saying that our existence is pointless and we really can't change a bloody thing. Many would logically conclude that if this is so, we should screw it all, live for today and forget the rest, awaiting our common demise. **As it is with the good man, so with the sinner, as it is with those who take oaths, so with those who are afraid to take them. This is the evil in everything that happens under   the sun; the same destiny overtakes all. For the living know that they will die, but the dead know nothing; they have no further reward, and even the memory of them is forgotten.** (Ecc. 9: 2-5). Are you sufficiently bummed out at this point?

The dead know nothing. They are just forgotten. Talk about fatalism! If this   is true, doesn't a "live for today" philosophy make the most sense? This crushing fatalism is fraught with nagging dilemmas for believers. The obvious is: Why be righteous? Why do good? Why worship God? Kinda like Job's dilemma. My guess is that if the Bible just ended here it would have never been a bestseller. In fact, the religion we all deal with on a daily basis would have been a colossal flop. But—without need of a spoiler alert—the story *does* get better as we go on. But we still have several chapters in between that are some of the most "awesome" and wacky in the Bible. Don't skip ahead for the "Good News" just yet. You are really going to love the rest of the Old Testament. Trust me.

"Your navel is a rounded Goblet that never lacks blended wine."
Song of Songs, the Bible's X-rated book is an embarrassment to the straight-laced.

Song of Songs

Let him kiss me with the kisses of his mouth.

I have an image in my mind of our dour forefathers back in Plymouth reading the Song of Songs and wincing. I likewise have an image of some backwoods Southern preacher snorting and blowing from his pulpit (pronounced pool-pit). He rants and rages on about the evils of our modern society while steering his motley congregation away from the Song of Songs and back to more suitable fare—like "The wages of sin is death!"

The Song of Songs (also referred to in older texts as the Song of Solomon) is by far the oddest and most incongruous book in the Bible. When Bible-believers are accused of being too straight-laced and puritanical by outsiders, they point to the Song of Songs to indicate that there is indeed some romance and eroticism in the Bible. Of course that is where it stops. It is in the Bible, but is rarely brought up or discussed. This book indeed falls into the category of materials that need "interpretation" by the theologians, scholars, and televangelist/preachers (of course).

In fact, it needs a lot of interpretation as no one seems quite sure what its purpose is and why it is even in the Bible in the first place. It is pretty racy stuff and I am sure that, given the chance, most modern church leaders would exclude it from scripture as "inappropriate." You may recall back in Leviticus when we looked at all those rules and regulations regarding sexual behavior and uncleanness. Whereas those decrees and commandments seem horrifying on one side, the Song of Songs is delightfully titillating on the other. Sex is such a difficult subject for religious people to deal with, and this book just makes it even more so.

Let him kiss me with the kisses of his mouth—for your love is more delightful than wine. (Song of Songs 1: 2). **Your cheeks are beautiful with earrings, your neck with strings of jewels. We will make you earrings of gold studded with silver. My lover is to me a sachet of myrrh resting between my breasts. How handsome you are, my lover! Oh, how charming! And our bed is verdant!** (S of S 1: 10,11,13,16). Ooh, verdant!

Can you picture the Puritans handling that? Can you imagine Solomon *writing* it? Oh sure, the guy with 700 wives and hundreds of lesser female concubines seems unlikely to say: "Let him kiss me with kisses of his mouth." I might expect that from his dad, David—but Solomon? Come on! Actually, I sort of imagine that a lot of this fluff was written by medieval monks in some dark dank scriptorium in some long-lost monastery somewhere in Northern Italy centuries ago; sort of like in the famous novel entitled, The *Name of the Rose*, by Umberto Eco. Great story ... and very telling. Anybody who has studied art of the Middle Ages has likely noticed the erotic, whimsical little cartoons that the monks hid in the text and in the margins. Haha. Those guys must have been as horny as any modern priest trying to remain celibate in our world today. Well, at least they were having fun, h u h ?

I also sort of see in my mind's eye the likes of Eleanor Rigby or the everyday housewife—middle-aged women, frustrated and overlooked—reading the *Song of Songs* and getting a tingle out of phrases like: **Awake, north wind and come, south wind! Blow on my garden that its fragrance may spread abroad. Let my lover come into his garden and taste its choice fruits.** (S of S 4: 16). Ooo... Choice fruits indeed. **All night long on my bed I looked for the one my heart loves; I looked for him but did not find him...** (But when she finally did, whew!) **Get this: I held him and would not let him go till I had brought him to my mother's house to the room of the one who conceived me.** (S of S 3: 4). Now, what's that all about? It beats me.

But the Song is not just written from the female perspective. The male lover has some spicy things to say as well. **How beautiful your sandaled feet, O prince's daughter. Your graceful legs are like jewels, the work of a craftsman's hands. Your navel is a rounded goblet that never lacks blended wine. Your waist is a mound of wheat encircled by lilies. Your breasts are like two fawns, twins of a gazelle. Your stature is like that of the palm, and your breasts like clusters of fruit. I said, "I will climb the palm tree; I will take hold of its fruit. May your breasts be like the clusters of the vine, the fragrance of your breath like apples, and your mouth like the best of wine?** (S of S: 7: 1-3; 7- 9). I will climb the tree? That seems a bit pornographic for Yahweh, huh?

Anyway, I think you get the picture. This is real poetry and is probably the most fun you can have when reading the Bible. But the problem remains:

Why is it there, and what does it mean? All this talk of a woman's breasts, her navel, and her "choice fruits" makes most clergymen uneasy because it is so counter to the whole spirit of the rest of everything we have encountered thus far on our tour. Women have been largely ignored or treated as plunder, property, or something to be carried away after a battle, along with the livestock. Bible readers and interpreters over the centuries have always been more comfortable with the Proverbs image of the noble woman. Remember? **She gets up while it is still dark; she provides food for her family and portions for her servant girls. She sets about her work vigorously; her arms are strong for her tasks.** (Proverbs 31: 15-17).

The patriarchal Jewish society—of which we have been reading thus far— and, later, the Christian, have both treated women as mere objects. This short section of scripture is the only example of real eroticism expressed in poetic, graphic detail; and most of it is from the female perspective or in praise of the female persona. Enjoy it but briefly. It does not last. We will soon enough be back to the old saw: "Women are evil bitches and are responsible for all the woes of the world." You'll see.

Commentators (like our dear Jerry Falwell) describe this as a *"challenge to an ardent devotion and fidelity to God and mate."* What? Obviously he just pulled that out of his ass. Others call it *allegory*, calling on the reader *"to look beyond the literal meaning of the text and to construct new and more spiritual meanings."* What? Since when are literalists allowed to even *consider* looking beyond the literal meaning of anything in the Bible, let alone to come up with *new* meanings? Heck, if they can buy the flood story as literal, why not this? Who needs new meanings anyhow?

Some Jewish scholars saw the songs as a message relating to the special union between Jehovah and Israel as a nation. And many of the early Christian Church fathers saw it as a message of God's love for the Church. This brings us to a topic that we will encounter from here on: The relationship between God and Israel—and, later, that of God and the "church"—is seen as a *bride and groom* affair. BTW, that is what we call a *metaphor.* LOL.

Fundamentalists and literalists have a great deal of trouble with metaphors and/or allegory. For the most part, they reject the very notion of it. However, all but the most diehard literalists concede that there is some allegory— some metaphor—in the Bible. When we finally wind up in the Book of Revelation you will see what I mean. But you can imagine that if you open the door to allegory, the next question is: Well, was the flood allegorical? How about Sodom, the plagues of frogs, gnats, and flies? What about the talking snake or Balaam's talking donkey? Were those real or just symbols? Did God really turn Mrs. Lot into a pillar of salt, or was that representative of a deeper concept? What was real and what was just symbolism? This is no small issue, and it has been debated again and again over the centuries. But we are not here to propose answers to these millennia-old questions, but are just passing through on our tour to have a look-see. But you do have to admit—it does make you wonder :-)

Part 7

Prophets
and
Principles

Isaiah

"I have more than enough burnt offerings ..."

Reading the Book of Isaiah is like riding a roller coaster. It has its high heights and its deep, crashing lows. It rises and falls rapidly, with wild swings and instant drop-offs. This is the first book of the following seventeen that are collected under the general banner called "the Prophets." As your tour guide, I have to steer us clear of repetition and redundancy. And if you thought Kings and Chronicles were redundant, wait till you read the Prophets. But, hey, wait, that's my job as your guide. You don't have to read all those zillions of chapters of the same old stuff. I will pick out the best for you, lest you go crazy. We will consider three of the "major prophets" and skip the rest. But don't get me wrong; if you really want to read Haggai, Nahum, Habakkuk, or Obadiah, feel free. Knock yourself out. LOL.

So, let's talk about Old Testament prophets. Their task was twofold. In addition to the obvious—foretelling future events—the prophet also was an oracle to warn the Jews of their misbehavior and to call on them to quit, repent, and return to the hardline legalism of the law upon which their society was based. The prophets whom we are to encounter now were special people, called by God in much the same way as was Moses (minus the burning bush, of course). Isaiah was called out in a most unique way.

In the year that King Uzziah died, I saw the Lord seated on a throne, high and exalted, and the train of his robe filled the temple. Above him were seraphs, each with six wings; with two wings they covered their faces, with two they covered their feet, and with two they were flying. And they were calling one to another: "Holy, holy, holy is the Lord Almighty; the whole earth is full of his glory." (Isaiah 6: 1-3). Isaiah is totally wowed :-)

"Woe to me!" I cried. "I am ruined! For I am a man of unclean lips, and I live among a people of unclean lips, and my eyes have seen the King, the Lord Almighty." (Is. 6: 5). Then one of the seraphs flew down, took a live coal, and placed it on his lips—whereupon his sin and guilt are excused. Properly cleansed, he was ready for God's famous question: **"Whom shall I send? And who will go for us?"** To which Isaiah properly answered: **"Here am I. Send**

me!" (Is. 6: 8). Thus began the career of the most famous of the prophets, and a tradition practiced by the Jews and later adopted by the Christians—with enormous consequences.

It is not a particularly easy task to foretell the future. The prophets and diviners of all ancient religions that were into such predictions were quite careful to hedge their bets. The Jewish prophets were no exception. But, in general, their task was not all that difficult as the handwriting was on the wall. A look at a map of the region tells the whole story…

The area in which the Jews had finally managed to migrate, settle, and build their temple and capital, is located on a narrow strip of arable land less than a hundred miles wide, between the Mediterranean Sea and the vast Arabian Desert. Egypt, the ancient and well-established kingdom of which we have heard and read so much already, lay to the southwest and always presented a potential threat. Stretching north and east around the vast Fertile Crescent, lay other potential enemies like the Assyrians and the Babylonians. In every case, they had to follow the same basic geographic path to interact with one another; whether it was for commerce or to wage war, Israel was right in the middle. Due to its geographic location, it was no wonder that everybody in the ancient world ended up marching right through Israel at one time or another over the centuries. Like, what other way *was* there to go? Across 1,000 miles of sand? Hardly. So, after the Jews had fought endlessly for generations to take over the "Promised Land" and kick out all the original inhabitants, they finally got to build their city and its palace and temple. Just when they managed to get everything the way they wanted it, the Assyrians began to press in on them from the north.

The Bible is quite ethnocentric. It appears that the Israelites are the center of the Universe—the entire world revolving around them and their god. If you take the Bible literally, this is quite true. If you just look at history alone and without the Bible, other nations and cultures were developing simultaneously as well. All these wars and struggles of one tribe against another and one army against another were certainly not confined to the area that we now know as Israel. The Egyptian civilization, which stretches back into dimmest antiquity, was already mature and quite evolved when the Israelites were still living in tents and slaughtering the Amalekites. We also know that the Chinese, for example, were highly developed and flourishing long before this, as were the Jews' other neighbors, like the Hittites and Phoenicians.

The Jewish prophets made the scene beginning around 740 BCE. This is well within the bounds of *recorded* human history. Unlike the tribal legends and hand-me-down stories of the Old Testament, we are now dealing with real names and real places and people. We are dealing in information that can be fact-checked and crosschecked from various accounts all over the region and the world. It makes events more human-sized. Notice that men are no longer living to be 900 years old like in Noah's time.

Notice the absence of rivers turning to blood, plagues of frogs and flies, fire raining down from the sky, pillars of salt, and the Sun standing still. Quaint, but questionable (except by modern fundamentalist literalists, of course, who take all those stories that we have encountered as totally true). But we already know that, so let's go on.

The ancient Israelites could get away with all those tall tales way back when they were living in tents, wandering in the wilderness, and getting stoned around the campfire at night. But times had changed; circumstances had changed. The Jews were now living in a world forming itself into nations with sophisticated mechanisms of government, and were being exposed to the thoughts, ideas, and religions of the civilizations around them. David and Solomon had brought the Jews into a civilized status in the world. Where they had once been nomads, shepherds, and warriors, now they were craftsmen, merchants, and literates. They wrote poetry, songs, and literature. Jerusalem, with its royal palace and magnificent temple, must have been quite the showpiece at the time. Unfortunately, their moment in the Sun was to be short-lived. Peoples far more aggressive and outward-looking were rising up as well, and far faster and with more momentum. That poor little pinched-up slice of land tucked right in the middle of a rapidly expanding world was doomed from the start to be the doormat of all the powerful nations around them in a constantly changing, broader world.

Isaiah rightly foresaw doom. He knew that Israel was going to be run over by the Assyrian juggernaut. He saw the kings of Israel and Judah (the northern and southern halves of the kingdom) turning the nation from a freestanding theocracy to a dependence on alliances with various surrounding peoples. He knew full well that it just wasn't going to work out well for them. And it didn't. But in all his prophesying over the years, he always held a view that is still in play today. That notion is that the destruction of Israel and the disasters visited upon it, were due to the *guilt* of the people and not due to outside forces far beyond their control. Israel, the northern half of the kingdom, was the first to go—swallowed up by the invading Assyrians. Judah, the southern half, held out longer. Isaiah continued to warn them. So God sent Isaiah on his mission.

"Go and tell this people: Be ever hearing but never understanding; be ever seeing but never perceiving. Make the heart of this people calloused; make their ears dull and close their eyes. Otherwise they might see with their eyes, hear with their ears, understand with their hearts, and turn and be healed." (Is. 6: 9,10). "Turn and be healed." This is a key phrase that is the cornerstone of much of the Judeo-Christian thought right up to our day. The belief is that the forthcoming disasters are the result of *improper behavior*, and that by doing something to change it, destruction can be avoided.

In the tradition of the earlier ancient tribal societies and agrarian civilizations that followed, when misfortune befell the populations, someone was called upon to explain why; and, also, what was needed to make it right again. When crops failed, when there was drought or disease, or when enemy armies stormed in—the people demanded to know why they were suffering, and whose fault it was, and what was to be done to fix things. That job fell to the witch doctor, the shaman, or the prophet. And as prophets go, Isaiah was definitely one of the best.

He dutifully preached Jehovah's party line: Follow the law exactly and worship Yahweh exclusively. But since y'all haven't been doing these things sufficiently, disaster is unavoidable. It is not the Assyrians that are going to destroy you; it is God! He is just going to use the Assyrians like he would use a broom to wipe you out and sweep you away. **Destruction has been decreed, overwhelming and righteous. The Lord, the Lord Almighty will carry out the destruction decreed upon the whole land.** (Is. 10: 23). On and on and on it goes. This theme gets a bit tired and beaten to death, but wait … there's a variation! Yeah.

If the people *repent* ... if they turn from their wicked ways ... if they return to God and follow his commandments, he will restore them and fight for them, routing their enemies. God and his people will be vindicated and the aggressor will be annihilated. **See, the day of the Lord is coming—a cruel day, with wrath and fierce anger—to make the land desolate and destroy the sinners within it.** (Is. 13: 9). Back and forth it goes, chapter after chapter. In all, there are numerous prophesies against Israel and Judah. But moreover, there are even all sorts of threats trashing the Assyrians, the Babylonians, the Moabites, Damascus, Cush, Egypt, Arabia, Tyre, and even the *whole Earth*! Isaiah was really on a roll (and that's just up to chapter twenty- four)! Wow.

Talk about hedging one's bets. Judah gets soundly warned of its impending destruction. And each of its potential invaders is warned that if they destroy what's left of Israel, they will in turn be destroyed themselves. So, no matter who attacked whom, there was a prophecy in place to cover it. That way, no matter what happened, Isaiah could say: "See, I told you so."

Isaiah spent a good deal of time as a prophet to King Hezekiah, the king of the rump state of Judah (which Assyria later absorbed anyway). In the meantime, he just kept on warning of impending invasion and disaster. No kidding! Assyria had a massive army poised in the north. Duh. Like, who couldn't see that coming? LOL.

Anyway, as part of his duty as prophet to the king, Isaiah *had a miracle healing ministry* as well—kind of like Katherine Kuhlman and Oral Roberts. King Hezekiah got deathly ill and called for Isaiah, who told him that unless he got his shit together he was going to die. The king whined and sniveled and cried and repented, begging Yahweh to heal him. Apparently, God was impressed with all his shameless groveling and authorized Isaiah to heal him. Then Isaiah said, **"Prepare a poultice of figs!"** (II Kings 20: 7). That should do the trick. Well, it always worked for my grandmother!

Isaiah tells Hezekiah that God heard his prayers and was sufficiently satisfied with all his self-flagellation and was going to heal him. But the king isn't sure of his prophet and wants a sign from the Almighty himself to prove it. So Isaiah pulls out all the stops and asks: **Shall the shadow go forward ten steps, or shall it go back ten steps?** (II Kings 20: 9). Whereupon Hezekiah points out that it is no big deal for a shadow to go forward—but backward? Now that would be a cool sign. **Then the prophet Isaiah called upon the Lord, and the Lord made the shadow go back the ten steps it had gone down on the stairway of Ahaz.** (II Kings 20: 11). Wow, is that a miracle or what? Heck, Joshua had enough clout with God to have him stop the Sun for twenty-four hours; but Isaiah had enough juice with the man upstairs to have him reverse its direction altogether. Imagine that!

Okay, time for a new transition. Isaiah introduces a new idea. **The Earth is defiled by its people; they have disobeyed the laws, violated the statutes and broken the everlasting covenant. Therefore a curse consumes the earth; its people must bear their guilt. Therefore earth's inhabitants are burned up, and very few are left.** (Is. 24: 5,6). What? Now this is something different, huh? This is a signpost on our tour. This is an indication of the direction in which we are headed. Notice what is happening here. Up to now, God cares nothing at all about anyone but the Jews. He considers the non- Jews as about on the level of swine, dogs or conies. Slaughter them. Kill them all. Push them out of the land. Kill all their cattle. And their little dogs too!

But now, all of a sudden, we are catching a whiff of something new. The *Earth* is defiled by its people! They have disobeyed the laws, violated the statutes, and broken the everlasting covenant. *What* laws, what statutes, what everlasting covenant? Up to this point God has made this deal with the Jews only, and everybody else can just go take a flying leap. Now there is talk of a more general law, a more universal covenant with all mankind. But, just like back in the flood story, it is undefined. We are simply not told what it is. Damn.

The Christians point to this as a true prophecy indeed. It foretells, they say, the coming of Christ and his universal message to mankind. They will refer to this and Isaiah in general as proof that God had a plan in mind all along for all peoples of the planet—not just the Jews. We are at a crossroads, a turning point. The Bible—at this juncture—takes on an entirely more universal tone. But that is just a *hint* so far. The most often preached and quoted of Isaiah's words are literally screamed at all of us by the wild-eyed born again Christians who believe that these words don't apply to them. Hah! It is to them—the "type" of Israel—to whom they are directly aimed.

"If you do away with the yoke of oppression, with the wagging finger and malicious talk, and if you spend yourselves on behalf of the hungry and satisfy the needs of the afflicted, then your light will rise in the darkness and your night will become like the noonday. You will be like a watered garden, like a spring whose waters never fail." (Is. 58: 9-11). The Almighty is simply telling the believers to get their collective act together.

Jeremiah and Ezekiel

Before I formed you in the womb I knew you ...

About 100 years after Isaiah did his thing as a prophet, Jeremiah came along; and we encounter another five chapters of similar warnings and predictions. Hot on Jeremiah's heels was Ezekiel. Sandwiched in between the two books is *Lamentations*, a poetic book of dirges. I have always quipped that the title is apropos—lamenting all the contradictions, blunders, and bloopers that we have seen in the Bible :-)

Anyway, both of these prophets could have used an editor. They were both wordy and windy, ranting on and on about the same thing. There was simply no doubt that the nation of Israel/Judah was in trouble. The Babylonians were gaining strength and expanding militarily, up and along the Fertile Crescent, from their capital in Babylon (now tasteful Baghdad). Other ancient peoples were being displaced as well. There was no doubt that sooner or later Israel would fall under the steamroller too. So the endless prophecies to that effect are taken for granted. Both Jeremiah and Ezekiel maintained Isaiah's notion that it could all be prevented if God's people would get with the program.

We read from all three prophets the same theme: God is sick and tired of all this sinning; and just sacrificing goats and bulls as guilt offerings is getting old. Obviously, over the years the Jews caught onto the "sin now, pay later" theory. The Christians have done likewise for years, and you don't have to read a hundred chapters to get the drift. The real big thing that God is pissed off about (as usual) is idolatry. God just never has liked any other gods, period. He has never liked man worshiping statues, the Sun, the Moon, the stars, animals, nature or anything other than him. He never changed his opinion about rival gods. They were simply out.

Israel was influenced by its neighbors and trading partners, so various other religions affected the way the Jews thought about the world around them. All mankind was pretty much in the same boat. Droughts, plagues, wars, and famines ravaged all the parties in the ancient world, and no one was immune. Using hindsight, I can't blame the Jews for dabbling in other religions. If you consider individuals, families, and communities dealing with life-threatening problems and events, without even a hint of modern science or medicine—in the face of human tragedies like starvation, sickness, and death—surely individuals would be tempted to try anything to help them understand and get through. Vocabulary word time again. *Syncretism is* a word used by theologians and anthropologists. It means to mix or blend thoughts, ideas, beliefs, and rituals from various religions into a new hybrid. Due to its central location on the way to just about anywhere and everywhere, it is no wonder that Israel was influenced by contending belief systems from various sundry sources. Yahweh just hated that! The prophets ranted and raved against it, and warned that it would be their downfall for sure. Again and again God spoke through the prophets, threatening that if they didn't purify themselves and stop dabbling with other religions—adopting and adapting them—their doom was at hand. Like, duh.

But, "If you will return, O Israel, return to me," declares the Lord. "If you put your detestable idols out of my sight and no longer go astray, and if in a truthful, just and righteous way you swear, 'As surely as the Lord lives,' then the nations will be blessed by him and in him they will glory." (Jeremiah 4: 1,2).

Then we pick up on a new wrinkle. A new theme begins slowly to emerge —One which, as we follow along, becomes of paramount importance. **Circumcise yourselves to the Lord, circumcise your hearts, you men of Judah and people of Jerusalem, or my wrath will break out and burn like fire because of the evil you have done—burn with no one to quench it.** (Jer. 4: 4). Huh? Circumcise your hearts? What the heck does that mean?

Jeremiah preaches a message of condemnation for the most part. But he introduces the use of this word "heart"—and uses it a lot. The notion of a personal religion is implied, and a personal relationship with God pokes its head up out of the sand. Up to now, we have known God to be sovereign and arbitrary. He can do whatever the hell he wants to. It is he who gives the commandments and decrees, and we just better comply—or else. Up to now there has not been much (if any) mention of a personal relationship between individuals and God (except for his pets). David, for example, related to God on a somewhat personal level. The Psalms indicate that David worshiped God because he genuinely wanted to. He really did get off on worship, singing, and dancing in the nude, and carrying on in praise of the Almighty.

But if you look back at Moses, Joshua, and the Israelites in general, their relationship to God was based on fear and intimidation. They behaved like children. They did what they were told without really understanding why, and when they were bad they were spanked. God made the rules; they obeyed blindly. And when they did not obey unswervingly, they were punished— simple as that.

Of course, we recall from Ecclesiastes that this is not altogether true. They often suffered whether they were good or bad, obedient or not. The whole system was not quite working. God spent the first few millennia doing all sorts of showy tricks and feats like sending floods and plagues, and raining fire down from heaven. This had everybody scared. They toed the line; but, as we know, they drifted too. They wanted kings, he gave them kings. Now he sent prophets, but they still flirted with other gods. Clearly this wasn't working either. How could God get man to worship him without threatening them? Ever so gradually a new idea seems to begin to dawn on God. IMHO, God was progressively getting the picture that these prophets—handy as they were— were still not getting through to the people.

Remember back in Exodus that God gave the original Ten Commandments? Then, in Leviticus he overwhelmed us with rules and regulations enough to choke a horse, governing everything right down to every little bodily function—like ejaculation. He made a covenant—an agreement with the Israelites. Do as I say and worship me only, and you will inherit the land and live until you die. He then raised up judges, priests, and prophets to enforce all these rules by constantly reminding everybody about them. They still failed. ...Now things are changing.

"This is the covenant I will make with the house of Israel after that time," declares the Lord. "I will put my law in their minds and write it on their hearts. I will be their God, and they will be my people. No longer will a man teach his neighbor or a man his brother, saying, 'know the Lord,' because they will all know me, from the least of them to the greatest," declares the Lord. "For I will forgive their wickedness and will remember their sins no more." (Jer. 31:33,34).

Wow! This is new. Is God mellowing out a bit? It sure looks like it. Up to now we have known him as the creator God; curser and murderer of wicked mankind; the sender of plagues and stopper of wombs; destroyer of armies, enforcer of laws—a real bad-ass cop in the sky. Now, almost imperceptibly, there is a subtle change. He is going to make a new covenant with *individual* persons. No longer is he going to chisel his laws on stone tablets and force everyone to obey them. He is going to try something different. He is going to write the laws on the hearts of men. (And women, I presume :-)

Now don't get me wrong. This isn't as revolutionary as it looks. First of all, it is still just for the Jews. Everybody else can just go suck out. So God is not really turning into Mr. Nice Guy. However, he suspects that because of this preprogramming of the laws into men's minds and hearts, they will then worship him naturally and dump the gods of stone and wood and gold and stuff, preferring to raise their voices of praise and adulation to him alone. Will it work? We shall see.

Jeremiah rants and raves, threatens and cajoles for another twenty-some chapters, and then writes those desolate chapters called Lamentations. I lament having to say it, but they are really not all that germane, as Ezekiel takes up the call at that point and continues on and on with the same theme for another seventeen chapters before the next quirk appears.

Do you remember when Noah passed out drunk in his tent? Do you remember what God told Solomon regarding the downfall of Jerusalem? Do you see what they have in common? Let's take a look to see if we can observe a correlation. **"You shall not make for yourself an idol in the form of anything in heaven above or on the earth beneath or in the waters below. You shall not bow down to them or worship them: for I, the Lord your God am a jealous God, punishing the children for the sin of the fathers to the third and fourth generation of those who hate me, but showing love to thousands who love me and keep my commandments."** (Exodus 20: 5,6). See—cursing or not cursing, blessing or not blessing succeeding generations based on the behavior of the forefathers, had been going on for eons. These are only a few examples of a tradition based on the notion that individuals are nothing themselves, but, rather, part of an ongoing family line or continuum. This is about to change.

For every living soul belongs to me, the father as well as the son—both alike belong to me. The soul who sins is the one who shall die. He will not die for his father's sins; he will surely live. But his father will die for his own sin, yet you ask "Why does not the son share the guilt of his father?" The soul who sins is the one who will die. The son will not share the guilt of the father, nor will the father share the guilt of the son. The righteousness of the righteous man will be credited to him, and the wickedness of the wicked will be charged against him. (Ezekiel 18: 18- 20). Woah! OOOooo. Can you see what's happening? As time goes on it is more and more apparent to the people that it is a rip-off religion that punishes three or four generations for the sins of the fathers.

Common sense would tell us that if we screw up our environment, our children will inherit the mess. But when God curses a whole line of people into slavery and misery due to the behavior of one man that is simply unfair. Maybe God realized at that point that this being the case so far, no wonder his chosen people were kicking the tires of other gods and religions. Perhaps they offered a better deal.

So right here God decides to improve the deal. From now on everyone is going to be responsible for his (or her) *own* sins. He who sins is going to die in them and the righteous will die righteously. Yea. But, of course—as you may recall—Solomon pointed out that they are all going to die in the end anyway; so what is the big deal really? Good question ... and, up to this point, one that God has not come up with an answer to. Yet.

As any tour of LA wouldn't be complete without a visit to its famous cemetery, Forest Lawn, our tour also has a graveyard smash. It is called the Valley of the Dry Bones, and I'll bet you can sing along with the lyrics. Dem bones, dem bones, dem dry bones. Remember? Well, this story is found right here in Ezekiel! Let's read...

God speaking: **"Son of man, can these bones live?" I said, "O sovereign Lord, you alone know." Then he said to me, "Prophesy to these bones and say to them, 'Dry bones, hear the word of the Lord.' ... So I prophesied as I was commanded. And as I was prophesying, there was a noise, a rattling sound, and the bones came together, bone to bone. I looked, and tendons**

and flesh appeared on them and skin covered them but there was no breath in them. (Ez. 37: 3,4,7,8).

Then God breathed life into them and they stood up—alive! Notice what God says next: **"Son of man, these bones are the whole house of Israel. They say, 'Our bones are dried up and our hope is gone; we are cut off.'** (Dead, remember?) **Therefore prophesy and say to them; 'This is what the sovereign Lord says; O my people, I am going to open your graves and bring you up from them; I will bring you back to the land of Israel.'"** (Ez. 37: 11-13).

I have heard lots of sermons isolating the phrase: *"I am going to open your graves and bring you up from them,"* as a reference to the resurrection of the physical body, that the fundamentalist Christians so look forward to. We'll talk about the "rapture" later on the tour :-)

Perhaps the most diehard literalists take this word for word, but even Jerry Falwell's LBC refers to it as "allegory," which it is. We are assured that it really is just a means for God to promise Israel that after they are destroyed by the Babylonians and carried away into captivity, they will one day be resurrected as a nation and will live again. But this little question keeps nagging at my mind... If *this* is allegory, who says the creation story isn't allegorical as well? Or the flood story, the story of Sodom, or the pillar of salt?

Oh no! Those are *literal*. So how do you know they are different—literal? Well, they just *are*! (I see.)

Well, literal or not—speaking of Babylon and allegory, there is plenty of that ahead on our tour in the story of Daniel, coming up next. You'll love it!

The story of Daniel, one of God's true pets, is full of excitement. Lions, fiery furnaces and totally cool visions. Something for the whole family!

Daniel

A fiery furnace, a den of lions, and dreams galore!

I think everybody likes this account because—unlike Isaiah and Jeremiah and Ezekiel—it is short, fun-filled, and to the point. It is easy reading and actually tells a story, instead of just railing on and on about the same thing. Besides that, we all seem to remember the stories from Daniel, don't we?

The Book of Daniel is one of the most well-known and oft-referred to in the Old Testament. The stories of the fiery furnace and the den of lions are great bedtime fare for small children (far more uplifting than the slaughter of the Amalekites, for example). But this book's popularity with adults stems from its introduction of a whole new theme in scripture—one that builds a bridge to the New Testament and to our day and beyond. Prophecy about us!

We may recall from our reading in the major prophets, that the notion of prophecy itself took the form of warnings and threats of destruction of Israel, and stuff like: **"Therefore this is what the sovereign Lord says: My anger will be poured out on this place, on man and beast, on trees of the field and on the fruit of the ground, and it will burn and not be quenched."** (Jeremiah 7: 20). Remember?

Well, actually that all happened. In fact, it happened again and again throughout those centuries. Israel, Judah, and that whole region were conquered and reconquered, ravaged and pillaged by various contending armies for years. So the prophesies of the likes of Isaiah, Jeremiah, and Ezekiel would not only apply to specific cases, but to just about anything—anytime. Modern preachers and televangelists haul out these Old Testament warnings and apply them to America, Europe, and just about any place on Earth!

When I was doing missionary work in the Philippines in 1975 or so, I recall hearing a visiting ding-a-ling American preacher use this particular verse in Jeremiah chapter 7 as a warning to the *Philippines*! Actually, I don't think he knew the difference between the Philippines and the Philistines :-) His tirade went on and on. "If the Philippines continue to flirt with communism and turn away from their democratic government..." then their land would experience the woes of the prophecy of Jeremiah. Actually, Marcos was in power at that time and the communists were nonexistent. And talk about democratic government! Hah! LOL all the way.

So, is a *warning* a prophecy? If you put your hand on a hot stove, you will get burned. If you don't repent, you're going to be overrun by the Assyrians or the Babylonians. The Major Prophets' warnings can apply to nearly any situation anywhere. Take your pick. On our tour we've already encountered dreams predicting future events; Joseph's dreams back in Egypt (Genesis 37) leap to mind. But Daniel introduces a new and different kind of prophecy. (A new vocabulary word.) *Eschatology* is a foretelling-the-future kind of prophecy, relating predictions and prognostications of the "end times" through signs and symbols, dreams and visions. Modern preachers, "teachers," theologians, and sundry other religious quacks and charlatans go apoplectic with the Book of Daniel, for—as they say—it predicts *our* future. And that interests us in these "end times" greatly. Besides, it sells books, DVDs, and all manner of other religious trinkets and memorabilia. LOL. It has a huge market of total suckers.

Daniel was one of the Jewish exiles living in Babylon. How ever did he get there? Well, when Israel and Judah were captured in about 600 BCE, all the valuables were systematically carted off back to Baghdad (I mean Babylon :-). But, unlike the Jews, who when they conquered somebody, simply killed them all (and the animals) ... Remember Joshua at Jericho, for example? Well, the Babylonians were more sophisticated. They not only took the booty—the loot—but they took all the people as well. What's the point of killing them when they would make dandy slaves? (Smart thinking, huh?)

But the Babylonians were even more together than that, as they actually sorted the captives into categories. Daniel must have scored pretty high on his IQ test, because he was chosen to be trained by the Babylonians as a civil servant...not a bad deal. He rose to the top when he interpreted a dream of the famous King Nebuchadnezzar. The king was overwhelmed by Daniel's "gift" and put him in charge of the kingdom's "wise" men. Cool, huh? Then he became "Chief of the Magicians." And we all know how much God likes magicians. Recall Exodus and other accounts calling for their elimination. LOL.

King Neb was mad at Daniel and had him cremated in the "fiery" furnace.
He was so pissed off that he had the flames stoked to 10,000 degrees Fahrenheit.
BTW, that's the temperature of the surface of the Sun! LOL.

Well, Daniel was in a good position at that point, to be sure; so, he wangled the appointment of three of his friends to his department. Shadrach, Meshach, and Abednego all got cushy administrative assignments in the kingdom as well. But, as you may recall from childhood or Sunday school, what happens next is not a prettypicture.

King Nebuchadnezzar made an image of gold, ninety feet high and nine feet wide. Then the herald loudly proclaimed, "This is what you are commanded to do, O peoples, nations and men of every language: As soon as you hear the sound of the horn, flute, zither, lyre, harp, pipes, and all kinds of music, you must fall down and the worship the image of god that King Nebuchadnezzar has set up. Whoever does not fall down and worship will immediately be thrown into a blazing furnace." (Daniel 3: 1, 4-6). BTW, this was particularly difficult to do because three of those abovementioned instruments had not been invented yet, but would be introduced by the Greeks 500 years later. Hmmm. Oh well, the Bible is inerrant, so let's go on. The three amigos wouldn't bow down to the golden statue. Bad move. They were summarily condemned to be thrown into the fiery furnace.

I've always gotten a kick out of the term "fiery furnace." Like, what other type is there? Anyway, Nebuchadnezzar was hopping mad at them. In fact, he was so pissed that he ordered the furnace to be seven times hotter than usual. Now that's really hot. In fact, astronomers have pointed out that it would make the temperature 10,000 degrees Fahrenheit (5500 C.) ... which is the temperature of the surface of the Sun. Yeah, sure. Nevertheless, they were tossed in. You know the story. Shazam! They didn't burn.

But the real import of the story is: **Then King Nebuchadnezzar leaped to his feet in amazement and asked his advisers, "Wasn't it three men that we tied up and threw into the fire?" He said, "Look! I see four men walking around in the fire, unbound and unharmed, and the fourth looks like a son of the gods."** (Dan. 3: 24,25).

This makes Christians just cream in their jeans, claiming that the fourth person in the furnace was none other than the great Jesus Christ himself! Up until now we have seen some other examples of a mystery personage appearing here and there. Remember this? "Let *us* make man in *our* image, let us go down to see ..." And in no case is it specific—just implied. God and Jesus, together up in the sky. But this is an important indicator on our tour ... a road sign pointing us forward on our journey. Well, Nebuchadnezzar was totally freaked out. Do ya think? He effusively praised the God of the Jews and said: **"Therefore I decree that the people of any nation or language who say anything against the God of Shadrach, Meshach and Abednego be cut into pieces and their houses be turned into piles of rubble, for no other god can save in this way."** (Dan. 3: 29). I can hear the sermons flying!

Daniel was resident in Babylon when the kingdom was conquered by Darius, King of the Medes (in our day we would call them *Iranians*). He maintained his administrative position with great esteem. But the other magicians were jealous of him and goaded the king into pitching him into the infamous den of lions. Well—as we all know—Daniel got the last laugh, as God shut the lions' mouths; and he got through the whole incident without a scratch. Like Nebuchadnezzar, Darius was wowed. He issued a proclamation: **"I issue a decree that in every part of my kingdom people must fear and reverence the God of Daniel."** (Dan. 6: 26). The Fundamentalists wet themselves over this verse too :-)

Well, once again, Daniel landed on his feet. Actually, he was still on the top of the heap under Cyrus the Persian. It is so clear that Daniel was another of God's pets. It doesn't mention how the rest of the Jewish captives fared. But my guess is that working in the Persian salt mines was no picnic. But that's just a guess.

The narrative changes abruptly after this ... beginning with chapter seven. Whereas, up to now, Daniel was being written about—then, all of a sudden, he is the writer. He had a vision. "In my vision at night I looked and there before me were the four winds of heaven churning up the great sea. Four great beasts, each different from the others, came up out of the sea." (Dan. 7: 2,3). Then it gets weird right away.

"The first was like a lion, and it had wings of an eagle. I watched until its wings were torn off and it was lifted from the ground so that it stood on two feet like a man, and the heart of a man was given to it." (Dan. 7: 4). Okay, anyway, it goes on like that... The second beast was somewhat like a bear; the third was a sort of hybrid leopard with four heads and four birdlike wings; the fourth monster had iron teeth that crushed and devoured its victims, and it also had ten horns. Whew. But it continues ... **"While I was thinking about the horns, there before me was another horn, a little one, which came up among them; and three of the first horns were uprooted before it. This horn had eyes like the eyes of a man and a mouth that spoke boastfully."** (Dan. 7: 8).

Fortunately for us, the interpretation of the dream is provided! **The four great beasts are the four kingdoms that will rise from the earth.** (Dan. 7: 17). **The fourth beast is a fourth kingdom that will appear on the earth. Different from all the other kingdoms and will devour the whole earth, trampling it down and crushing it. The ten horns are the kings who will come from this kingdom.** (Dan. 7: 23). Are you still with me? **After them another king will arise, different from the earlier ones; he will subdue three kings. He will speak against the Most High and oppress his saints and try to change the set times and the laws. The saints will be handed over to him for a time, times and half a time.** (Dan. 7: 24,25). Got that?

Well, thousands of pages have been spilled out over the centuries, attempting to explain the vision of the ten horns and all. The Jews would obviously disagree, but the Christians have always maintained that Daniel's vision had (and still has) apocalyptic meaning, referring to the end of time and the second coming of Christ. Looking back from the Christian period to Daniel, it is easy to build such a case in view of verses like: **"In my vision at night I looked, and there before me was one like a son of man, coming with the clouds of heaven. He approached the Ancient of Days and was led into his presence. He was given authority, glory, and sovereign power, all peoples, nations and men of every language worshiped him. His dominion is an everlasting dominion that will not pass away, and his kingdom is one that will never be destroyed."** (Dan. 7: 13,14).

Several more visions follow. These are interpreted by Daniel himself, as well. They refer specifically to Babylonia, Persia, and Greece—which has led critics for years to speculate that none of this was written by Daniel in the first place, but by some cleric about 500 years later. But to quote Rhett Butler: "Frankly, my dear, I don't give a damn." Besides, as you may have noticed, all along the tour I have not even brought up the issue of authorship. (Well, Moses, not withstanding.) Pretty much everything in the Bible is of disputed authorship anyway, so why spoil your tour fussing around with things that are completely unknowable? There is little evidence that any of the writings that we have read so far were written by any of the men to whom they are ascribed—so why quibble over Daniel?

Fuggettaboudit. Besides, we are moving into more modern times now, and events that we are presently talking about were actually documented by not only the Jews, but by other civilizations as well. And—I might point out— many of these left far more reliable histories for us to examine.

We dare not get bogged down here. We could. The last four chapters of the Book of Daniel are so convoluted and arcane that they are virtually unintelligible. Stopping our tour here to analyze them would be like touring the Library of Congress and stopping to read everything in one particular section, like antibiotics or Mongolian equine husbandry. We've got to move along. This is just a look at what's in the Bible—not an explanation. If you are looking for an explanation of the visions of Daniel—by all means—ask your minister, priest, or rabbi. But be prepared for a snow job. Believe me, they don't know.

Poor Daniel. Even *he* didn't get it. **I heard, but I did not understand. So I asked, "My Lord, what will the outcome of all this be?" He replied, "Go your way, Daniel, because the words are closed up and sealed until the time of the end. As for you, go your way till the end. You will rest, and then at the end of the days you will rise to receive your allotted inheritance."** (Dan. 12:9,12,13).

Obviously, this is a reference to a forthcoming resurrection at some future time—or so they say. But, you have to admit, it is juicy material for religious hucksters who claim that since these are indeed the End Times, these mysteries have *already* been opened. And it is *they* who can explain it all to you :-) ...For a small donation, of course.

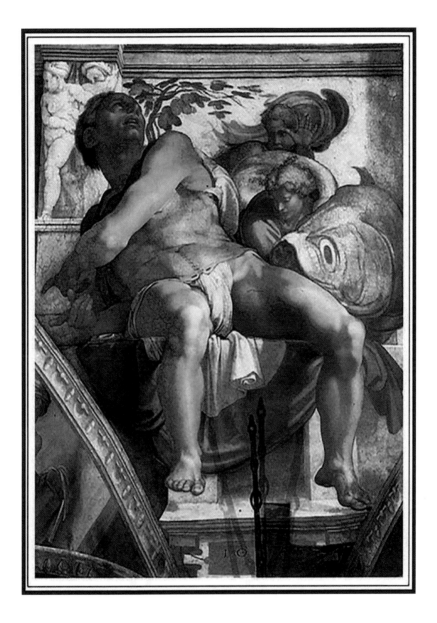

The big fish arrived on cue and swallowed poor Jonah. It burped him up on the beach three days later. The Fundies try and try to make this fish tale plausible. LOL.

Jonah

What a fish story!

This is, by far, one of my personal all-time favorites :-) This is another of those classic tales that most people are aware of, but couldn't tell with any degree of accuracy if called upon to do so on a quiz show. All we seem to recall is that Jonah got swallowed by a whale and survived in there for three days. There is much more to the story.

One of the reasons that I feel the Book of Jonah is important is that it is one of those clear works of fiction that the fundamentalists are stuck trying to defend as fact. Even though the true Bible believers do accept as literal the real chokers—like the talking donkey, Noah's ark, and the Sun standing still—they don't usually try to defend them as fact by citing scientific evidence to prove their possibility. Instead, they ignore the impossibility factor and tell us to look at the lessons that they teach. What a copout! However, Jonah's story is borderline. "It *could* have happened" ... they claim. "God could have created a special fish just for the purpose of swallowing him." Few hold to the whale theory anymore after we've learned that whales are not fish, but mammals, and live on plankton (and don't swallow men alive). Besides, the Bible says *fish*, so it was a big fish. Period.

Before we get down to the "one that got away" part, let's review why Jonah was on that trip in the first place. **The word of the Lord came to Jonah son of Amittai: "Go to the great city of Nineveh and preach against it, because its wickedness has come up before me." But Jonah ran away from the Lord and headed for Tarshish.** (Jonah 1: 2,3).

This is the revolutionary idea found in this book. Jonah was a Jew. The Jews were totally exclusive in their attitudes toward non-Jews, aka "Gentiles." God never gave a damn about anybody outside the Jewish circle. Outsiders were only wicked bystanders in God's big play featuring the Hebrews. God manipulated them, destroyed them with fire and floods and plagues, and ordered their slaughter and extermination regularly. Now, all of a sudden, God is doing a flip-flop. "Go to Nineveh and preach against it!" What? The obvious shocker here is that he is apparently going to give them a warning. He is going to extend them a courtesy. Instead of just killing them with a flood, a rain of fire and sulfuric acid from the sky, or with a conquering army, he is going to give them a chance to alter their wicked behavior first and maybe forestall disaster. Wow, this *is* something different!

This presents the same problem that faced those killed in the big flood, the plagues of Egypt, and the destruction of Sodom and Jericho (for example). The law, with all its multitudinous commands and decrees, was designed for the Jews. It was never even addressed to the other people inhabiting the planet. The law had by now defined wickedness (for the Jews). We know full well by now what the no-nos are. But even if Jonah *did* follow instructions and go to Nineveh (modern Mosul, Iraq)—probably the largest city in the world at the time—how would he preach to them? What would he say?

Would he preach a message like Jeremiah or Ezekiel did, warning them to stop being wicked—or else? Would he promise them that if they changed they would not be vaporized in some creative cosmic maelstrom? Would he insist that they conform to Jewish laws and commandments? Would he, in fact, be trying to make Jews out of them? Would he attempt to *convert* them? This is wild. Judaism is not a missionary religion. Where else have we seen, heard, or had any inkling of God caring one iota about the Gentiles? No wonder Jonah was totally freaked. He just wasn't programmed for that kind of an assignment. He didn't know what to do, so he just ran the other way.

He got on a ship heading west across the Mediterranean. A ferocious storm ensued. The sailors were terrified and, of course, had to find out whose fault it was that they were in such a predicament. They cast lots and God revealed to them that Jonah was to blame. Modern, pious churchgoers decry gambling as "of the devil," but God used this method to reveal Jonah to them. I have always wondered where all this fervor against gambling comes from. Proverbs even points out: **The lot is cast into the lap, but its every decision is from the Lord.** (Proverbs 16: 33). Sounds like God likes having his hand in every decision ... every throw of the dice ... every turn of the cards... every pull of the slot machine:-)

At Jonah's own insistence they tossed him overboard, whereupon the big fish arrived on cue and swallowed him. He was in there for three days and nights. That is amazing. Furthermore, he was awake and conscious. Beyond even that, he waxed eloquent. From inside the fish, Jonah prayed to the Lord his God. He said: **"In my distress I called to the Lord, and he answered me. From the depths of the grave I called for help, and you listened to my cry. You hurled me into the deep, into the very heart of the seas, and the currents swirled around me; and all your waves and breakers swept over me."** (Jonah 2: 1-3). I think you get the drift. It goes on and on. I have always wondered who recorded those poetic statements. Was somebody else down in there with him? Who brought the ink and paper? LOL.

In any case, the Lord commanded the fish and it burped Jonah up on the beach. God commanded him again to go to Nineveh and preach. He wasted no time complying at that point. In fact, he made the journey in three days flat. Nineveh (Mosul) is like 600 miles from the Mediterranean Sea. Without the aid of motorized transportation and a good freeway—I have no idea how he managed it. But I guess that is just one of those little mysteries along the way on the *Biblical Mystery Tour*:-)

The other reason I like this story is that it gets right to the point. **Jonah started into the city, going a day's journey, and he proclaimed: "Forty more days and Nineveh will be destroyed." The Ninevites believed God. They declared a fast, and all of them, from the greatest to the least put on sackcloth.** (Jonah 3: 4,5). Oh, if only God had offered that courtesy to Sodom! **When God saw what they did and how they turned from their evil ways, he had compassion and did not bring upon them the destruction he had threatened.** (Jonah 3: 10).

Well, Jonah was pissed. Do you know why? He didn't want them to repent. He wanted them destroyed. He was angry at God for sparing them. He didn't see any point at all in including those awful Ninevites in his exclusive club. What are we seeing here? A kinder, gentler Yahweh? It sure looks that way.

Keep in mind—the Bible that we have in hand here is not arranged in chronological order. We find ourselves, nevertheless, in the final few pages of the Old Testament. The crazy quilt of the other short books around Jonah are referred to as the Minor Prophets. They fit into the cracks concurrently, with some of the Major Prophets. Why God chose to put them in this order is about as clear as why he made the plants in Genesis before he made the Sun. Oh well, another mystery.

So, looks like we have run out of Old Testament on our "once over lightly" tour of the Bible. For those of our Jewish tour members who wish to depart at this point, it has been a pleasure. Of course, you are certainly welcome to remain on the tour if you like, as you might really enjoy familiarizing yourself with some of the weird territory that lies ahead in what we call the New Testament. Actually, it might really help you understand your wacked-out Christian neighbors and friends better ...But don't count on it!

Rest Stop

Where do we go from here?

The Old Testament ends in a whimper, not a bang. The Jews are in captivity in Babylon, which is overrun by the Persians under King Darius. He allows the Jews to return to Jerusalem to begin putting things back together again. The account of this "long walk home" is found in the books of Ezra and Nehemiah. Despite their chronological position, these books are physically located back before Job. Who ever arranged this hodgepodge anyway? Whoever it was must have been drinking too much wine or smoking something. Anyway, the whole story just sort of fades. But this is not a "happily ever after" ending.

Hundreds of years pass and Israel is absorbed into a new and far more exciting world ... a Greek world. The biblical view had always been ethnocentric. Yahweh and the Israelites were, in their eyes, the center of the world—the Universe in fact. With the arrival of the Greeks, Israel's position in the world as a whole became more irrelevant. The center of the world was Greece. Alexander probably didn't much even remember conquering the Jews. They were just a sort of speed bump en route to Egypt and all points East, as well. Like modern Americans in many ways, the Greeks spread their culture wherever they went. I just don't think that Yahweh and the Jews were quite ready for the Greeks. The ancient nations and peoples of antiquity—their languages, customs and cultures ... their gods, priests and prophets—gradually began melting into a new and more enlightened world order. The Jews fought integration, of course. But a civilization as powerful and dynamic as the Greeks simply overwhelmed them.

The Jews, by then, were just one more group in an expanding world, shuffled to the sidelines of history as the world looked westward. Rome inherited the foundations of the Greek culture and greatly expanded on it. The Romans may not have been as creative as the Greeks, but were they ever extraordinary administrators! Wow, could these guys ever run an empire! Now, within the greater Roman province of Palestina, Israel was just a tired little corner of the massive Roman Empire.

But in this unimportant small province in a backwater little podunk district called Galilee, and in a one-horse-town named Bethlehem, our next biblical hero is born. His story is a good one! Our story picks up in a manger... Let's go on.

Part 8

Parables
Prophecy
and
Punishment

Mary underwent ritual purification after the birth of Jesus. If she was without sin, as we are led to believe, why would she have to?

The Gospels

Jesus... the early years

There are plenty of examples throughout the Bible of stories being retold twice or, in some cases, three times. These are called doublets (and triplets). But Jesus gets his story told *four* times! Of course, the problem with having different people retelling the same story is that the accounts can conflict. Four different people with four different points of view undertake to recount the birth, life, and untimely death of Jesus Christ—purported king of the Jews.

Now, there was no question that the Jews needed a deliverer. It seems that they were just about always in need of someone to deliver them from oppression. Moses did a great job getting them out of Egypt, as we have seen. And, of course, we can't forget others like Joshua, Samuel, and David—to name a few that we have met along our tour route. Now, the Jews were struggling under the yoke of the oppressive Romans. And they didn't like it. They needed a savior, a deliverer, a *messiah*.

There were plenty of references to promised deliverers throughout the Old Testament in the past. So many, in fact, that even though they may not have been intended as description of latter pretenders, they could be applied to just about anyone. Written decades after Jesus' passing, the four Gospels (as we know them) attempt in different ways to cast Jesus of Nazareth in the role of savior and promised deliverer. The four Gospels are focused on different aspects of Jesus' persona, to appeal to different social and anthropological groups. Matthew's gospel is very Jewish in focus, Mark's is targeted to the Romans, and Luke's to the Greeks. John's gospel—the "odd man out"—is what most refer to as a kind of "universal" message. I don't think I have to make the point again that there are contradictions.

Instead, let's try to get a feel for the spirit of the New Testament's message, before we get down to the details. So, let's start with this well-worn verse ...

In the beginning was the Word, and the Word was with God, and the Word was God. He was with God in the Beginning. (John 1: 1,2). Now, this is theology! The Word (Logos in Greek) was with God and, in fact, was God, or his equivalent. This title is used in several places in the New Testament. It implies an equal status with God. Whereas we read in Deuteronomy: **Hear, O Israel: The Lord our God, the Lord is one.** (Deut. 6: 4) ... now we are confronted with a plural. Someone was with God in the beginning—someone equal to him! Huh? Well, which is it? One, or more than one? Let's go on... **Through him all things were made; without him nothing was made that has been made.** (John 1: 3). This "whomever" (mystery entity) was responsible for creation, along with the creator of whom we read in Genesis chapter 1. Remember? But it goes on.

In him was life, and that life was the light of men. The light shines in the darkness, but the darkness has not understood it. (John 1: 4,5). All this esoteric symbolism! Life, light, darkness, understanding. It is all so new, so different, so un-Yahweh! Back in the Old Testament, Yahweh just roared out demands, commands, and threats from on high—rained down fire from the sky and drowned millions. Now we are talking about understanding? What is this? Is this the dreaded killer sky God that we have all gotten to know along our tour? What's going on here? But it just keeps getting better.

There came a man who was sent from God; his name was John. He came as a witness to testify concerning that light, so that through him all men might believe. (John 1: 6,7). Keeping in mind that this was written decades after John's untimely demise, it is still revolutionary. All men might believe. *All* men? Wow. Take a breath. We are painfully aware of Yahweh and his exclusive Jewish club. So what's this talk about all men? All of a sudden the sender of floods, fire, plagues and the stopper of wombs is extending favors to all mankind? Are we talking about the same God here? **The true light that gives light to every man was coming into the world.** (John 1: 9). Whoa, I'm speechless (and skeptical).

And the Word became flesh and lived for a while among us. We have seen his glory, the glory of the one and only Son who came from the Father, full of grace and truth. (John 1: 14,15). This notion of God becoming flesh— taking on the form of a man for a while, in order to interact with mankind—is not unique to Christianity. The Greek gods regularly left Olympus and spent time among men on Earth. Other ancient religions have similar accounts. The Jews regularly borrowed from pagan religions as we have seen. God had never been pleased with that, and the response was swift and heavy-handed, for sure.

Although they all longed for a Moses-style deliverer to appear on the scene, to liberate them from Roman tyranny, the Jewish hierarchy knew full well that they were living in a precarious situation indeed. Despite their desire for a messiah to boldly dispense with the Roman occupation army, as had been done to Pharaoh's, the realistic leadership of the Jews knew better than to rock the boat.

Into this delicate balance Jesus was born. During the census of Caesar Augustus, Joseph and Mary went to Bethlehem to register. **He went there to register with Mary, who was pledged to be married to him and was expecting a child. While they were there, the time came for the baby to be born, and she gave birth to her first born, a son. She wrapped him in strips of cloth and placed him in a manger, because there was no room for them in the inn.** (Luke 2: 5-7). You know the story, so I'll skip the part about the shepherds, the angels, the wise men from the East, and all that, as it has been done to death already—wouldn't you say? Besides, we are inundated with this whole tale every Christmas, without fail.

Anyway, Mary was expecting, but they were not married. The child was born. It was a boy. Sounds pretty straightforward to me. After all, we all know where babies come from. (Fucking.) Joseph and Mary underwent ritual purification according to the Law of Moses (Leviticus 6-8). I have always wondered why she had to be purified if it were so that she was a virgin, as is claimed. If she knew that she had been impregnated artificially by the Holy Spirit and all, why would she submit to ritual cleansing? After all, she would not be impure in that case, would she?

I can hear their tiff already. Mary says: "Joseph, why should I go to the temple and sacrifice two (young) pigeons? After all, I am still a *virgin*, you know. You know we haven't done anything. You remember I told you how this all happened in the first place; I was just sitting alone by myself, minding my own business, when this angel came to me and said: **"Greetings, you who are highly favored! The Lord is with you. Do not be afraid, Mary, you have found favor with God. You will be with child and give birth to a son, and you are to give him the name Jesus. He will be great and will be called the Son of the Most High."** (Luke 1: 28,30,31). Honestly, Joseph dear, that's just how it happened. Just as I said. And no, dear, I was not ever with another man. It is only you I love. Surely you know that—don't you, Sweety Pie?"

Well, if Joseph was gullible enough to buy that line, I think he would have been an ideal candidate to invest in property down in that alkali wasteland where Sodom and Gomorrah once stood. But he was likely a bit swifter than that, and probably told her to button it up and get on with the cleansing. BTW, this ritual purification after childbirth comes from Leviticus (surprise)! Typical Biblical sexism here—a baby boy renders the mother ceremonially unclean for forty days, and a girl twice as long. Why doesn't that surprise me? Anyway, another ritual: **On the eighth day the boy is to be circumcised.** (Lev. 12: 3).Ouch.

Okay, on with the story... **On the eighth day, when it was time to circumcise him, he was named Yeshua bar Yosef** (AKA Jesus), **the name the angel had given him before he had been conceived.** (Luke 2: 21). After the forty-day period of purification had ended, Joseph and Mary took Jesus to Jerusalem to dedicate him to the Lord and to offer a sacrifice of two young doves—in keeping with the law. Actually, the law requires the sacrifice of a lamb, but here is the caveat: **"If she cannot afford a lamb, she is to bring two doves or two young pigeons, one for a burnt offering and the other for a sin offering. In this way the priest will make atonement for her and she will be clean."** (Lev. 12: 9). IMO, if Mary really had wanted everybody to buy the virgin birth story, she would have absolutely refused to make a sin offering. After all, she had not sinned at all. I would have refused. How about you? ...Just a thought.

I also like the next part. Yearly, Joseph and Mary went to Jerusalem to celebrate the Feast of the Passover. You remember the Passover, when the angel of death passed over the Jewish houses in Egypt, while murdering the firstborn of all the Egyptians? (Just checking. *There will be a test at the end of the tour* :-) During one of these visits (when Jesus was twelve) they accidentally left him behind in Jerusalem when they left to return to Nazareth. After three days of frantically searching, they found him in the temple with the teachers. Mary was furious. **"Son, why have you treated us like this? Your father and I have been anxiously searching for you."**

Jesus replied condescendingly: **"Why were you searching for me? Didn't you know I had to be in my Father's house?" But they did not understand what he was saying to them.** (Luke 2: 49,50). Duh, like, they just didn't get it. I can hear it all now: "Come on, Mom—think. Remember when the angel visited you?

Remember what it said? **He will be great and will be called the son of the Most High. The Lord God will give him the throne of his father David, and he will reign over the house of Jacob forever; his kingdom will never end.** (Luke 1: 31-33). Didn't that make any impression?

Think about it, Mom. I'm the son of God—remember? Obviously, I am going to be in my father's house, the temple! Why did it take you three days to figure that out and think to look for me here?" But it says that they didn't understand. Maybe Mary should check out some of that property in the alkali flats herself.

No matter how you cut it, neither Joseph nor Mary was any too bright. But Jesus was a genius. You know the story. Mark's Gospel recalls his baptism in the Jordan River. It was spectacular. **And so John came, baptizing in the desert region and preaching a baptism of repentance for the forgiveness of sins. The whole Judean countryside and all the people of Jerusalem went out to him. Confessing their sins, they were baptized by him in the Jordan River.** (Mark 1: 4,5). What? Where did this come from? Baptism? WTF? New rule!

Out of the clear blue sky we are introduced to a new concept—baptism. I have a copy of the much quoted *Cruden's Complete Concordance*. This handy little book is designed to help the reader locate words in the Bible, and let one know where they are found. I note with interest that the word "baptism" is found exclusively in the New Testament. What was going on out there in the Jordan River anyway? This crazy person, John the Baptist, was out in the desert region, preaching a baptism of repentance for the forgiveness of sins. Did he just make this up? We have no previous reference to baptism whatsoever. Now, all of a sudden, everybody wants to get wet.

Another thing I really like about this story is that John the Baptist is a real odd kind of guy. Get this... **John wore clothing made of camel's hair with a leather belt around his waist, and he ate locusts and wild honey. And this was his message: "After me will come one more powerful than I, the thongs of whose sandals I am not worthy to stoop down and untie. I baptize you with water, but he will baptize you with the Holy Spirit."** (Mark 1: 6-8). More new stuff.

Here's this weird guy doing this baptism thing that we have to assume he made up himself, as it has no Old Testament traditional precursor. People are coming from all over to repent and be baptized in the Jordan River. Jesus gets baptized by John, despite John's self-proclaimed unworthiness. Then, well, wow! Total wow! **As Jesus was coming up out of the water, he saw heaven being torn open and the Spirit descending on him like a dove. And a voice came from heaven: "You are my Son, whom I love; with you I am well pleased."** (Mark 1: 10,11). Ta-da ... In one move, Jesus eclipses John and takes over the show from there. We are definitely in uncharted territory now. But you remember how the story proceeds, right?

At once the Spirit sent him out into the desert, and he was in the desert forty days, being tempted by Satan. He was with the wild animals, and the angels attended him. (Mark 1: 12,13). So Satan reenters the picture. It is unclear which of the many forms Satan was taking at this point: a snake, as from the curse in the garden; a snobby gadabout, as in Job; or some hideous creature, as depicted by medieval artists in Dark Age Europe. Not that it matters much, I suppose. In any case, he's still that wily character whose job it is to try to get Jesus to reject God and the plan for his life, throw all caution to the wind, worship Satan, and get all the kingdoms of the Earth in return. But Jesus isn't buying.

"Get thee hence, Satan!" (Matthew 4: 10). (Note: I just had to quote that from the King James Version. Sometimes I really miss 1611.) Strong words, no matter what. So Satan flies the coop and we won't hear from him again for a spell. BTW, if you want a review, go back to Job for a refresher :-)

By now, John the Baptist has been put in prison. It probably seemed a logical place to put a weirdo like that. Today we would probably put him in a psychiatric hospital under proper medical care and chemical treatment. But— camel hair, leather, and beeswax aside—he did set the stage for the entree of the son of God, so he could truthfully proclaim: "Mission Accomplished." Yea! From that time on, Jesus began to preach, **"Repent for the kingdom of heaven is near."** (Mt. 17: 17). His ministry had begun!

If your right hand causes you to sin, cut it off and throw it away. (Mt. 5:30)

Parables (New Rules)

If your right eye causes you to sin, gouge it out and throw it away.

In addition to beginning his ministry on Earth with a few flashy miracles, early on, Jesus started to teach a whole new set of concepts quite unlike anything we have encountered on our tour through the Old Testament so far. This will really seem like unfamiliar territory. We have encountered Psalms and Proverbs, but the Parables are different. Jesus was kind of like Aesop and his famous "fables." These are the closest thing in western culture that we can point to paralleling the Jesus-teachings. Of course, the Chinese, for example, have zillions of really great illustrative little stories that seek to instruct and inform proper conduct. How should we treat others? How do we want to be treated? Simple enough. But some of the stuff that Jesus taught would likely freak out poor Aesop:-)

Some of his parables are allegorical in nature, using metaphor to communicate ideas to his simpleminded (mostly peasant) audience of the day. In other cases he speaks in a straightforward manner, addressing issues that need no symbolism whatsoever. I have always loved the parables, as I think they apply as aptly to the religious self-righteous of our present day as they did to the dimwits way back when. The fundamentalists, dripping with modern bigotry and prejudices—who piously claim to accept and believe every word of Scripture as is—ought to spend a bit more time reading the parables. Nonetheless, like the self-righteous bastards of Jesus' day, likely, they would simply fail to see *themselves* in these passages.

Let's begin to read in Matthew, where we encounter the "Beatitudes." As simple and obvious as they are, they proved a tremendous stumbling block for certain religious folk of the first century. And they still do today. Imagine that. Let's start with this famous one: **Blessed are the poor in spirit for theirs is the kingdom of heaven. Blessed are the meek, for they shall inherit the earth.** (Matthew 5: 3-5). For years it has been pointed out that these verses were ideally suited for the administrative hierarchy of the Catholic Church to subjugate and control the uneducated and simpleminded masses. By promising rewards later for pain and suffering incurred now, those who were suffering could, for the first time, look forward to a reward in a *future* life. This is a big shift from the "we're all going to die and rot" theme of Ecclesiastes, wouldn't you say? Wow, an afterlife ... with *rewards*! Cool and a half:-)

Rejoice and be glad, because great is your reward in heaven (Mt. 5: 12) as opposed to Solomon's famous: **For the living know that they will die, but the dead know nothing; they have no further reward, and even the memory of them is forgotten.** (Ecclesiastes 9: 5). Remember that? Kind of a drag, huh? I definitely prefer the uplifting message of Jesus, don't you? Of course, the contradiction is glaring; but the Bible contains no contradictions, remember? Three cheers for inerrancy :-)

What are we seeing here? As far as I am concerned, it is nothing short of a revolution. Jesus begins to completely restructure the entire way the world was to be perceived. This is only the first of many bombshells that he dropped on the whole Jewish worldview. Up to now we have seen the here-and-now mindset of the Jewish people. From the ten commandants through all the laws, rules and regulations, decrees and instructions, nothing was ever mentioned about an "afterlife." The message of the Old Testament could be summed up as: "Life's a bitch and then you die." But now this man Jesus introduces that and more! *Rewards*! Yea! But how un-Jewish. For sure.

Obviously, this was mighty revolutionary for the Jews. But most ancient peoples had developed this idea eons before. The Egyptians, for one, had elevated the quest for the afterlife to an art form. The pyramids are a testament to their belief in life after death. For them, life was just a dress rehearsal.

Jesus makes a big point of saying that he is not on Earth to abolish the law of the Old Testament. Consider this: **Do not think that I have come to abolish the Law or the Prophets; I have not come to abolish them but to fulfill them. I tell you the truth, until heaven and earth disappear, not the smallest letter, nor the least stroke of a pen, will by any means disappear from the Law until everything is accomplished.** (Mt. 5: 17,18).

No sooner does he tell us that nothing at all in the law can be changed, then he immediately begins changing it! LOL. Jesus usually prefaces a change in things by saying: "You have heard it said ..." When you hear that, be prepared.

For example: **"You have heard it said, Do not murder, and anyone who murders will be subject to judgment. But I tell you that anyone who is angry with his brother will be subject to judgment."** (Mt. 5: 21, 22).

And how about this: **"You have heard it said, Do not commit adultery. But I tell you that anyone who looks at a woman lustfully has already committed adultery with her in his heart."** (Mt. 5: 28). Or, try this one out for size: **"Again, you have heard it said, Do not break your oath, but keep your oaths you have made to the Lord. But I tell you, do not swear at all: either by heaven, for it is God's throne, or by earth, for it is his footstool; or by Jerusalem, for it is the city of the Great King."** (Mt. 5: 33-35). And the hits just keep on comin':-)

On and on, Jesus systematically reverses rule after rule, law after law, and idea after idea. In place of well-defined consequences for various types of behavior—and misbehavior—he substitutes very esoteric and confusing alternatives. Like: **If your right eye causes you to sin, gouge it out and throw it away. It is better for you to lose one part of your body than for your whole body to be thrown into hell. And if your right hand causes you to sin, cut it off and throw it away. It is better for you to lose one part of your body than for your whole body to go into hell.** (Mt. 5: 29, 30). Hell? What the hell is that? Oh, another new concept! Yea!

Back to one of our tour's main themes for a minute. The fundamentalist Evangelicals among us insist that the Bible is literal. God did creation in six literal days, the animals literally went into the ark, and the Sun literally stood still. So then, is all this talk of gouging out eyes and cutting off hands literal or not? Quoting our dear Bible commentary author and fine Christian, Jerry Falwell: *"The statement of cutting off one's hand or plucking out one's eyes definitely is not to be taken literally. What Jesus implied is..."* (LBC pp. 1889). Aha! Jesus *implied*! Hmmm.

For those willing to take as literal fact talking donkeys, manna falling out of the sky, and the Sun going backwards, why not accept as literal Jesus' command to gouge out the offending eye or to cut off the offending hand? At least that would be consistent. But I think I know why. The Bible bangers themselves have all lusted with their eyes and done quirky things with their right hands from time to time, whether they admit it or not (snark snark).

So, let's pause a moment on our journey to talk a bit more about this problem. And a helluva problem it is. Hell, that is. What is it and where is it? First of all, we have already experienced the Old Testament version of hell, called *Sheol* (the place of the departed). You may recall Saul and the witch, Endora, calling Samuel up from the dead. Presumably he was in Sheol. Samuel, as we recall from our earlier reading, was a righteous prophet and all; so it was unlikely that he was burning and roasting in a Christian hell. He was simply "away" resting in Sheol. But Jesus introduces this new twist. Better lose a body part than go into *hell*. The New Testament begins using a different word for hell: *Gehenna*. It is like a bonfire, a rubbish dump, a miserable and disgusting place where garbage is burned and destroyed. *Cruden's Concordance* calls it "the place of retribution for evil deeds" (p. 297). Oooo.

This really changes things! In total contradiction to centuries of Jewish thought and tradition, Jesus singlehandedly changes the world. With the introduction of the concept of reward or *retribution* for earthly behavior, he sets the stage for the triumphs and tragedies of our modern world. All the rest of his teachings about giving to the poor and caring for the sick and being good, are founded on an immovable cornerstone: *fear of hell*. Nothing before or since has had quite the power to persuade or, at least, to cause question. The notion of a literal burning hell or Gehenna certainly got their attention. And it still gets ours today!

By introducing this absolutely new idea to his audience of simpleminded uneducated provincial blockheads, Jesus sets the stage for the establishment of a totally new religion—one with him as the center. The focus changes to a simple A or B choice: reward or punishment. And here come the rules ... Accept 'em and fly or reject 'em and fry.

"Do not store up for yourselves treasures on earth, where moth and rust destroy, and where thieves break in and steal. But store up for yourselves treasures in heaven, where moth and rust do not destroy, and where thieves do not break in and steal. For where your treasure is, there your heart will be also." (Mt. 6: 19-21).

Jesus reforms the way his followers are supposed to look at life. He introduces bold and unconventional ideas, teachings, and doctrines so completely at odds with everything that had gone before, that they really bear no resemblance at all to the original. Now there is a difference. Personal comportment is now the factor that determines one's destiny. Whereas Solomon wrote "the dead know nothing," Jesus says the dead will either bask or burn, depending on the ways they act, think, and feel. With a few miracles to prove his point, he changed the world.

"Enter through the narrow gate. For wide is the gate and broad is the road that leads to destruction, and many enter through it. But small is the gate and narrow the road that leads to life, and only a few find it." (Mt. 7: 13).

In contrast to the old thinking that rewards and punishments are in the here and now, Jesus holds out the first twig to tempt mankind to consider the idea of *eternal* bliss. "Life" he calls it. Narrow is the road that leads to life. We have not yet been well-acquainted with the idea of eternal life, but it is coming. And we turn to John's Gospel for more on that. Quick—let's go see what it is all about :-)

There is a lot of talk these days about being "born again." The third chapter of John's gospel is where it all comes from. Jesus gets a visit from a Jewish clergyman (called a Pharisee) in the dead of night. Nicodemus sneaks out to talk to Jesus on the sly, personally, because he has caught wind of all the things that Jesus has been teaching, and—above all—the miracles that he has been performing. He opens himself up to Jesus with a sort of "What's it all about?" questioning attitude. Now, this guy was no unschooled dummy, so Jesus lays it on the line: **"I tell you the truth, unless a man is born again, he cannot see the kingdom of God."** (John 3: 3). Whereupon Nicodemus says, "Huh?" So Jesus continues: **"You must be born again."** (John 3: 7). **But Nicodemus persists: "How can this be?"** (John 3: 9). Like, come on, what are you saying *exactly*? Finally Jesus comes to the point and answers the question and establishes himself right then and there as the link between God and mankind. He is the bridge. He is both God and man himself. **No one has ever gone into heaven except the one who came from heaven—the Son of Man.** Then those famous words... **For God so loved the world that he gave his one and only Son, that whoever believes in him shall not perish but have eternal life.** (John 3: 16). In one sentence and in one fell swoop, Jesus explains it all. *Whoever believes!* Wow.

Whoever believes? The *Old Testament* is now on its ear. In a few words and phrases Jesus opens the door to eternal life—not just to the Jews, but to whoever believes! Anyone. The world just became a different place. **For God did not send his Son into the world to condemn the world, but to save the world through him. Whoever believes in him is not condemned, but whoever does not believe stands condemned already because he has not believed in the name of God's one and only son. This is the verdict: Light has come into the world, but men loved darkness instead of light, and will not come into the light for fear that his deeds will be exposed. But whoever lives by the truth comes into the light, so that it may be seen plainly that what he has done has been done through God.** (John 3: 17-21).

At this point we run into one of the great paradoxes of the New Testament. In John's gospel we are informed that belief is the prerequisite for life eternal. But this everlasting life is not to be lived here on this Earth. It is to be lived in a place called heaven. But we have to die to go there. Well, since we all have to die anyway, why not go to the place that's the best? But not everybody gets to go. And here comes the issue—the dividing line—the ultimate question. Who is going to get eternal life in heaven and who is not? And of those who are not going, what of them? Answers please. Jesus, please tell us.

Jesus is not handing out free tickets to heaven—the Kingdom of God. And from now on along our sojourn, we will be considering this issue thoroughly. But let's start with one of my favorites. Modern churchgoers should pay close attention. **"Not everyone who says to me, Lord, Lord, will enter the kingdom of heaven, but only he who does the will of my father who is in heaven. Many will say to me on that day, Lord Lord, did not we prophesy in your name, and in your name drive out demons and perform many miracles? Then I will tell them plainly, I never knew you. Away from me, you evildoers!"** (Mt. 7: 21-23).

So who is in ... and who is out? Let's zip on ahead and find out, alright?

Ministry and Miracles

I am the way, the truth, and thelife.

Trying to sort out the chronology of events that define the life and ministry of Jesus, from the four accounts we know as the Gospels, is enough to give us a headache. The authorship of all four accounts is in question. No one knows for sure who actually wrote any of them, as they are quite contradictory. Mark and Luke could certainly not have been eyewitnesses to any of these purported events, and whether or not Matthew or John actually wrote the books ascribed to them is totally up in the air. Apparently, most of these accounts were written several decades or more after the fact, and hundreds of years passed before any continuity could be established by Italian monks and scribes (unless you count the Counsel of Nicea). So, legally speaking, these events are just hearsay. But, as with any other tour you might take, the guide is required to inform the tourists that this is mostly fiction.

So, for that reason, I will not try to pick at the obvious questions and inconsistencies between the accounts. Instead, let's look at the events just as they are presented and try not to chase back and forth comparing details, which I assure you are a jumble. Modern evangelical Christians get all pissed and bent out of shape when you point this out. They play their big ace card called Josephus. This fellow was a Jewish "historian" living in Rome around 75 CE (AD for you fossils). He wrote this massive tome about the history of the Jews. It is like 1,000 pages long and boring. Somewhere, buried in about page 726 or so, there is a passing reference to a certain Yeshua Bar Yosf, a guy who was crucified around 30 CE. Somehow that proves something to them. Like trying to prove the scientific existence of Noah's ark by climbing around mountains in Turkey, Fundies claim that this conclusively verifies the existence of the "historical Jesus." Of course, it does no such thing, as Josephus lived over two centuries after the "fact." So, obviously, he was not on the scene and, in fact, never left Rome in his life. So what the hell did he know? He listened to hand-me-down stories and legends, and simply wrote them down. And likely read old Roman records of thousands of crucifixions during that time. Anyway, let's just look at the stories with the same dose of reality as we did when we read of Moses throwing the magic chunk of wood into the poison well back in the wilderness. Okay :-)

Sometime after Jesus was baptized and did his temptation-in-the-wilderness gig, he chose his disciples. The following day he showed up at Cana for a wedding with the disciples in tow. His mom, Mary, was there too. We all know what happened next. The wedding party was rolling along when the host ran out of wine. OMG, what to do? Mary was in a frenzy. Dizzy woman that she was, she was in a tailspin and implored Jesus to do something. Just like back when he was twelve in the temple, he talked down to her: **"Dear woman, why do you involve me?" Jesus said, "My time has not yet come."** (John 2: 4). Obviously, Jesus didn't even want to deal with her problem. But he did.

Nearby stood six stone water jars, the kind used by the Jews for ceremonial washing, each holding from twenty to thirty gallons. Jesus said to the servants, "Fill the jars with water," so they filled them to the brim. Then he told them, "Now draw some out and take it to the master of the banquet." (Jn. 2:6-8).

They did so, and the master of the banquet tasted the water that had been turned into wine. He did not realize where it had come from, though the servants who had drawn the water knew. Then he called the bridegroom aside and said, "Everyone brings out the choice wine first and then the cheaper wine after the guests have had too much to drink; but you have saved the best till now." (Jn. 2: 9,10).

We simply must evaluate this more carefully. John's gospel says: **This is the first of his miraculous signs, Jesus performed in Cana of Galilee. He thus revealed his glory, and his disciples put their faith in him.** (Jn. 2: 11,12). I have heard hundreds of sermons about this miracle, and in each and every case, the preacher was careful to point out that this was not "literal" wine. That's rich, huh? Literalists saying that something in the Bible was not literal. LOL. After all, Jesus would never make real wine, and would certainly never actually drink any himself! OMG, no. Drinking alcohol in Evangelical circles is a sin worse than murder. The very notion of Jesus, the perfect son of Christians, stomaching genocide and slaughter with no problem, and drinking wine—let alone making it—is unthinkable. The killing of everyone in Jericho or the annihilation of the Amalekites does not raise an eyebrow. They can handle the brutal slaughter and bloodletting, murder and mayhem, and killing of everything with breath in its nostrils. But drinking wine? That is intolerable. And Falwell really weighs in here as well:

"The symbolism is clear. The power of Christ filled the emptiness of the water pots and that same power is able to fill the emptiness of Judaistic religion" (LBC, p. 2080). Who's kidding whom? What a crock!

So the first miracle out of the bag is *symbolic*. When Moses threw the staff down and it turned into a snake—that was literal. When the Nile turned to blood, that was literal too. When fire rained down onto Sodom that was literal. But, when the water was turned into wine that was instead symbolic! Total bullshit.

Shortly thereafter he did another symbolic act lost on our fundamentalist friends. He drove the hucksters and con artists out of the temple. The center of religious life in Jerusalem was the temple, which had become a perverted scene of religious fundraising and snake handling. Sort of like Christian television broadcasting today, the temple was full of all manner of pseudo-religious marketers. Jesus flew into a rage and threw them out. This did not go down well with the religious hierarchy of the day, aka the "Sanhedrin." In addition to his renunciation of the clergy, the Pharisees and Sadducees, he pointed out the hypocrisy of the common folk as well. Then, to add insult to injury, he began opening a dialogue with non-Jews! Heaven forbid.

The Samaritans were Gentiles living in the region of Samaria. The Jews looked down on them as sort of *Untermenschen*—subhumans. Kind of like how southern white Baptists look down on persons of color, the Samaritans were untouchables (to the Jews). Jesus tells a parable about a "good" Samaritan. We even use this as a reference to this day. As the story goes, thieves, robbers, and thugs had robbed, rolled, and beat up a person along the road, leaving him in a heap. The righteous and pious citizens just walked by or stepped over him. Referring to the Jews, but applying to modern Christians as well, everybody just ignored a fellow human being in pain and misery. Then a hated loathsome Samaritan with no religious background or Biblical training stopped and ministered to the needs of the unfortunate wayfarer. The point of the story is obvious. But why can't the self-righteous among us today see themselves in this story? Beats me.

Pay attention now, because the serious miracles are about to begin. Turning the water into wine or walking on water was cool and all that, but, quite frankly, the tricks Moses did with snakes, frogs, gnats, and flies were really more awesome than the water-to-wine trick. In John we read of an event that points out the calcified hypocrisy of the religion of the time and sets the stage for the problems ahead. Jesus was in Jerusalem. There was a pool there near the Sheep Gate, called Bethesda. The lame, blind and infirm used to lie around the pool waiting for an angel to "trouble" the waters, whereupon they were to plunge in and be healed. I have always wondered what ever happened to that magic pool. I guess it went the way of the flaming sword flashing back and forth in the Garden of Eden or the flaming fire pot of Abraham. We just don't seem to have any of these kinds of neat things around anymore :-(

Anyway, Jesus talks to an old fellow who has been infirm for thirty-eight years. (Wonder if Josephus noted that specific detail.) When Jesus saw him lying there and learned that he had been in this condition for a long time, he asked him, **"Do you want to get well?"** Like duh. I can't help it—but what a dumb question! What is the guy going to say? "Oh, not really. I'm really not here for healing, but just for the entertainment." Sorry. Well, of course the guy replies in the affirmative, but there is a problem...

"Sir, I have no one to help me into the pool when the water is stirred. While I am trying to get in, someone else goes down ahead of me." (Jn. 5: 5-7). What kind of a weird arrangement is this? Where in the hell did this pool come from? Who set it up? And, above all, why didn't the Romans know of it or put it into one of their innumerable reports? And where in the world do we get this "first cripple into the pool gets healed" notion? If you think about it a while—and try to imagine all these assorted handicapped, blind, and sick individuals waiting for the angel to "trouble" the waters—it does make you wonder, huh? Anyway, Jesus learns that no matter how fast the old geezer was, somebody always "went down" faster. What a bummer. But Jesus felt sorry for him. Then Jesus said to him, **"Get up! Pick up your mat and walk." At once the man was cured; he picked up his mat and walked. Later Jesus found him at the temple and said to him, "See you are well again. Stop sinning or something worse may happen to you."** (Jn. 5: 8,9,14). BTW, that healing was done on the Sabbath, which was a major offense—punishable by death, sort of like being gay or working on Sunday.

In the chapters that follow, Jesus heals all manner of diseases and teaches all sorts of revolutionary new doctrines. He is gaining a tremendous following. "He's dangerous!" chant the darkly robed figures representing the Pharisees in the rock opera, *Jesus Christ Superstar*. The religious leadership saw potential disaster in what was coming if they let Jesus get away with all these showy miracles and stuff. They went straight to the Romans and tattled on Jesus. They wanted the Romans to arrest him immediately. Like the Romans cared. What was his crime? He healed on the Sabbath, and did all sorts of other stuff that totally pissed the Jews off. The Romans were the occupying power, but cared nothing about these petty religious squabbles. So Jesus just kept on goading the Jews by proclaiming himself as equal to God (by word and deed). Oh, they just hated that. Jesus said, **"When you lift up the Son of Man, then you will know who I am and that I do nothing on my own but speak just what the father has taught me. The one who sent me is with me; he has not left me alone, for I always do what pleases him."** (Jn. 8: 28, 29). Can't you just see it? The priests and all those high holy men in their long dresses are so mad they are about to blow up. They roar at him: **"The only Father we have is God himself."** (Jn. 8:41).

You have to admit, Jesus is cool. He just lays them out: **"If God were your father you would love me, for I came from God and now am here. I have not come on my own; but he sent me."** (Jn. 8: 42). Then he really rubs their faces in it: **"You belong to your father, the devil, and you want to carry out your father's desire."** Holy crap! Do you have any idea how incendiary that remark is? Trust me—it is dynamite. Boom.

Following on the heels of this outrage, he takes the heaven and hell idea out of the parable stage, and states as fact: **"I tell you the truth, if a man keeps my word, he will never see death."** (Jn. 8: 51). The Pharisees are spitting mad at this point, and hiss at him like snakes: **"Are you greater than our father Abraham? He died, and so did the prophets. Who do you think you are?"** (Jn. 8: 53). To which Jesus replies causally but confidently: **"I tell you the truth, before Abraham was born, I am!"** (Jn. 8: 58). Melt down! I just love that line: "Who do you think you are?" Who indeed? Wow.

As we read all four accounts we conclude the same thing. Jesus spoke in metaphor about his identity, origin, work on Earth, and his destiny. He alluded to his end and what his passing would accomplish. But most people ended up just scratching their heads. As time went on, Jesus spoke more directly. Finally, there was no doubt. **"I and the Father are one."** (Jn. 10: 30). This person is actually claiming to be God himself. At this point the Sanhedrin shit a collective brick. *Thud.* This guy is dead already—doomed.

If we can accept any of this as factual at all, one thing is becoming apparent: Jesus is on a roll. He has been teaching, preaching, healing, and exhorting for quite a while now. He has taken his show on the road, and his fame is now spreading all over Israel. He is no longer making any pretense. He is God and his triumphant entry into Jerusalem proves his popularity. **"Hosanna!"** shout the masses. **"Blessed is he who comes in the name of the Lord! Blessed is the King of Israel!"** This spectacle was not lost on the Jewish religious leadership. Not one bit.

So the Pharisees said to one another, "See this is getting us nowhere. Look how the whole world has gone after him!" (Jn. 12: 19). They were afraid. They knew good and well what was happening. What were at first the offbeat teachings of a backwoods carpenter from Galilee began taking the shape of a national movement. The masses saw Jesus as a liberator. They saw him as the deliverer who would singlehandedly throw off the yoke of Roman oppression. The Sanhedrin, the top dogs of the Jewish establishment, knew better. This Jesus was upsetting the delicate balance of power in the province and beyond. The implications were dire. **"What are we accomplishing?" they asked. "Here is this man performing many miraculous signs. If we let him go on like this, everyone will believe in him, and then the Romans will come and take away both our place and our nation."** (Jn. 12: 47, 48).

The historic decision to eliminate Jesus was a conspiracy between the Jewish leadership and the Roman occupation authorities, using one of his inner circle —namely, a certain Judas Iscariot—as go-between and ultimate fall guy. The story of the betrayal, the trial, and crucifixion of Jesus has been told to death for centuries. Meanwhile, Jesus was laying the groundwork for his own demise, and simultaneously establishing the foundation of an entirely new religion. He had already introduced the idea of a judgment day—a literal burning hell—and a place called heaven where he was getting ready to go. He points out that although he is going to be heading on his upward way soon, he is actually planning to come back! Yea!

What a hell of a way to spend Easter!

"Do not let your hearts be troubled. Trust in God; trust also in me. In my Father's house are many rooms; if it were not so, I would have told you. I am going there to prepare a place for you. And if I go and prepare a place for you, I will come back and take you to be with me that you also may be where I am. You know the way to the place I am going." (Jn. 14: 1-4). But Thomas, one of the disciples, insists that they do not in fact know exactly where he is going and, much less, how to get there. Whereupon Jesus puts in place the cornerstone of the new religion. **"I am the way, the truth and the Life. No one comes to the Father except through me."** (Jn. 14: 6). The new religion is born.

Did Jesus intend to found a whole new religion? Well, if in fact he was God, and God is omniscient, of course he would already know the outcome of his actions as a man. Up to now we have seen God as the creator of the Universe, the exclusive deity of the Jews. He roars and rumbles, bluffs and blusters, rains down water and drowns everything, rains down fire and destroys whole cities; he commands the destruction of whole civilizations and races of people. Then he rests. He appears in burning bushes, wrestles with mortals, and speaks through asses. He makes wagers with the devil, betrays old friends and then restores their fortunes. He raises up prophets, judges and kings, and puts down others. He sends people on errands, curses some and blesses others. The whole nature and character of this god is arbitrary and irrational. He is totally inconsistent and impossible to predict. Like other ancient civilizations whose gods sent plagues and floods and volcano's fire, the poor little Jews were constantly offending their god and trying again and again to appease him so he would not send an invading army or a flood or a plague on them.

Now Jesus speaks of Yahweh as a "father." In my father's house are many rooms (The KJV calls them mansions. Way better, I reckon). How sweet. Jehovah is not really a monster after all. He's not a crook; he's a daddy. This is the new, kinder, gentler Yahweh. Jesus is God. Like father, like son. Well, all this is just fine and dandy. Jesus is a groovy person who is really beautiful, kind, and sincere. He is a man and he is a god and he is just perfect. To quote the rock opera again: *"You've got to say one thing, Jesus is cool."* However, the problem he presents to the status-quo is short-lived. They arrange for his arrest, trial, and execution. He is out of the picture. But before departing the scene, he planted one more small seed that soon enough reared its tiny head for the first time. Here goes...

"Go into all the world and preach the good news to all creation. Whoever believes and is baptized will be saved, but whoever does not believe will be condemned. And these signs will accompany those who believe; In my name they will drive out demons; they will speak in new tongues; they will pick up snakes with their hands; and when they drink deadly poison, it will not hurt them at all; they will place their hands on sick people, and they will get well." (Mark 16:15-18).

Well, so much for the exclusivity of the Jewish club. Jesus simply gives the god of the Jews to everybody! Gee, thanks. And, in the same breath, he establishes the new religion as a missionary endeavor. Go, preach, teach, baptize! The foundation for a new world order had thus been formed. *Mission accomplished.* **"It is finished"** ... and the post-crucifixion, resurrected Christ is beginning his ascent into the clouds, like the Wizard of Oz in his hot air balloon. He waves to the cheering crowd and promises to come back soon :-)

You know, all of this is so lala, but I doubt that it would have had much staying power as is. In fact, after that last hallelujah had died away and everybody left and went home to cook dinner, likely the whole show would have ended in a fizzle. But that would be a rather boring ending, huh? Well, the story is far from over and we are about to meet a most amazing man—a Jew of the highest order—a Pharisee named Saul. His story, the next stop on our tour, makes the whole life, message, and challenge of Jesus work. He's the one who really gets everything spinning. Hold on tight. It's going to be a bumpy ride.

Jesus ascends back up to heaven, leaving the Apostles to figure out a way to make his message work.

Acts

You shall receive power when the Holy Spirit comes upon you.

The Book of Acts is officially called the *Acts of the Apostles*. It is a narrative about the goings-on right after the death and resurrection of Jesus, and the early development of the new religion. It was presumably written by Luke—or so they say—and contains all sorts of fun and interesting material. It starts off explaining what happened to Jesus right after the crucifixion. **After his suffering, he showed himself to these men and gave many convincing proofs that he was alive. He appeared to them over a period of forty days and spoke about the kingdom of God.** (Acts 1: 3).

During that time he told them to wait in Jerusalem until they received the promise of the Father, namely the Holy Spirit. To make matters more complicated, the third person of the trinity is introduced obliquely in Acts chapter 1: **But you will receive power when the Holy Spirit comes on you and you will be my witnesses ... to the ends of the earth.** (Acts 1: 8). Now, what is this all about? Well, this is an area of great debate among Bible believers. What is involved here is the direction that the new religion is going to take.

Jesus has been crucified but not taken back up to heaven yet. He is still hanging around the Earth, interacting with various disciples and other people. He charges the disciples not to leave Jerusalem until they have been empowered by the Holy Spirit, the newly introduced third party of the Godhead, aka "the Trinity." Empowered to do what? To carry the message of the Gospel throughout the world. As we have seen in abundance, the Jews were exclusive. They had their own God and their own laws and their own system. They slaughtered non-Jews left and right without a thought, and were in turn slaughtered, enslaved, and bound into captivity themselves. This had been going on since they first left Egypt under Moses, back in Exodus.

Now things are quite different. The macho, chest-thumping Yahweh of the Old Testament is being eclipsed by the gentle, passive, longsuffering Jesus whom we first encountered in the Gospels. As the story goes, Jesus opened the door to a whole new way of thinking. He introduced the notion of *eschatology*, events that will take place in the future. He spoke a great deal about the coming of the kingdom of God, future strife and struggles on Earth, and future judgment, or final reward and condemnation for the inhabitants of Earth. This had had no place in Jewish history or thinking. Even though, since the time of Isaiah, a messiah deliverer had been promised, for the most part Jesus failed to convince the mainstream that he was in fact *that* messiah. He did his preaching, teaching, and healing, but in the end he was arrested, tried, and executed as a criminal, a lunatic, and general troublemaker. His disciples fell apart after his death but later regrouped and bumbled around Jerusalem until the day of Pentecost. Then things changed.

Finally Jesus departed the earth. After he had said this, and a cloud hid him from their sight. (Acts 1: 9). He went back up above the blue dome in the sky. **They were looking intently up into the sky as he was going, when suddenly two men dressed in white stood beside them. "Men of Galilee," they said, "Why do you stand here looking into the sky? This same Jesus, who has been taken from you into heaven, will come back in the same way you have seen him go into heaven."** (Acts 1: 10). The notion of Jesus' return is a theme we will encounter on our tour throughout the remainder of the Bible, and it permeates most current religious and political discussion in the US and around the world to this day. "Jesus is coming! ... Look busy!"

On the day of Pentecost the remnant of the original Gospel disciple band got together and had quite a hoedown. Jerusalem was teeming with visitors from all over the Empire. It was like a convention. The wine was flowing. The Bible recalls: **Suddenly a sound like the blowing of a violent wind came from heaven and filled the whole house where they were sitting. They saw what seemed to be tongues of fire that separated and came to rest on each of them. All of them were filled with the Holy Spirit and began to speak in other tongues as the Spirit enabled them.** (Acts 2: 2-4). All this commotion freaked out the visitors and some asked "What's all this about?" (Whereas others noted that they all had been drinking quite a bit already that early in the day.) In any case, Peter, one of the original twelve, stood up and claimed that this phenomenon was not just a drunken orgy, but was in fact the fulfillment of a prophesy of the minor prophet, Joel.

He quotes: **In the last days, God says, I will pour out my spirit on all people. Your sons and daughters will prophesy, your young men will see visions, old men will dream dreams. I will show wonders in the heaven above and**

Peter and the Goofy Gospel Gang took to speaking in tongues, and freaked out the whole town.
Likely drunk, they established the first communist financial system ever!
And we all know how successful that was! :)

signs on the earth below, blood, fire and billows of smoke. The sun will be turned to darkness and the moon turned to blood. (Acts 2: 17, 19-20).

Well, since the Moon *didn't* turn to blood right then and there, it is unlikely that this was the actual fulfillment of Joel's prophecy after all. But that didn't stop Peter any. Simpleminded fisherman and uneducated hick that he was, he really thought that he was participating in the ushering in of the end times. 2,000 plus years later ... we're still waiting :-)

No matter what actually happened there that day, several of the participants in the merriment felt "empowered" and got wound up and spun out from there. In a fit of emotional euphoria, a couple of the partiers began preaching wildly in what would become known as the "Pentecostal style"—loud, fast, high, and totally whacked-out :-) But they had fun. They weren't the brightest bunch. In fact, they were for the most part, a collection of hillbillies and dunderheads (except maybe Matthew, who worked for the IRS). But Jesus had chosen *them*. And, I admit, that is part of the charm of the whole thing. I guess if God can speak through a talking donkey, using this motley crew isn't so out of reason. Peter was a perfect example. He was a thug and a bully. He was sort of a religious Rocky Balboa, well-meaning but ham-handed. The religious intelligentsia did not take him seriously, especially after his performance in the "upper room" and after the celebration of Pentecost was over. In fact, the disciples were all hopped up with nowhere to go. Running hither and yon around town, they ran afoul of the law and were in and out of jail during those early post-Jesus times. There just wasn't much focus or direction. But that was about to change.

A new society was being formed out of all this chaos. The early "church" as they called it, was truly communist in nature. **All the believers were one in heart and mind. No one claimed that any of his possessions was his own, but they shared everything they had. There were no needy persons among them. For from time to time those who owned lands or houses sold them, brought the money from the sales and put it at the apostles' feet, and it was distributed to anyone as he had need.** (Acts 4: 32-25). Karl Marx would have been proud! :-)

The Bible deals with property and ownership issues immediately after the giving of the Ten Commandments. Clear back in Exodus chapter 22, we have seen that the ownership of property (and people) are addressed as of paramount importance. Suddenly we are now dealing with *communal* ownership concerns. Karl Marx probably would not have been able to make a case against the church had the early Christians continued to develop a communist system as they started to. However, quickly, it became a matter of control—and Peter took control. He instituted a practice of having believers sell their land and bring the proceeds forward and put them at his feet. (Acts 4: 37). Right here in the Book of Acts, the church lays the groundwork for the accumulation of its incredible wealth. Check this out...

Now a man named Ananias together with his wife Sapphira, also sold a piece of property. With his wife's full knowledge he kept back part of the money for himself, but brought the rest and put it at the apostles' feet. (Acts 5: 1,2). Trouble ensued. He kept some of the cash for himself and his wife. Big mistake. Do you know what happened next? Well, he dropped dead right on the spot! Wow. And then, when Sapphira came in, she was struck dead as well. **Great fear seized the whole church and all who heard about these events.** (Acts: 5: 11) Well, I guess so! Holy shit! ... But what makes me think that this little anecdote was inserted much later, when the church was expanding its wealth and position, or needed to raise money for various papal wars? Just a thought. Anyway, fear is a most effective means of mind control, huh?

For the most part, Acts is a history of the early church. By *church* I mean the fledgling Christian religion. There is much debate as to the actual meaning of the word "church." Perhaps its meaning can be clarified by the events that happen next, and with the introduction of a new character whose role ahead is as profound as that of Moses, Joshua, or David. His name is Saul (later changed to Paul), and he was a total bastard.

Saul was perhaps a member of the Sanhedrin. He was a Pharisee and a Jewish clergyman, with all the clerical and religious training to take over operation of the new movement—kind of the CEO. One problem: He had a heart of stone. He hated everything to do with Jesus and his spin-off religion, which was a heresy to pure Judaism. His persecution of the new church was legendary. We read of his seething hatred in Acts chapters 8 and 9. But all the while, God is planning his conversion experience.

One of the first converts to what we would now refer to as "Christianity" was a boy-next-door type of young man, named Steven. European Christian painters, for centuries, have depicted him as the blond beautiful Aryan Nordic Adonis type. He is portrayed as kind of a GQ model beauty. Saul, the evil power-hungry Jewish Simon Legree villain type character, oversaw the execution of this saintly martyr. Saul, the hideous, despicable Darth Vader type character, wanted nothing more than to totally destroy and eliminate this new heretical doctrine, which was invading pure Judaism like poison ivy.

He set about doing this with fervor. **Meanwhile, Saul was still breathing out murderous threats against the Lord's disciples. He went to the high priest and asked him for letters to the synagogues in Damascus, so that if he found any there who belonged to the Way, whether men or women, he might take them as prisoners to Jerusalem.** (Acts 9: 1,2).

So, as the account goes, Saul was riding to Damascus when a bright light from heaven knocked him off his ass. Unlike in the story of Balaam, the donkey did not speak. Instead, Saul heard a voice from heaven speaking to him: *"Saul, Saul, why do you persecute me?"* Needless to say he was freaked out and did it in his pants. **"Who are you, Lord?" Saul asked. "I am Jesus whom you are persecuting,"** He went on, **"Now get up and go into the city, and you will be told what you must do."** (Acts 9: 3-6). So he did. And in Damascus he falls in with the local church where he is baptized and begins his ministry. He is well-educated, well-known, and connected. He has all the ingredients necessary to make this new religion fly. The other apostles were simply lacking in credibility, and had Saul not converted, the whole thing would have likely dwindled and pooped out. But Saul, now renamed Paul, sets out with the fire and zeal of a new convert—*a true believer!*

The remainder of Acts recounts Paul's missionary journeys throughout the Roman world. He was full of piss and vinegar—energy and enthusiasm—and had the tenacity of a bull dog. In the following chapters he gets into one scrape after another, preaches the new doctrine tirelessly, and travels hundreds of miles all over what is now Greece and Turkey. He gets into endless debates, fights and fracases; gets beaten up and bashed, shipwrecked and thrown in jail;

and dragged before all manner of officialdom—but just keeps on ticking! He was a real fireball, to be sure!

But despite all of his incredible stamina and his superhuman dedication to his task, it is unlikely that Paul, by himself, would have made anything more than a tiny dent in the ancient world through his evangelistic efforts alone, despite his dogged determination. Paul did, however, make a lasting impact on mankind! How did he do it? In addition to his unflagging zeal as a missionary, and his stunning oratory as a preacher, he rocked the world most of all with his writing.

Somehow between traveling all over the Eastern half of the vast Roman Empire—preaching the new message of Christ to the Jews, Greeks, Macedonians, Galatians, Colossians, Thessalonians, and Romans (to name a few)—he established new churches in various locations as well. He mentored an apprentice named Timothy (who later wrote his own stuff), and taught and expounded like a madman. And in his spare time he managed to write lengthy thought-provoking letters—which we call *Epistles*—that have come down to us today.

These letters were sent to various individuals and churches of the day. In them, Paul gave the new religion form, substance, and—even more importantly—a systematic theology. This organizing of ideas and codifying of concepts served to legitimize the new religion in a way that nothing else probably ever could have.

As we leave Acts, we leave Paul in Rome, the center of the Western Universe at the time. The original Gospel band, for the most part, are never heard from again. But Paul has picked up on a new trend, and made a name for *himself* by promoting a revolutionary theology with himself as its chief operating officer and proponent. He takes the reins from here and tirelessly makes his mark on history. Of course, we are all paying a price for his worldview now, whether we like it or not. But from here on, it is all Paul's show. So take it away, Paul the Apostle!

Paul simultaneously frees us from the Old Testament law and then binds us to it more tightly.
He never did know for sure what he was writing about. We are still scratching our heads today.

Epistles

If anyone is in Christ, he is a new creation.

The next section of the Bible—commonly called "the Letters,"—are by far the most complex and detailed area of the entire body of Scripture, simultaneously laying the groundwork for the new Christian faith and sowing the seeds of endless conflicts to come. Giving a tour of the Epistles would be like giving a guided tour of the Smithsonian. Word by word, verse by verse, chapter by chapter, Paul systematically creates an entire new religion, and clearly, carefully organizes it. There is simply no way to adequately analyze the intricacies and subtleties of the books of letters on a first time quickie tour. They are too detailed. So let us approach them in broad topics. Although these missives are all written to different fledgling churches in diverse social and geographic positions, certain themes are common. These are the basis for the new religion that Paul created out of what Jesus started.

Let's start with the concept of eternal life that Jesus introduced back in the Gospels. It was all very new, basic, and easy. **For God so loved the world that he gave his only son, that whoever believes in him shall not perish but have eternal life.** (John 3: 16). Neat and sweet. Unfortunately it is too simple. Not only does it contradict everything we have ever known about dear Yahweh; but it is way too namby-pamby, broad, and easy, to suit Paul, a Pharisee and scholar of the highest degree. He just couldn't accept the simplicity of the message. He just had to fill in the blanks and write in the fine print. It is his nature; he needed to. A total compulsive, he needed to expand and expound. And boy did he ever!:-)

Keeping in mind all that we have read thus far, we can plainly see that God appears to have changed his mind again. He seems no longer to be the angry, jealous, furious God of the Old Testament who thundered down from Mt. Sinai and wrought murder and mayhem from the flood through all those bloody battles and plagues and sulfuric rains of fire.

Do you remember what God said back in Genesis just before he sent Noah into the ark with all those animals? **"I will wipe mankind whom I have created from the face of the earth—men and animals, and creatures that move along the ground, and birds of the air—for I grieved that I have made them."**

225

(Genesis 6: 7). There was no talk then of second chances, forgiveness, or promises of life eternal—just swift and final punishment. We have come a long way since then, huh? Now God is born again! Suddenly he is the "Father," the giver of gifts, the healer, the forgiver. Where did we get all this "For God so loved the world" stuff?

Jesus opened the door to the notion of everlasting life. Obviously Solomon's analysis was incorrect. If no matter what we do, no matter how we act, and no matter how we think, in the end we are all going to die and rot ... then what is the point of life anyway? All those live-for-the-moment philosophers were the smart ones, and the law-followers the fools. After chewing on this paradox for centuries, a new kinder gentler Yahweh is introduced. Unfortunately, the new covenant, as presented by Jesus, was too vague (or too difficult for the peasants and other dunderheads to understand). All this talk of the kingdom, hell fire (Gehenna), and eternal life was an attention getter, but what are the details? Paul gladly supplied them :-) Yea!

Paul also supplies new details about the concept of sin. In the Book of Romans we read in the fine print: **We have already made the charge that the Jews and Gentiles alike are all under sin. As it is written: There is no one righteous, not even one: There is no one who understands, no one who seeks God. All have turned away, they have together become worthless; there is no one who does good, not even one."** (Romans 3:9-12).

Jews and Gentiles alike? In this same chapter, one of the most oft-quoted in the entire New Testament, this famous verse appears: **There is no difference, for all have sinned and fall short of the glory of God.** (Rom. 3: 23).

Sin is no longer defined as an act like disobedience or working on Sunday; it's a *condition*! Men are "in sin" ... and the result of sin is death. **Therefore, just as sin entered the world through one man** (Adam), **and death through sin, and in this way death came to all men because all sinned.** (Rom. 5: 12). Then logic follows... **For the wages of sin is death.** (Rom. 6: 23).

Wow. Now all men are the same! All men are sinful by nature and that is due to what we call "original sin" ... that is, the sin of Adam and Eve in the garden

(Remember the serpent and the tree and the fruit?). They ate the forbidden fruit despite God's stern warning not to. So God condemned all mankind to death as a result. Seems fair. But Paul redefines death as not a simple physical death of men and animals and plants, but a *spiritual* death of the "soul." Hmmm. Interesting, huh? New idea.

Paul hereby introduces a new concept of death as well. Both life and death are being redefined. They had to be. The Old Testament notion was entirely too passé. Even a fool could figure out that if there was no reward or punishment for earthly behavior, then why not just live it up for a while and die? Solomon showed us back in *Ecclesiastes* just how pointless it was to even bother trying to live righteously according to the law. Since we're all going to die anyway, so what?

Now this is a whole new bag. We are all doomed—Jews and Gentiles alike. We are all going to be cast into the fire. No matter what we do, it is insufficient. We cannot save ourselves. What are we to do? **But the gift of God is eternal life through Jesus Christ our Lord.** (Rom. 6: 23). God is going to save us by his "grace" because he is such a good guy and because he loves us oh so much :-) But wait—there's a hitch. (Surprise!) More rules. We have to do things *his* way. Oh, this again. Yes, yes, shades of the old Yahweh.

And there is salvation in no one else, for there is no other name under heaven given to men by which we must be saved. (Acts 4:12). Oh, gee, a *new* exclusivity! There is only one way, one truth, and one door to God ... Jesus Christ! For those Jews who are still on the tour ... take that! Hah. But the good news is that the door is open to everybody. The bad news is that if they don't hear about the magic door, or don't understand it or accept it wholeheartedly, they are not able to use it. Sorry. They will have to be lost forever and die unsaved; and they will have to go to a literal burning hell in their ignorance. Kind of like back in the flood; all humanity is going to be doomed en masse again. But this time, the big wipe out will come without warning ... (in the twinkling of an eye).

Are you still with me? Cheer up—it gets more complicated. Paul's got some new ideas about the law too. Leave it to a Pharisee to get back to legalism sooner or later. Paul writes: **So, my brothers, you also died to the law through the body of Christ. But now, by dying to what once bound us, we** have been released from the law so that we serve in a new way of the spirit, and not in the old way of the written code. (Rom. 7: 4-7). So we are *released* from the law! Hey, that works for me :-) So we can throw out all that stuff about clean and unclean foods, sin and guilt offerings, and all those sexual rules from Leviticus and Deuteronomy, right? Well, no, not really. Bummer. Paul is a Jew and clergy at that. It would be impossible for him to trash the entire Old Testament and his entire tradition even though he acknowledges that it is really bankrupt. So he compromises and states that Jesus didn't come to abolish the law, but to *fulfill* it. What the heck does that mean?

Well, Paul natters on and on about the war between the law and the spirit, the spiritual and the carnal nature of man, and the new life in the Spirit as introduced by Jesus. It gets all so very complex and convoluted. In the end, Paul seems totally unable to make up his mind. Which is more important—the law or the spirit? His frustration is carried up to this day by our friends, the Evangelicals, who similarly believe that the law cannot be abolished without pulling down the whole house of cards. "Jesus came to set us free from the law," they chant, and meanwhile seek to impose their law on everyone they don't like (take gay people, for example). See the dilemma? Are we free from the law or not? No one knows.

Paul's frustration with this enigma winds itself down into trivial day-to-day matters. For an example of Paul's ambivalence and borderline schizophrenia, try this on for size: **Do not let anyone judge you by what you eat or drink ...** (Colossians 2: 16). But then: **Do not get drunk with wine, which leads to debauchery.** (Ephesians 5: 18). Sounds like back in Proverbs, huh? But throughout Colossians and Corinthians, Paul sides on the word of the law. Take for example: **Wives, submit to your husbands, as is fitting in the Lord.** And the biggie: **Slaves, obey your earthly masters in everything; and do it not only when their eye is on you.** (Col. 3: 18, 22) And the ever popular: **Women should remain silent in the churches. They are not allowed to speak, but must be in submission, as the Law says!** (I Cor: 14: 34). As the law says! And take that, you uppity women.

What? Old prejudices, old bigotries, and inequities are still in place? Didn't we fight a civil war about slavery? Both Catholics and Protestants of the Confederacy ran pell-mell to Paul in Colossians to adjudicate their ownership of "darkies." The

Emancipation Proclamation may have freed the Southern slaves, but it didn't change the immutable Bible. Slavery is still right there, in Paul's words. We just ignore that today, kind of like the command to kill all homosexuals. That is still there too. Of course, there are still some loving Christians that secretly long to exterminate the "fags."

Women present a problem of the first order. Paul is adamant: women are to sit down and shut up. Some modern churches ignore that clear declaration completely while others totally comply with it. But that is an issue that won't be solved anytime soon—will it? But even racial prejudices are not absent from the New Testament. Whereas the Old Testament is rife with all manner of racial profiling by God, most moderns are totally unaware of a cute little verse in Paul's letter to Titus. Paul had visited the Mediterranean island of Crete during his missionary journeys and found the local yokels to be ... Well, let Paul speak for himself: **Cretans are always liars, evil brutes, lazy gluttons.** (Titus 1: 12). Truly inspired ... right from the mouth of God.

The letters have something for everybody. But much like Psalms and Proverbs, taken verse by verse, just about anything at all from Paul's Epistles can be "proven." The problem is focus. Our modern church splits and schisms, doctrines and denominations, are all—in part—due to this banquet of discordant information dished out by Paul the Apostle. What is important? What is subordinated? What is to be believed, followed, and enforced? And what can be ignored, left out, and avoided? It's anyone's guess. But preachers and teachers and evangelists of myriad persuasions all know the answers. Hah.

And finally! Paul clarifies a teaching of Jesus that baffled and bamboozled the disciples and early church folks like crazy. Jesus made constant references to his impending return to Earth. But as usual, those dingbat fishermen and peasants just didn't get the drift. But Paul really got it all. Or maybe he just made it up. But in any case, this talk of the end times and future rewards for believers makes our Christian friends and relatives just wet themselves in anticipation.

The gist of the matter is that Jesus himself—in glorified form—will at some point in the future show up in the sky unannounced, and whisk away all his followers. He will return "as a thief in the night." And those who have an advanced reservation get to fly up in the sky with him. And the rest of mankind will be shit out of luck. Here is how things will transpire according to Paul …

Listen, I tell you a mystery; we will not all sleep, but we will all be changed—in a flash, in the twinkling of an eye, at the last trumpet. For the trumpet will sound, the dead will be raised imperishable, and we will be changed. For the perishable must clothe itself with the imperishable, and the mortal with immortality. (I Corinthians 15: 51-53). What? Now it is Paul who sets the stage for all future "coming events" … This is so cool. Not only has Paul singlehandedly taken the vague, otherworldly teachings of Jesus and redefined them as we have just seen; but is now addressing the end of time. He introduces a bizarre new concept, which still psyches up the Bible thumpers of our day. They call it the "rapture of the church."

I have to interject a bit here as tour leader. The term "rapture" is *not* found in the Bible. The first popular use of the word in an eschatological (futuristic) context is in the mid-19th Century in America (naturally). It is kind of contemporaneous with the rise of the Mormon cult. Lots of weird stuff going on back then, huh? Okay, back to Paul …

According to the Lord's own word, we tell you that we who are still alive, who are left till the coming of the Lord, will certainly not precede those who have fallen asleep. (I Thessalonians 4: 15). Jesus spoke often of his return—the "second coming," as it is popularly known. Naturally, everyone in the ancient world wanted more information about that promised event. Paul supplies that information, thus setting the stage for the final chapter of the Holy Bible and the last stop on our tour.

Paul really leaves the stage with a bang. Check this out: **For the Lord himself will come down from heaven, with a loud command, with the voice of the archangel and with the trumpet call of God, and the dead in Christ will rise first. After that, we who are still alive and are left will be caught up with them in the clouds to meet the Lord in the air. And so we will be with the Lord forever.** (I Thes. 4: 16,17). I can hardly wait :-)

If you find that your "born again" Christian relatives, neighbors, friends, and coworkers are arrogant and smug, perhaps this is the reason. Even though the

The Rapture of the Church (though not found in the Bible), was hinted at by Paul in the
Epistles. Even though it is a total fabrication, it still makes
Christians just cream in their jeans :-)

modern Christian believer so wants to be kindhearted and humble—caring for the sick, feeding the hungry, and clothing the naked—they just can't. They are too enamored with Paul's promises of their future glory and reward. They are just gaga waiting for the rapture. I have heard sermons for years promising the imminent return of Christ. I look back now and realize that even at the time, I thought those predictions that J.C. was going to show up almost any day were bogus. I even hear tell of whole churches fleeing out into the parking lot, hands and eyes skyward in utter "rapture." ... Any moment now! LOL.

For these true Biblical literalists, the rapture is kind of like the big California earthquake. In the twinkling of an eye, Christ will appear in the sky above and everything we know here on Earth will be over. It will be too late. And—like those caught in the big quake without proper food and bottled water, medical provisions, bandages and flashlights—they will be out on their own. *Sayang naman*. Too bad. When Christ appears on the scene this time it will not be as a humble baby in a manger, but a wrathful vengeful judge. Woe be unto anyone caught at the second coming with his pants down!

There will be a loud sound, a trumpet and a *shout*! Yea! Christ shall appear in the sky (presumably above Jerusalem, or Dallas, Texas, for the Southern Baptists). Remember now, the writers of this stuff were flat-Earthers. To them this all would make sense. Anyway, the "dead in Christ" will be raised first. All the Christians from centuries past will rise up out of their graves and their bodies will reassemble themselves en route upward. They will all be gathered together with Christ "in the clouds." For those of us accustomed to looking at the Earth from Landsat satellite photographs, we know that the Earth's atmosphere is quite thin. So all those real, physical reconstituted bodies of the dead will be squeezed together in the stratosphere, as clouds cannot be found any higher than that. Shortly thereafter, the Christians who are alive at the time of the triumphal return will fly up and join their long-dead, departed brethren in the clouds too. Whoopie!

No matter how absurd and implausible this may sound, it's one of the major doctrines of modern fundamentalist Evangelical Christianity, called "the Blessed Hope." Someday soon, the Christians will have the last word and, above all, the *last laugh*. Christ will come back and immediately snap them up, out of this world (perhaps through the hole in the ozone layer), to heaven, where God lives. Woo.

But what about the rest of us on the tour? What's going to happen to us? Well, that is coming! In fact, it is really a super-dooper end of the line for us all. For those of us who don't "get raptured," our fate is sealed. The horror and terror awaiting us is so unthinkable that it had to be revealed in a dream, as no conscious human could possibly make up such a thing. Paul has set the stage and has gotten us all wound up for the grand finale. And what a finale it is! The Bible ends with a bang! Fireworks. It is called the *Revelation* (the revealing), and how revealing it really is!

Angels, demons, fires, and flood. Earthquakes, burnings, plagues, and blood.
All of us are going to die. After that, we're going to fry.

Revelation

Talk about four aces!

Oh no. Just when we were beginning to think that maybe there was hope for a nice reformed Yahweh, he decides to end the world once and for all. The first time he destroyed everybody it was rather straightforward. He sent a flood and everyone was drowned (along with all the animals, birds, reptiles and amphibians). This time it is far more epic, more theatrical, more Hollywood :-)

According to modern Bible believers, the next event on God's divine calendar is the rapture of the church. We have no idea when it may happen. Shortly thereafter, the events foretold in the Book of Revelation will begin to take place. And, believe me, those of us who do not get to go up in the rapture will wish we had! It was Mark Twain who wrote of the smugness of the "Christian with four aces." If you believed with all your heart that you are destined to fly up in the sky and be whisked away from the final hellish days on Earth, you might likely be a smuggie too.

If Psalms is a tossed salad, and Proverbs are like jelly beans, then Revelation is definitely most of all like coleslaw. It is a mixture of detail so fine and confusing that it is impossible to pick out anything individual at all, or with any meaning of its own. Purportedly written by John, the Gospel writer, on a tiny insignificant island in the Mediterranean, called Patmos, in about the year 90 CE—it contains either the ravings of a totally demented old geezer, or the concoction of a wild collection of drugged out Italian scribes years later. Either way, it really doesn't matter who is responsible for this incubus; the fact is that millions of people around the world actually believe its prognostications. And those who do believe it as actual fact wait gleefully for their fulfillment. After all, those who so ardently believe and anticipate these prophecies, aren't planning to be around here on planet Earth to experience them firsthand. They plan to observe all the hideousness from their mansions over the hilltop with Jesus and Yahweh, and smugly scoff: "They should have listened!"

It begins: **On the Lord's Day I was in the Spirit (or in his cups) and I heard behind me a loud voice like a trumpet, which said: "Write on a scroll what you see, and send it to the seven churches ..." Write what you have seen,**

what is now and what will take place later. (Revelation 1: 10,11,19). So, here are just a few highlights. See if you can follow them. There might be a pop quiz later on.

I looked and there before me was a door standing open in heaven. And a voice I had first heard speaking to me like a trumpet said, "Come up here, and I will show you what must take place after this." At once I was in the Spirit, and there before me was a throne in heaven with someone sitting on it. (Rev. 4: 1,2). After some description about rainbows, emeralds, jasper and carnelian, John continues: **In the center, and around the throne, were four living creatures, and they were covered with eyes, in front and in back. The first living creature was like a lion, the second was like an ox, the third had a face like a man, the fourth was like a flying eagle.** (Rev. 4: 6,7). **Each of the four living creatures had six wings and was covered with eyes all around, even under his wings!** (Rev. 4: 8). Wow, some bad acid trip, huh? Weird enough for you? Oh, but we've just begun.

Then I saw in the right hand of him who sat on the throne a scroll with writing on both sides and sealed with seven seals. (Rev. 5: 1). **Then I saw a lamb, looking as if it had been slain, standing in the center of the throne, encircled by four living creatures and elders. He had seven horns and seven eyes, which are the seven spirits of God sent out into all the earth.** (Rev. 5: 6). I'll capsulize for a while, okay? So the lamb opens the scroll. That's a big deal to Bible expositors, who just love to explain what all this means. Then John envisioned four horsemen atop four horses (each of a different color). The first horse was white and the rider rode out as a conqueror. The second— a fiery red one—had a rider given power to take peace from the Earth and to make men slay each other (as if they haven't been doing so already for millennia). The third—a black one—had a rider with scales in his hand. And the fourth was a pale horse with a pale rider named death. Hades was following close behind. Remember him—the Greek god of the underworld? **They were given power over a fourth of the earth to kill by the sword, famine and plague, and by the wild beasts of the earth.** (Rev. 6: 8).

I told you it was theatrical. But wait—it just keeps getting better. **There was a great earthquake. The sun turned black like sackcloth made of goat hair, the whole moon turned to blood, and the stars in the sky fell to earth.** (Rev. 6:13).

Well, I suppose this was believable stuff in the first century CE, but hardly appropriate for science class today—even though there are Fightin' Fundies nationwide, campaigning constantly to have it taught in our public schools, right next to science as equal! Try to envision those cute little lanterns hanging up there on the blue dome sky. That earthquake really must have been at least a 9.0 or more to knock all of them off at the same time! Yowzers!

Then the kings of the earth, the princes, the generals, the rich, the mighty, and every slave and every free man hid in caves and among rocks of the mountains. They called to the mountains and rocks, "Fall on us and hide us from the face of him who sits on the throne and from the wrath of the Lamb!" (Rev. 6: 12-16). OMG, who is this "Lamb" anyway, and why is it so pissed off?

Well, the Lamb is Jesus, of course. Like, duh—the Lamb of God. And he is angry at mankind because they did not believe him when he came the first time as a humble carpenter from Galilee. So no more Mr. Nice Guy. This time he is coming like a mondo meat grinder and is ushering in all this astronomical destruction. Like father, like son. Then seven angels roll in with seven trumpets. This is great. I have always loved this part. Don't skip it. Look what your pious Christian Aunt Doris is avoiding as she watches down from on high while you put up with all this shit. "Should have listened!"

The first angel sounded his trumpet and there came hail and fire mixed with blood, and it was hurled down upon the earth. A third of the earth was burned up, a third of the trees were burned up, and all the green grass was burned up. (Rev. 8: 6,7). Christians have been accused over the years of being anti-environmental (which, of course they are); but no wonder! If their deity has no more respect for the Creation than to destroy it thusly, is it any wonder that his followers have such contempt for "God's footstool" as well? I have always thought of this as being like the little kid who builds a cool sand castle, then kicks it all down. Such fun destroying things, huh?

The second angel sounded his trumpet and a third of the sea turned into blood, a third of the living creatures in the sea died and a third of the ships were destroyed. The third trumpet sounded, and a great star, blazing like a torch, fell from the sky on a third of the rivers and on springs of water—

the name of the star is Wormwood. The fourth sounded and a third of the sun was struck, and a third of the moon, and a third of the stars, so a third of them turned dark. (Note: Kind of hard since according to Revelations 6:13 all of the stars had already fallen to Earth!) A third of the day was without sunlight, and also a third of the night. (Rev. 8: 12). Like, isn't the night without sunlight anyway? Just asking.

Anyway, *almost* done with all the falling stars and smoke and fire and blood and plagues and destruction. But one more of my favorites, please. Then an eagle flew by calling **"Woe woe woe to the inhabitants of earth..."** (Rev. 8: 13). I say woe woe woe myself, reading all this weirdity. It is supposed to symbolize future events, and libraries have been spilled out by Christian "scholars" down through the ages trying to explain the meaning of all these visions. Like, why sink only one third of the ships? But above all, why all the symbolism? Why didn't God just treat Brother John like Moses, and take him up to a mountain, and give him some stone tablets with *specific* warnings and *clear* instructions? Like Nostradamus', some of the visions and symbols can be interpreted—sort of, sometimes, maybe. I think that John was never on that island, but those drunken monks centuries later just thought it would be a great gag to write a real elaborate hoax just for fun.

You have to be thankful that this is just a once-over-lightly tour. There are twenty-two chapters of this, and some clergy have invested their entire lives picking at every word in an attempt to understand it all. And they all come to different interpretations. It is like gypsy fortunetelling, to me. But there are a few more elements that we have to encounter before we conclude our tour, because they are taken so seriously by our friends, the Evangelicals.

Okay, moving right along... More falling stars, more darkening of the Sun and Moon ... more fire and smoke, more plagues and destruction. Alright already; we get it; we get it. But here comes another wrinkle that really has the Fundies in an uproar. Enter the flying locusts as big as horses, that sting like scorpions. But the weird thing is that they can only sting the folks without the seal of God on their foreheads! What? Who would that be? I thought all those lucky bastards had been raptured already and were watching the play from heaven. Nobody can explain it. Of course, many claim to. But if you read their books, they all disagree. Gee whiz, no kidding.

But the humorous part to me is that the stinging locusts were only allowed to sting the unlucky for *five* months. Why not six?

Next come four different angels who are "bound" at the River Euphrates (which is still in Iraq, BTW :-) Their assignment: Kill one third of mankind. **A third of mankind was killed by the three plagues of fire, smoke and sulfur that came out of their mouths.** (Rev. 9: 18). Why is Jesus doing all this to mankind? Why has he gotten so mean lately? Well, here's why: **The rest of mankind that were not killed by theses plagues still did not repent of the work of their hands; they did not stop worshiping demons, and idols of gold, silver, bronze, stone and wood—idols that cannot see or hear or walk!** (Rev. 9: 20). OMG, not this old saw again. Sounds like Yahweh of old to me. ... How about you? Still fixated on those idols that can't see, hear, or walk. (Sigh)

Oh, you'll be able to envision this next part, for sure. The seventh angel blows his final trumpet and shouts: **"The kingdom of the world has become the kingdom of our Lord and of his Christ, and he will reign for ever and ever."** Then, *The Raiders of the Lost Ark* revisited: **God's temple in heaven was opened, and with his temple was seen the ark of his covenant. And there came flashes of lightning, rumblings, peals of thunder, an earthquake and a great hailstorm.** (Rev. 11: 15-19). Just like in the movie! Only Spielberg left out the hail. But basically he nailed it :-)

Shortly thereafter... **A great and wondrous sign appeared in the sky. A woman clothed with the sun, with the moon under her feet and a crown of twelve stars on her head. She was pregnant and cried out in pain as she was about to give birth. Then another sign appeared in heaven: an enormous red dragon with seven heads and ten horns and seven crowns on his heads. His tail swept a third of the stars out of the sky and flung them to the earth.** (Rev. 12: 1-4). (How many stars could possibly have been left at this point?) Come on, John, get it together! Anyway, she gave birth and God immediately snatched the child up to his throne. The woman fled to the desert for 1,260 days, and a war in heaven ensued. (Note: You can't imagine how modern "eschatologists" worry and scurry around about the number of days that the "woman" was out there in the desert. It is hysterical. Anyhow, the dragon was "hurled down" to Earth with his angel entourage. Apparently, he couldn't catch the woman, so he went off to make war against her other "offspring" ...whomever they are. Skip, skip... I'll compress the rest of John's pipe dream for you. Trust me—it's a whole lot more of the same. Actually, it's like watching back-to-back film trailers for about ten-in-a-row different monster flix, with lots of dragons, krakens, transformers, terminators, and other sundry hairy beasts and winged monsters—accompanied by lots of earthquakes, falling buildings, and miscellaneous pyrotechnics that appeal to fourteen-year-old boys. Awesome!

But next comes the thing that scares the shit out of Fundamentalist Evangelical Christians. He is called "The Beast" (and he is *really dear* old Satan whom we have already met in Genesis, Job, and the Gospels ... remember?). But he's in disguise. You visit any fundamentalist church worth its salt, and you will hear a sermon or two from Revelation 13. I can't skip over this, as it is so critical to their whole worldview. Now pay attention. This is serious stuff ... **And I saw a beast coming out of the sea. He had ten horns and seven heads, with ten crowns on his horns, and on each head was a blasphemous name. The beast resembled a leopard, but had feet like those of a bear and a mouth like that of a lion.** (Rev. 13: 1,2). Then the world was astonished and followed the beast. No one could stand against it. Gawd, I wouldn't want to even try. He (or it) was given authority over the people of the world (those still left standing after all the plagues and locust and all, that is). He has a cohort—another beast. Alas, it only has two horns. But it speaks like a dragon! Ooo! (Assuming that we all know what a dragon speaks like :-)

The dreaded beast does all manner of magic signs and wonders. He, like, totally wows the remaining Earthlings, and makes them all take a *mark* on the right hand and on the forehead. **So that no one could buy or sell unless he had the mark, which is the name of the beast or the number of his name. This calls for wisdom. If anyone has insight, let him calculate the number of the beast, for it is the man's number. His number is 666!** (Rev. 13: 17,18). Now, hold on a minute. After all these plagues, fire bombings of sulfur, hailstorms, and blood; the annihilation of the entire agricultural base; the darkening of the Sun and Moon and millions of stars impacting on Earth ... *what*, pray tell, would there be left to buy or sell anyway? I kid you not; most modern Christians are

Hell is a total bummer. Our Christian friends get to watch us from on high
while we wriggle and writhe in misery forever!

terrified of the *mark of the beast.* They are horrified that *social security numbers* are indeed that very mark! Stop laughing ;-)

We're getting there. A final round of plagues is announced. **I saw in heaven another great and marvelous sign: seven angels with the seven last plagues—last, because with them God's wrath is completed.** (Rev. 15: 1). (Finally!) **"Go, pour out the seven bowls of God's wrath on the earth." The first angel poured out his bowl on the land, and ugly and painful sores broke out on the people who had the mark of the beast and worshiped his image.** (Rev. 16: 2). Moving right along...

Then the second angel turned the *entire* sea into blood ... Not just a third of it like before. This is the real deal. **The third did likewise to all the rivers; the forth poured out his bowl on the sun, which scorched all the remaining people on Earth!** (The end of human life as we know it!) ... But, what's this? **The fifth angel plunged the beast's kingdom into darkness, and "men gnawed their tongues in agony!"** Wait a minute here. Didn't the Sun just scorch all the remaining people on Earth? You know, this reminds me of the creation story where God creates the plants before the Sun. Now the Sun scorches what's left of mankind but there are still people gnawing their tongues away! Oh well, *inerrancy.* Sorry to bring that up one last time at this late date in the Holy Scriptures. My bad. **So, the sixth angel poured its bowl into the great Euphrates River, thus drying it up to prepare the way for the advance of the "Kings of the East."** Didn't the second angel already turn all the world's rivers into blood? But there's more ... (naturally). What of the seventh angel?

The seventh angel poured out his bowl into the air. Then, out of the temple (what temple?) **came a loud voice booming: "It is done!"** Finally! But—hate to tell you—it *wasn't* done! There's more :-(More lightning, more blood, more earthquakes, and—of course—more hail! After all that other shit, hail actually doesn't seem so bad after all—does it?

Then, enter the great Prostitute, aka the *Whore of the Earth.* This is one wicked bitch. She is dressed in purple and scarlet (a very poor color combination). A total fashion victim, she is bedecked with gems and jewels, holding a golden chalice filled with *abominable* things. But it fails to mention *what* things. Damn, I'd like to know. Anyway, she rides in on the beast with the seven heads and ten horns. Remember him? BTW, this is *super* important to the Fundies. Why? Who is she and what do they say she represents? The *Roman Catholic Church*! What? I kid you not.

"The Kings of the earth committed adultery with her, and the merchants of the earth grew rich from her excessive luxuries." But her doom is sealed. She will be consumed by fire, for mighty is the Lord God who judges her. (Rev.18: 3,8). BTW, the Holy See does not agree with this interpretation. Likeduh.

Well, more woes; more white horses; angels and all that stuff; a big battle called Armageddon that the shouting preachers love to go on and on and on about, even though ... who would fight it? Weren't all the remaining inhabitants of the planet Sun-crisped back there by the fourth angel? Anyway, it really doesn't much matter as even the Fundies fight among themselves about everything from here on out.

Let's face it. At this point (no matter how it was done), the Earth is total toast. But just leaving everything like that would be a real downer, wouldn't it? What a bummer ending. But wait... There's more! From his heavenly throne, Jesus proclaims: **"I am making everything new!"** (Rev. 21: 5). Of course, it is all over for the trashed Earth and everybody but the born-again, spirit-filled, Bible-believing Protestant Fundamentalist Evangelical Christians. This is their new home and they have it all to themselves. Yea!

Then—pure *deus ex machina*—a holy city, "the new Jerusalem," glides slowly down out of the sky. And is it ever a groovy place! It is brilliant like crystal— just like the Crystal Cathedral :-) It has twelve gates with the names of the twelve tribes of Israel inscribed on them. It is 1400 miles square, with walls 200 feet thick. Wow. The walls are made of jasper and the city is made of gold. The foundations are made of sapphire, emeralds, sardonyx, carnelian, chrysolite, beryl, and all those awesome shiny blings.

Nobody but the Fundies gets to enter. The rest... And I mean *everybody* else, i.e. **The cowardly, the unbelieving, the vile, the murderers, the sexually immoral, those who practice magic arts, the idolaters and all liars—their place will be in the fiery lake of burning sulfur.** (Rev. 21: 8).

It is called "the city built foursquare," and the streets are really paved with gold. The Bible says so. And, as we have seen on our tour, it is such a reliable source. But, hey, nothing impure will ever enter the city. Nor will anyone who does what is shameful or deceitful... **But only those whose names are written in the Lamb's Book of Life!** (Rev. 21: 27). Hallelujah! Glory!

Whew! Talk about four aces!

As You Leave Our Tour...

Please watch your step!

I really hope you have enjoyed your journey through the Bible. And it's been a delight having you along. And as you leave the bus, please note that there is a small box available where you can make a charitable donation to your favorite televangelist. (I'll make sure he gets it ;-)

And hopefully this tour has added to your Biblical knowledge and wisdom. But remember ... To quote our old friend, Solomon: **For with much wisdom comes much sorrow; the more knowledge the more grief.** (Ecclesiastes 1:18).

Good grief!

Bye :-)